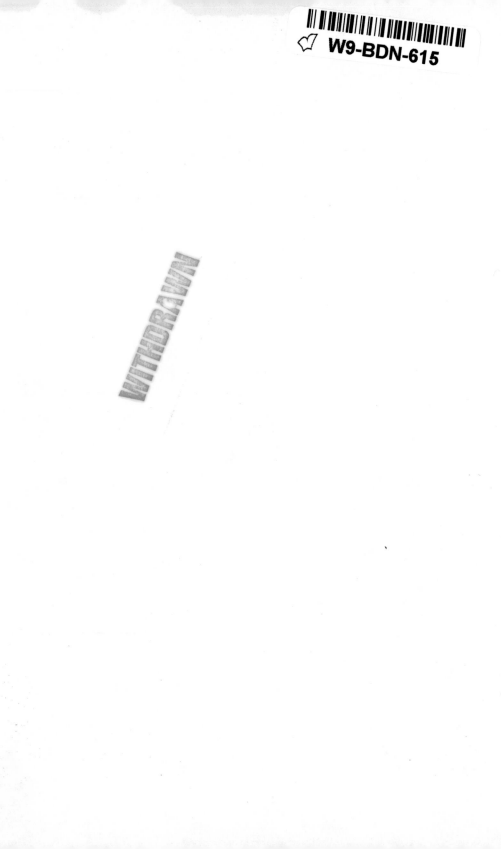

Reading and Dyslexia

How information on the page is transmitted to the brain is one of the key questions underlying the search for exactly how children, both normal and those experiencing difficulty, learn to read. Specifying the role of different visual processes and the moderating effects of attention is critical to our understanding of this question; both of these issues are addressed in *Reading and Dyslexia*. In addition to new research in the area, the book provides a thorough review of the most important work to date.

A team of leading international researchers discuss investigations of different visual pathways and neuroanatomical areas, the involvement of eye movements, fixations and the visual span, the interactions between movement and vision, and the effects of attentional processes such as focus, interference and inhibition. Each chapter considers explanations of reading ability and their importance in understanding why some individuals experience problems with the acquisition of literacy skills.

Reading and Dyslexia provides a convenient, concise and scholarly resource for all those interested in reading ability. It will be especially useful for researchers and academics in psychology and education.

John M. Everatt is Lecturer in Psychology at the University of Surrey, UK.

Reading and Dyslexia
Visual and attentional processes

Edited by John Everatt

London and New York

First published 1999 by Routledge
11 New Fetter Lane, London EC4P 4EE

Simultaneously published in the USA and Canada
by Routledge
29 West 35th Street, New York, NY 10001

Routledge is an imprint of the Taylor & Francis Group

© 1999 John Everatt: selection and editorial matter;
individual chapters, the contributors

Typeset in Times by Keystroke, Jacaranda Lodge, Wolverhampton
Printed and bound in Great Britain by Redwood Books, Trowbridge, Wiltshire

British Library Cataloguing in Publication Data
A catalogue record for this book is available from the British Library

Library of Congress Cataloging in Publication Data
Reading and dyslexia : visual and attentional processes / [edited by]
    John Everatt.
        p.   cm.
    Includes bibliographical references and index.
    ISBN 0–415–12327–5 (hc.). — ISBN 0–415–20633–2 (pbk.)
    1. Dyslexia. 2. Visual perception. 3. Reading—Physiological
aspects. 4. Reading disability—Physiological aspects. 5. Visual
learning. I. Everatt, John.
LB1050.5.R362   1999
371.91'44—dc21   98–41321
                                                                        CIP

ISBN 0–415–12327–5 (hbk)
ISBN 0–415–20633–2 (pbk)

Contents

Illustrations

Figures

Tables

Contributors

Yalchin G. Abdullaev, Louisville Health Sciences Center, Department of Psychiatry and Behavioral Sciences, Louisville, KY, USA

Denise Baker, School of Psychology, University of Wales, Bangor, UK

Monica Biscaldi, Brain Research Unit, Institute of Biophysics, University of Freiburg, Freiburg, Germany

Mark B. Bradshaw, Department of Psychology, University of Surrey, Guildford, Surrey, UK

Francis Culverwell, Department of Psychology, University of Surrey, Guildford, Surrey, UK

Barbara D'Entremont, Department of Psychology, Dalhousie University, Halifax, Nova Scotia, Canada

Delyth Evans, School of Psychology, University of Wales, Bangor, UK

John Everatt, Department of Psychology, University of Surrey, Guildford, Surrey, UK

Burkhart Fischer, Brain Research Unit, Institute of Biophysics, University of Freiburg, Freiburg, Germany

Martin H. Fischer, Department of Psychology, University of Massachusetts, Amherst, MA, USA

Gadi Geiger, Media Laboratory and Research Laboratory of Electronics, Massachusetts Institute of Technology, Cambridge, MA, USA

John A. Groeger, Department of Psychology, University of Surrey, Guildford, Surrey, UK

Maureen Kay, School of Psychology, University of Wales, Bangor, UK

Raymond M. Klein, Department of Psychology, Dalhousie University, Halifax, Nova Scotia, Canada

Jerome Lettvin, Media Laboratory and Research Laboratory of Electronics, Massachusetts Institute of Technology, Cambridge, MA, USA

William Lovegrove, Department of Psychology, University of Wollongong, Wollongong, NSW, Australia

Bruce D. McCandliss, Learning Research and Development Center, University of Pittsburgh, Pittsburgh, PA, USA

Barbara McCorquodale, Department of Psychology, University of Surrey, Guildford, Surrey, UK

Sue McNamara, Department of Psychology, University of Surrey, Guildford, Surrey, UK

Karen Pepper, Department of Psychology, University of Wollongong, Wollongong, NSW, Australia

Alexander Pollatsek, Department of Psychology, University of Massachusetts, Amherst, MA, USA

Michael I. Posner, Department of Psychology and Institute of Cognitive and Decision Sciences, University of Oregon, Eugene, OR, USA

Keith Rayner, Department of Psychology, University of Massachusetts, Amherst, MA, USA

Erik D. Reichle, Department of Psychology, University of Massachusetts, Amherst, MA, USA

Sara C. Sereno, Department of Psychology, University of Glasgow, Glasgow, UK

Julie Smith, Department of Psychology, University of Surrey, Guildford, Surrey, UK

Alan Wilks, School of Psychology, University of Wales, Bangor, UK

1 Associations between reading ability and visual processes

John Everatt, Barbara McCorquodale, Julie Smith, Francis Culverwell, Alan Wilks, Delyth Evans, Maureen Kay and Denise Baker

Introduction

Reading is a complex skill which is often taken for granted. It is only when the varied skills involved are considered in detail that we find ourselves in a complex world of learnt operations and mental processes. The act of reading can be thought of as comprising two basic processes: (i) decoding of the written form; and (ii) comprehension of the message presented by the written form. It could therefore be argued that reading is word decoding plus language comprehension. However, this view hides a multitude of subprocesses necessary for the successful completion of decoding and comprehension. The accurate decoding of the written form, for example, requires a visual system capable of precise perceptual processing and recognition of letters and/or combinations of letters in numerous and disparate writing styles. Visual processes therefore are vital components of reading, and it is upon these that the present book will concentrate. In particular, the book will focus upon those processes related to visual attention and eye movement control, given recent research and theoretical viewpoints which have focused upon these processes and their potential as explanations of reading behaviour and reading problems (see for example Conners 1990; Dykman and Ackerman 1991; Fergusson and Harwood 1992; Fischer and Weber 1990; Gernsbacher, Varner and Faust 1990; Geiger and Lettvin 1989; Herdman and LeFevre 1992; Lundberg 1991; Pennington, Groisser and Welsh 1993; Rayner *et al.*, 1989; Shaywitz, Fletcher and Shaywitz 1994; Stein and Walsh 1997; Whyte 1994). Consideration will also be given to motor, linguistic and memory processes, particularly when they are relevant to the theoretical views explicated, or present alternative explanations to the phenomena discussed. Motor processes are obviously important when considering eye movement control, although further links with reading can be made when considering visual-motor functions and theories relating attention to a process of selection for action (e.g. Allport 1987). Linguistic processes (such as the conversion of the written form into a sound, or phonological, representation) are often proposed as the main alternative to visual-based explanations for the phenomena observed within studies of reading. Finally, memory is related to both linguistic and visual-attention aspects. The long-term retention of written information is often discussed in terms of linguistic processes, whereas short-term storage of the same text is associated with sound-based representations.

However, the functions performed by working memory, particularly in terms of the hypothesised central executive, are often considered as analogous to those performed by attention (see Baddeley 1993).

The present chapter will introduce some of the themes covered in subsequent chapters. Its purpose is to provide the reader with the background to understand the phenomena discussed in the book while, at the same time, presenting new data on specific topics and posing questions for which subsequent chapters may provide answers.

Visual processes

The visual processing of lines of individual words is made possible by the movement of the eyes across that text; the eyes progressing in a series of fixations and saccades. Fixations occur when the eyes are stationary, saccades when the eyes move. Both are important aspects of text processing: fixations are necessary because it is during these that new information is taken from the page (Ishida and Ikeda 1989; Latour 1962); saccades are important because reading would prove very difficult if the reader were forced to fixate on one place and read with the corners of the eyes (Rayner and Bertera 1979). Fixations and saccades are therefore part of the process of extracting information from the text. Also, both eye fixations and saccadic movements are related to processes involved in attention and parafoveal/peripheral vision. Fixations occur on virtually every word, usually within the first half of the word, often referred to as the preferred viewing location (the point where the eyes actually land in a word; see Rayner 1979); though this may be distinguished from the optimal viewing position (O'Regan and Jacobs 1992), the position at which processing of the word is optimal. For eye movements to locate the next word, or preferred/optimal viewing position, parafoveal or peripheral processes must be utilised. Furthermore, eye movements bring the most sensitive region of the eye, the fovea, to bear on each word, thereby increasing the chance of that word being processed in detail. There is evidence that most word processing occurs within the fixation on that word, or, if it is not fixated, within the fixation prior to it (Carpenter and Just 1983; Hogaboam 1983; Rayner and Pollatsek 1981), giving the impression of attention being focused on the fixated word, perhaps as part of identification and integration processes. This idea is supported by findings for a restricted area of processing (the perceptual span) which extends little beyond the boundaries of the fixated word. Certainly, for English language readers, little seems to be visually processed beyond the left-hand boundary of a fixated word, and although word identification may extend beyond its right-hand boundary, it may be restricted in some way (Rayner and Pollatsek 1987). For such focusing operations to occur, attentional processes must play a vital part in reading. Perhaps if attentional or parafoveal/peripheral processes are deficient in some way, then reading will either not be optimum or not possible. If this were so, we would expect to find that these processes are related to reading ability, or coincide with reading disability; possibilities which will be considered in the present chapter.

The remainder of this chapter will concentrate on phenomena related to attentional and parafoveal/peripheral processes, since the following chapters of the book will concentrate upon this area. The chapter will be divided into sections discussing, in turn, (i) foveal/peripheral visual processes and the perceptual span, (ii) processes involved in movements of the eyes, (iii) visual attentional effects related to interference and inhibitory mechanisms, and (iv) resource implications of dual task procedures. Each section will be further divided into sub-sections reviewing research related to the development of reading; individual differences between experienced, able readers; and reading disabilities.

The perceptual span

Reading development

First, if there is a relationship between focusing attention and reading, we would expect a supposed feature of attentional focusing, such as the perceptual span, to be related to increases in reading ability with age. It is certainly the case that the span seems to develop with reading experience (Rayner 1986), being between a half and two-thirds its adult size in beginning readers. It is also possible that this development may be associated with developments in attention since there is evidence that selective and sustained attention improves from pre-school into early teens, and certainly over the initial reading years (Brown 1982; Hagen 1967; Higgins and Turnure 1984). However, as the reader becomes more experienced, so the perceptual span becomes larger, indicating that the area over which information can be retrieved is increased. This suggests that the inexperienced reader may need to focus attention more than the experienced reader, possibly because of poorer word processing capabilities. For example, Rayner (1986) found that as text difficulty increased, older readers (in the 4th grade) showed perceptual spans akin to younger readers (in the 2nd grade) and that compared with adult readers, reading rate in beginning readers was increased much less when information around the fixated word was removed. These findings indicate that: (i) reading difficulty affects the size of the span, with more difficult text requiring more focused attention; (ii) attention among beginning readers is focused on the word to a greater extent than in the adult reader; and (iii) during reading, parafoveal information is ignored more in the inexperienced than the experienced reader. This is certainly not evidence that the novice reader cannot focus attention while reading, and suggests that if attention plays a part in beginning reading it is to aid word identification/integration processes. The development of the perceptual span thus seems to be related to the difficulty of processing the fixated word (Rayner and Pollatsek 1987), with increases in reading experience allowing attention to be spread further into the periphery of vision. The use of parafoveal information may thus be a feature of more able reading, and suggests the possibility that reading ability is related to increases in the size of the perceptual span.

Individual differences in reading ability

There is scant evidence that the ability to extract information further into peripheral vision is related to increased reading ability in normal adult readers. Jackson and McClelland (1975, 1979) presented adult subjects with the task of identifying letters at varying degrees of separation within central and peripheral vision. Performance in this task was unrelated to comprehension ability or reading speed. Perceptual span size does not appear to predict reading ability.

One group of readers which claims to be both expert readers and to use larger perceptual spans is speed readers (see Brim 1968), and their progress through text at incredible speeds may be indicative of exceptional reading ability. However, any individual can move their eyes from the beginning of a page to the end of it at speed. The question is, have they comprehended any of the written information on the page while doing this? The claim for the speed reader being an exceptional reader requires that they also comprehend at least as much of the written information as the normal reader who does not use peripheral vision in this extended way, and most of the evidence does not support the speed readers' claims. Individuals using speed reading strategies often show poorer comprehension than normal readers, with comprehension levels being little more than those of normal readers who skip read (see Carver 1985; Just and Carpenter 1987; although see also Underwood and Everatt 1992). Thus an extended perceptual span does not necessarily lead to a better reader.

Reading disabilities

If the increase in the perceptual span was related to reading ability, those individuals who have poorly developed reading abilities should therefore possess smaller spans. However, Underwood and Zola (1986) found no difference in the size of the perceptual span between good and poor readers (5th grade children at or above reading grade or 1 year or more below reading grade). Poor reading ability does not appear to be related to under-developed, small perceptual spans (but see Levinson 1989). Although there is some evidence that impaired readers perform poorly when letters are embedded within distractor letters, this may not be specific to parafoveal vision since poorer performance exists when the items are presented to foveal vision (see Bouma and Legein 1977).

A second possibility is that if attentional focus (as evidenced by smaller perceptual spans) is necessary for the beginning reader to process each word, then a lack of attentional focus (non-fixation) may lead to problems in the initial stages of learning to read. Such a possibility is supported by evidence for increased peripheral information processing, or larger perceptual spans, within disabled readers. Geiger and Lettvin (1987) found that, compared with control subjects, dyslexics were more successful at identifying letters presented in the periphery of vision; a finding which has been replicated in subsequent studies (Geiger, Lettvin and Zegarra-Moran 1992; Perry *et al.* 1989), and extended to include increased peripheral identification of colour (Dautrich 1993; Grosser and Spafford 1989).

Such increased influences of peripheral information may be linked to the development of attention: the more developed the attentional processor, the better able the individual is to focus attention. However, other findings are inconsistent with the simple conclusion that dyslexics show increased peripheral processing. For example, Klein *et al.* (1990) found no evidence of increased peripheral processing when the dyslexic could not predict the direction in which the item was to be presented; Goolkasian and King's (1990) dyslexics showed increased peripheral processing for embedded letters, but not for isolated letters; Slaghuis and Pinkus's (1993) dyslexics presented increased peripheral processing only when items were seen briefly and followed by a pattern mask; Solman and May (1990) found that dyslexics were poor indicators of the position of an item presented to peripheral vision; and Raymond (1994) found that dyslexics performed less well than controls in tasks related to peripheral movement perception.

These findings might be explained by the recent views that argue for a transient/magnocellular deficit within dyslexics and either (i) the differential processing that the transient/magnocellular pathway performs compared with the sustained/parvocellular pathway, or (ii) the mutual inhibitory influences of these two visual pathways (see discussions by Breitmeyer 1993; Chase 1996; Hogben 1997; Lovegrove and Williams 1993; Lovegrove, Martin and Slaghuis 1986; Stein 1993). Although the transient/sustained distinction derives from relatively older neuroanatomical studies of the visual system of the cat, and the magnocellular/parvocellular distinction derives from more recent studies of primates, a commonly held view is that the functions of the these systems are analogous, and comparable with the human visual system (e.g. see Breitmeyer 1993). The transient/magnocellular system responds to faster stimulus changes, supposedly related to faster conducting Y-cells, which respond to gross (low frequency) detail. It has been posited as playing important roles in guiding eye movements, integrating information across fixations and movement perception (see Cornelissen *et al.* 1995; Stein and Walsh 1997). The sustained/parvocellular system, on the other hand, is related to X-cells which are more sensitive to slower stimulus velocities and higher spatial frequencies. This system seems to respond to finer details, and has been associated with central, foveal vision, and the extraction of information during fixations. In relation to reading, it is hypothesised that reading disabled individuals have a normally functioning sustained/pavocellular system, but an abnormally functioning transient/magnocellular system. The dyslexic's enhanced processing of colour and form within peripheral vision could be explained by considering that the visual pathways mutually inhibit each other (Breitmeyer 1993). In the normally functioning system, the transient/magnocellular pathway has dominance in the periphery of vision and inhibits the sustained/pavocellular pathway, thus peripheral vision is better able to detect fast changing stimuli. The converse is that central vision is better able to detect form and colour. If the transient/magnocellular system's inhibition of the sustained/parvocellular system were deficient in some way, then the latter's activity in peripheral vision may be enhanced, and so form and colour perception would be increased. Thus peripheral letter form identification would be increased, leading to peripherally presented words being processed more than usual, causing interference of centrally fixated words. This may be the source of the dyslexic's complaint that words seem blurred or jumbled-up. If this were the case, the disabled reader should become an able reader when text is presented one word at a time, and a couple of studies, both on individuals and groups of disabled readers, suggest that removing parafoveal words may aid poor readers in some cases. Hill and Lovegrove (1993) presented reading disabled and control subjects with text either one word or one line at a time. They found that their reading disabled subjects showed better reading performance in the single word presentation condition, in contrast to the reading able subjects who showed better performance when a whole line was visible (similar findings have been presented by Patberg and Yonas 1978, and Rayner *et al.* 1989, although not necessarily from the same theoretical standpoint). However, under single word reading conditions, dyslexics do not suddenly become able readers. If presented with a single word to read, the dyslexic reader will continue to experience difficulty learning to read that word, and, even when they have learned to read it, they may still take longer to name it (see Hulme 1988, and reply by Lovegrove 1991; also see van der Leij 1993). A second problem with this explanation is that Burr, Morrone and Ross (1994) have presented evidence suggesting that within the normally functioning visual system, the magnocellular pathway is less efficient during saccadic movements, whereas the operations of the parvocellular pathway seem to be relatively unaffected by the movements of the eyes, and may even be enhanced. Such evidence contradicts views regarding the mutual inhibitory influences of the two visual pathways, and their hypothesised roles within eye movements.

Whereas some have suggested that increased peripheral processing within dyslexics is due to abnormal cellular distributions (e.g. Grosser and Spafford (1989) have suggested that the dyslexic may have an extended fovea due to increased numbers of cones within peripheral vision), Geiger and Lettvin (1987, 1989) have argued that this is due to attentional strategies, based upon their findings that reading disabled individuals could be trained to produce more normal identifications across the visual field. It may be that whereas the normal reader focuses upon a word, the disabled reader views the scene in a more global way, processing information from a wider area. Training reduces the use of this strategy and increases the dyslexic's ability to focus attention on the appropriate information. Geiger and Lettvin (1989) also argue that such training was accompanied by descriptions of improved reading; although it is a pity that this was not formally accessed. Further evidence that this effect may be better explained in terms of a visual strategy rather than a neurological abnormality is provided by Geiger *et al.* (1992) who found that increased peripheral identification is only evident in the direction of reading (i.e. to the right of centre for Latin-natives, but to the left of centre for Hebrew-natives). It is difficult to see why abnormalities in peripheral identification should only occur in the direction of reading if they are due to a transient/magnocellular deficit. The Geiger *et al.* (1992) finding, if reliable, is better explained as a consequence of reading experience, unless we assume that an English disabled reader taught Hebrew would be an able Hebrew reader!

Increased peripheral processing by dyslexics would obviously support a relationship between attention and reading but, given inconsistent findings, further evidence is necessary. We sought this evidence by comparing able and disabled readers on a measure of interference, rather than identification. This was to avoid the criticism that Geiger and Lettvin's (1987) procedures might allow the dyslexic to deliberately improve peripheral identification by simply moving the centre of fixation towards a peripheral item rather than fixating the centre of the screen as instructed (see Goolkasian and King 1990; Klein *et al.* 1990). Such movements of the centre of fixation would not be intentionally chosen in the present paradigm since they would increase interference thereby reducing performance. The task chosen in these studies was a modified version of the Stroop effect (Stroop, 1935) which comprised a centrally placed block of colour (e.g. the colour red) paired with a centrally or peripherally placed interfering colour-word (e.g. 'blue') or non-colour control word (see Everatt, in preparation, for details). Given that the colour-word refers to a different colour concept, interference would be expected on most tasks that require a response based on the block of colour, although it would be expected to reduce as the incongruous colour-word is moved away from the colour (see Flowers and Stoup 1977; Gatti and Egeth 1978). If disabled readers show increased peripheral processing of letter information, then they should process the peripheral colour-word to a greater extent than non-dyslexics, and thus show less effect of the separation between incongruous colour-word and colour. Note that the disabled reader should have no choice but to process the peripheral word, since this is the proposed reason for their problems in normal reading; if they could avoid processing the word in this paradigm, why would they not do the same when reading text?

The studies included five groups of teenage/adult subjects. One group comprised a severe reading disabled group (13 to 16 years of age). Many of the subjects in this group had barely reached the level of reading individually presented high frequency words, and most could not read connected discourse. (A number of subjects within the same group were excluded from the present analyses since they presented little evidence of any word decoding skills, and showed no Stroop interference effects; the reported data were obtained from the remaining 24 subjects). Subjects within this group also had low IQs and, as such, they would not usually be diagnosed as dyslexic (see special issue of the journal *Dyslexia*, 1997, volume 3, issue 1, for a discussion of this point). The severe reading disabled group were presented with the task of sorting colours since they performed more ably in this task than within the more traditional naming task. In addition to the severe reading disabled group, two other groups of teenagers (13 to 16 years of age) were given the sorting task; one comprised 12 diagnosed dyslexics, the other a control group of 21 able readers. These latter two groups differed in their ability to name pseudowords (novel, unknown strings of letters; e.g. BLASP), and in terms of the time needed to name individually presented words, but produced equivalent average scores on the Ravens matrices. The final two groups consisted of adult subjects (aged 18 to 50), 18 of whom were reading compensated dyslexics drawn from college undergraduate courses. These subjects had been diagnosed as dyslexic during childhood and adulthood, but their

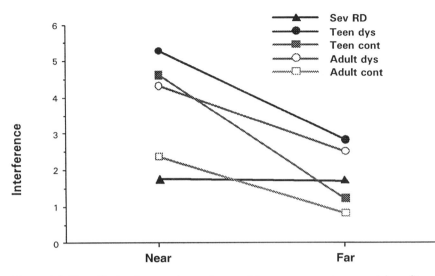

Figure 1.1 The effects of separating colour and incongruous colour-word in a Stroop interference task for five groups of subjects: the severe reading disabled group (Sev RD), the teenage dyslexics (Teen dys) and controls (Teen cont), and the adult reading compensated dyslexics (Adult dys) and adult controls (Adult cont).

Notes

The level of interference was calculated by subtracting non-colour word control from the incongruous colour-word conditions. Colours were presented singly at the centre of the white card with incongruous colour-words or non-colour words. In the near condition incongruous colour-words were presented directly above colours, whereas in the far condition words were moved to the right so as to avoid any overlap with the blocks of colour. Subjects sorted/named four sets of cards; one per condition.

timed reading of single, high frequency words was commensurate with that of 30 non-dyslexic college students who comprised the final group of subjects. Spelling performance among the adult dyslexics was, however, still well below that of the non-dyslexic adults. A feature of adult dyslexics seems to be that reading ability may improve considerably compared with childhood, but that spelling often remains poor (see Miles 1993). Also, the dyslexic adults were impaired compared with their non-dyslexic peers in a pseudoword rapid naming task (see similar findings in Everatt 1997). These adult subjects were given the same stimuli as the teenage groups, but were required to name the colours.

In accordance with the view that the ability to ignore peripheral information is related to reading ability, the severe reading disabled group showed equivalent interference from peripheral colour-words compared with centrally placed distractors, whereas control subjects and reading compensated adult dyslexics presented evidence of an ability to inhibit peripherally presented items (see Figure 1.1). However, the teenage dyslexic group also showed evidence of reduced interference from peripheral compared with central words, this reduction being similar to that shown by the teenage control subjects; findings more consistent with those of Klein *et al.* (1990) and Goolkasian and King (1990). The ability to ignore peripheral interfering information seems to be related to reading ability, but these findings suggest that it is only when problems with reading are severe that increased peripheral processing is obvious within such a task. Similar results are apparent within the card presentation task of Vrana (1980), who compared interference produced when target and distractor information were intermixed with interference produced by separated targets and distractors. A group of younger (8 to 10-year-old) subjects with learning disabilities within reading, spelling and/or mathematics were compared with a group of control subjects. Differences in distractor interference were found between the groups only within the combined condition. There was scant evidence of a difference between the groups when targets and distractors were separated. This learning disabled group were not as disabled as the severe reading disabled group in the present study, though they were younger, and showed results more consistent with the teenage dyslexic group. Reading ability may have to be very poor to show increased interference effects within peripheral vision.

A conundrum which develops from these findings is that Geiger and Lettvin's (1987) paradigm indicates that reading disability is associated with increased processing of peripheral information, whereas findings related to the development of the perceptual span suggest that inexperienced reading is related to decreased processing of information outside of the fovea (Rayner 1986). The Geiger and Lettvin (1987) findings also seem contradictory with the claims of the speed reading fraternity. How these two aspects of the relationship between attention and reading (i.e. increased parafoveal/peripheral processing relating to experienced or superior reading *and* disabled reading) can be reconciled is not obvious. For example, if we argue that the disabled reader has innate abnormal peripheral vision, we should find aspects of this affecting early eye movement behaviour, particularly in terms of the perceptual span. This is not so, the spans of disabled readers being no different from able readers (Underwood and Zola 1986). Indeed, the eye movements of reading disabled children are similar to those of younger, inexperienced readers (Olson 1985). It is also unlikely that the perceptual span starts off normally, but continues to expand within the disabled reader beyond the level at which its expansion ceases in the able reader. Suggesting that this is the cause of dyslexia is inconsistent with reading problems which manifest early in the career of a disabled reader (before about 8 or 9 years old when the size of the span corresponds with those in adults). Their implication that reading progresses normally until the span reaches the adult level when non-fixated words start to interfere with fixated ones is implausible.

Alternative explanations suggest some problem with the generalisation of the findings or with the methodology used. It could be that findings for increased peripheral processing are due to some experimental confound and that disabled readers can focus attention as well as able ones; i.e. there is no correspondence between attentional problems and reading disability. A related idea is that the disabled readers tested by Geiger and Lettvin (1987) constitute an atypical population. There is evidence to suggest that dyslexics/reading disabled individuals do not form a homogeneous group (Boder 1971; Satz and Morris 1981; Watson, Goldgar and Ryschon 1983), with some showing phonological problems and others visuo-spatial deficits. However, those showing signs of visuo-spatial deficits form only a small proportion of the samples studied (about 20 per cent), making it unlikely that they would produce the effects found by Geiger and Lettvin (1987) and others (Dautrich 1993; Grosser and Spafford 1989; Hill and Lovegrove 1993; Perry *et al.* 1989; Slaghuis and Pinkus 1993), without the added problem of some form of sampling error. This view, that findings differ due to distinct categories of poor readers, is consistent with our findings in the peripheral Stroop studies where the subjects with severe reading problems were a non-typical dyslexic group – showing general learning difficulties as well as those specific to reading. It may therefore be the case that attentional abnormalities are related to atypical or severe reading problems.

Alternatively, the perceptual span may not be a satisfactory measure of attentional focus, unlike the measure of peripheral processing in the Geiger and Lettvin (1987) study. Fixation location and the perceptual span could simply indicate word processing operations which proceed regardless of attention, and there is a wealth of experimental evidence that attention and fixation are separable (see Posner 1980). Attention would then be free to move about as it sees fit, sometimes ahead of fixation, sometimes lagging behind the movements of the eye. In fact, it has been argued that switches of attention take some 300 to 500 ms (Raymond, Shapiro and Arnell 1992). If this is the case, then the fact that fixations last on average only 250 ms may mean that it is necessary for attention to dissociate itself from the point of fixation. However, the complete separation of attention from the centre of fixation seems too bizarre a situation to contemplate and, in terms of the present discussion, would mean that measures of the perceptual span are not indicative of attentional processes in reading and should not, therefore, be considered.

A final explanation implies that an over-developed perceptual span is a consequence of reading problems for which the disabled reader tries to compensate (Geiger and Lettvin 1987, 1989). There are two major consequences of this possibility: first, although there is a relationship between attention and reading disability, there is no reason to assume that this relationship will tell us anything about normal reading. Second, attentional abnormalities will not necessarily inform us of the underlying cause of reading problems – the attentional abnormality is now simply a consequence, not a cause. Such a consequence may occur in some disabled readers and not others, and may be more likely in older dyslexics, particularly if it is due to some learnt compensatory strategy. It may even be confined to certain tasks. As such, the relationship between reading and attention will remain difficult to pinpoint.

Saccadic movements

A second possible relationship between reading and visual processes is suggested by the idea that saccades to the next fixation have to be programmed and that some mechanism must initiate those saccades and programme their structure. It is possible that reading suffers due to poorly constructed programmes or inaccurate representations of peripheral locations. In such cases eye movements may end at the wrong location, leading to inefficient reading. Alternatively, movements of the eyes could be uncoordinated leading to different images being formed on the two eyes.

Reading development

In terms of reading experience, younger readers show patterns of saccades which are different from adults. Compared with the adult, the beginning reader uses shorter saccades and more regressions back through the text, requiring larger numbers of eye movements to process the same amount of text. However, there is little evidence to show that such saccadic movements are inappropriately programmed in the beginning reader (leading to movements in the wrong direction, or to an unintended word), and then develop to be correctly programmed in the experienced reader. A more likely explanation is that changes in the number and length of saccadic movements follow the development of processes involved in word identification and text integration, with saccades becoming more adult-like as word recognition and integration processes improve. For example, saccadic movements in non-reading situations seem to become adult-like early in infant development (see Shea 1992), with saccadic latencies (the time taken to initiate an eye movement) being the only feature which may not develop full adult-like characteristics until adolescence (Ross and Ross 1987).

Individual differences in reading ability

Similarly, studies based on the monitoring of eye movements of readers with differing abilities suggest that variations in saccades may poorly explain variability in reading ability. There is some relationship between fixation length and reading ability, particularly as assessed by reading time (see Everatt and Underwood 1994), but this is more parsimoniously explained as due to the difficulty of processing the fixated word, and hence as a feature of the language system rather than eye movement programming or the interplay between visual and motor processes. Evidence also exists that regressive saccades are related to reading ability (see Kennedy 1987). Again, however, this may have little to do with the effects of visual-motor processes involved in saccadic programming or peripheral processing. Kennedy (1987) suggests that inefficient regressive movements may be due to poor memory concerning the locations of words within a text; an effect perhaps better explained in terms of linguistic processes than visual factors.

Finally, evidence for a relationship between reading ability and saccadic processes may be provided by the view that locating the convenient/optimal viewing position aids word recognition (see O'Regan and Jacobs 1992), and that this position may vary as a function of redundancy (O'Regan and Levy-Schoen 1987; Underwood, Hyönä and Niemi 1987). It seems, therefore, plausible that variations in processes designed to locate this position (either peripheral identification processes or eye movement programmes) will be related to reading ability. Again, however, the evidence is inconclusive. Everatt and Underwood (1994), for example, found scant evidence for the process of locating informative areas within words (and so avoiding redundant areas) being related to reading comprehension ability or speed of reading in adult able readers.

Reading disabilities

As with beginning readers, the eye movement patterns of disabled readers differ substantially from those of adult, able readers. Disabled readers show shorter saccades and more regressions, and such abnormalities have led to the view that reading problems stem from erratic eye movement behaviour (Pavlidis 1981). However, this view appears to predict that the severity of the reading problem should be related to the degree of abnormality in eye movements, whereas it appears not to be (see Rayner and Pollatsek 1989). If abnormal eye movements do cause reading problems, they should be found in non-reading situations, yet a number of studies have found no differences between reading able and reading disabled subjects' eye movements in non-reading situations (Fields, Newman and Wright 1993; Olson, Kliegl and Davidson 1983; Stanley, Smith and Howell 1983). Variations in eye movements seem simply to be a function of reading difficulties, rather than a cause, and may indicate underlying word recognition processes rather than attention.

There are, however, three areas of research where potential differences between able and disabled readers may suggest some eye movement related dysfunction within the disabled readers. First, differences have been found between good and poor readers in terms of the optimal viewing location discussed in the previous sub-section (Brysbaert and Meyers 1993). Similarly, Everatt, Bradshaw and Hibbard (in press) found that the information location effect, which showed little relationship with reading ability in normal, able readers, did correlate with reading ability in a group of dyslexic subjects. More severe reading problems may therefore be related to problems with representing/locating information yet to be fixated or programming accurate saccades to that information.

A second possibility is presented by the findings of Stein and colleagues (e.g. see the review by Stein 1993) for reading disabled subjects to show variation in eye dominance and characteristics similar to individuals with visual neglect. The former data suggest that images processed by each eye may not be as coordinated within the reading disabled individual as within the normal reader. This may be the source of the dyslexic's complaints that text seems jumbled or blurred. However, the means of assessing eye dominance used by Stein and colleagues (the Dunlop test) may be unreliable when discriminating able and disabled readers (see Goulandris *et al.* 1998), suggesting that the measurement tool requires further development or that not all dyslexic individuals present evidence of fluctuations in eye dominance. Our own research in this area (see Everatt, Bradshaw and Hibbard, in press), presents evidence for a number of dyslexic adults with poor stereo vision, but these dyslexics formed only a small sub-group (20 to 30 per cent) of the dyslexics assessed.

Stein and colleagues (see the recent review by Stein 1996; Stein and Walsh 1997) have further elaborated their views by proposing that variations in eye dominance are related to problems with eye movement control, and that both of these behavioural manifestations may be based on deficits within the magno-cellular visual pathway (see previous section on the perceptual span). This possibility is given credence by evidence for associations between measures of magnocellular pathway processes (such as flicker threshold) and binocular stability (Evans, Drasdo and Richards 1996), and the hypothesised dominance of magnocellular projections to the posterior parietal cortex which is involved in the control of normal eye movements (Stein and Walsh 1997). Deficits within the magnocellular pathway of the dyslexic may lead to the visual processing deficits discussed in the previous section and poor eye movement control. If the posterior parietal cortex is also involved in the orientation of spatial attention, magno-cellular deficits may also lead to attentional problems consistent with some form of neglect (Stein and Walsh 1997). For example, individuals with Balint's syndrome usually have posterior parietal lesions and present evidence of spatial neglect, particularly when eye–hand coordination is required (see Jeannerod 1997).

A final line of evidence which also relates attention and saccade programming to reading problems is that presented by Fischer and Weber (1990) who found that dyslexic readers show increases in the proportion of quickly initiated eye movements, termed express saccades. Express saccades have been posited as a measure of the ability to engage attention at a particular location. Those showing unusually large numbers of express saccades may be unable to engage attention to a location for sufficient time to enable complete information processing. Thus inappropriate handling of engaged states may be a fundamental problem for disabled readers; the eyes moving away from the word before complete integration of the word has been possible. Although the reliability of express saccades has been questioned (see Kingstone and Klein 1993), this view does connect the unusual eye movement patterns shown by disabled readers to problems with reading via a common underlying attentional malfunction. Such a relationship between attentional engaging/disengaging, eye movement programming and reading disability is also suggested by the transient/ magnocellular pathway deficit hypothesis (Breitmeyer 1993), potentially combining this effect with the findings for increased peripheral processing of information by the dyslexic (e.g. Geiger and Lettvin 1987). Further-more, if we assume that an engaged state is necessary for processing individual words, it might also explain why disabled readers have problems reading isolated words. Such an explanation for single word reading problems would suggest poor attention within tasks other than reading. We should find evidence for attentional problems, or increased distraction, in non-reading situations, and school children who are classed as poor readers and/or learning disabled are often described as easily distracted in class (Richey and McKinney 1978; Sinclair, Guthrie and Forness 1984). However, classroom distractibility can also be seen as a strategy rather than an attentional malfunction. A child experiencing difficulties with a task may assist her/himself by glancing around to see what other children are doing thereby gaining extra information (Turnure 1970). Thus, as with those arguments which posit eye movements as a cause of reading problems, dysfunctioning engaged and disengaged states need to be shown to occur outside the reading environment if they are to be considered as a precursor to reading problems rather than as a consequence. Given the questions raised about the procedures of Fischer and Weber (1990) by Kingstone and Klein (1993), we shall seek additional support from other paradigms.

Interference effects and inhibitory mechanisms

One such paradigm is the effect of interfering information on word and non-word (colours, objects, digits, etc.) processing. Increased selective attention should reduce the impact of information which is to be ignored. The degree of interference produced by such irrelevant information should provide some measure of how successful selective attention is. Consistent with this, groups who show large interference effects also show other features of attentional deficits; for example, schizophrenics, children with attention deficit disorders, patients with frontal lobe dysfunctions and those suffering from Parkinson's disease. Examples of measures of interference are numerous, but the best known, and perhaps the most appropriate to consider in the present discussion, is the Stroop interference effect (Stroop 1935). One reason for considering this effect above others is that the Stroop effect has been widely researched (see MacLeod 1991) particularly in relation to group differences (see Dempster 1991). We have already presented evidence for a relationship between Stroop interference and reading (see the section on perceptual span). The second advantage of the Stroop procedure is that this relationship can be examined in paradigms which are increasingly divorced from reading. The basic Stroop effect (which we will refer to as the colour-word paradigm) consists of presenting a word written in coloured ink, and requiring the subject to name the colour of the ink. Interference is caused by using a word which refers to a colour different from that of the ink (the word 'red' written in blue ink, for example). Colour naming times in this situation are slower in comparison to a situation where a block of colour is presented, or a non-meaningful string of letters (e.g. XXXX). The size of the Stroop effect may therefore be seen as an indication of the subject's ability to ignore the word and simply process the colour. Variations of the Stroop effect occur when subjects are required to name pictures which are presented with words referring to different but related concepts (e.g. the word 'horse' and a picture of a cow); this will be referred to as the picture-word condition. Manipulations which do not require word reading involve the subject counting digits, the number of which is different from the referent of the digit (e.g. counting 222), or naming colours presented as incongruously coloured objects (e.g. a blue banana); these will be referred to as the numerical Stroop and colour-object effects respectively. Given that there are a number of different experimental procedures, all of which should show effects of attentional processing, we will consider the evidence for the relationship between interference and reading, predicting that if reading and attention are interrelated, then there should be reliable signs for such a relationship across several versions of the Stroop task.

Reading development

There is a complex relationship between Stroop interference and reading experience. Initially, this relationship is such that interference increases with reading experience (Schiller 1966). As with findings related to the perceptual span, this is probably due to the development of word identification processes rather than changes in attention itself. For example, Ehri and Wilce (1979) gave beginning readers practice with unfamiliar words and found that interference from those words increased. Such interference is often viewed as the increase in the automatic encoding of the word, or the reduction of attentional processes within word identification. Attentional mechanisms may, therefore, form an important aspect of learning to read, but may play little part in reading once it is fully developed. However, once interference has reached some optimum level (around the age of 6 or 7 years), it starts to reduce through the rest of childhood until late teens/early adulthood, possibly increasing again from about 60 to 70 years of age (Comalli, Wapner and Werner 1962). These latter effects seem less likely to be due to the increased automaticity of word processing, since we would expect increased interference. More plausibly, reductions in interference are produced by improved attentional processes inhibiting a word response or focusing upon a colour response – i.e. the increased ability to control interference (see Ellis *et al.* 1989; Dulaney and Rogers 1994; Tzelgov, Henik and Berger 1992). Does this latter aspect of the Stroop effect tell us anything about reading ability?

We investigated the relationship between Stroop interference and reading ability within 24 subjects aged from 8 to 10; the age range within which interference should be maximum and decreasing. Reading ability was assessed by reading age as well as comprehension. The comprehension task involved subjects reading a short (approximately 100-word) age-appropriate passage (taken from Taylor, Morris and White 1994) and answering 10 questions related to the passage's content. Comprehension was based on the number of questions correctly answered out of a maximum of 10. Reading age was assessed by asking the subject to read a series of sentences aloud, the task stopping at the sentence where the child made their sixth reading error (previous errors being corrected by the researcher). The sentence at which the task stopped was converted into an estimate of reading age based on test norms. Subjects' reading ages varied from 8 to 10, consistent with chronological age.

For each of the Stroop conditions, the time taken to name the colour of 24 items presented on large pieces of card in four by six arrays was assessed. In the first condition, the items were coloured rectangles (six instances of red, blue, green and yellow) providing a measure of baseline colour naming. Subsequent conditions required the naming of the ink colour of incongruous colour-words (six instances of red, blue, green and yellow; Stroop interference), non-colour words (six instances of four words matched in terms of the number of letters and syllables, and word frequency with the colour-words; non-colour word interference), or line drawings of common objects (six repetitions of four line drawings taken from Snodgrass and Vanderwart 1980) presented in incongruous colours (e.g. a blue banana; colour-object interference). Interference was assessed by subtracting the three interference conditions from the baseline colour naming condition. The level of reverse Stroop interference produced by each subject was also assessed via the time taken to read the colour-words red, blue, green and yellow presented in black ink (baseline) or incongruous coloured ink (reverse Stroop interference); again the subtraction method was used to assess the magnitude of interference produced. (See Everatt, in preparation, for details of results.)

Correlations between the reading and interference measures are presented in Table 1.1. Increased interference was associated with lower reading scores, though the relationship was more consistent when comprehension rather than reading age was considered.

Table 1.1 Pearson correlation coefficients between the reading age or comprehension and the interference measures: traditional Stroop (Stroop), non-colour word (Non-col), colour-object (Object), and reverse Stroop (Reverse)

	Stroop	*Non-col*		*Object*		*Reverse*	
Reading age	0.03	−0.25		0.12	(0.36)	−0.17	(0.21)
Comprehension	−0.25	−0.05	(0.33)	−0.23	(0.30)	−0.39	(0.46)

Note
Figures presented in brackets present curvilinear correlation coefficients where these are larger than the linear correlations.

In a subsequent study, we further assessed the relationship between reading ability and the level of interference produced by Stroop-like tasks devoid of words across different ages to investigate developmental trends in the relationship between interference and reading. Subjects were aged from 6 to 12, and comprised three year groups: 31 year 2 school children, aged 6 to 7, 35 year 4 children, aged 8 to 9, and 32 year eight children, aged 11 to 12. Words were removed from the interference tasks to avoid the problem of the use of words in the traditional Stroop task producing spurious correlations with reading ability. Two interference tasks were used:

1 A version of the numerical Stroop task (based upon Francolini and Egeth 1980) in which subjects were required to count the number of coloured items in an array of letters and digits which were incongruous to the answer required (e.g. A33A). In the first condition the incongruous digits were coloured red and letters were presented in black ink, while in the second the letters were coloured and digits were in black. These manipulations varied

whether the incongruous information (the digits) had to be counted or not. A control condition excluding digits was also included (e.g. AXXA).

2   A task in which an array of letters formed the shape of a different letter, thereby producing two possible letter names from the same array (see Navon 1977). For example, a series of Ts arranged to form the shape of a letter H; the subject's task was to name the local feature – the letter T in the example. This condition was compared with a second in which letters formed larger non-letter shapes; e.g. a series of Ts forming a square shape – again the subject's response would be T.

Within both tasks, the number of items correctly completed per unit of time was measured – the unit of time was varied per year group to avoid ceiling/floor effects. In comparison with the control conditions, red digits, but not black digits, and global letter shapes showed reliable levels of interference which reduced across the age ranges assessed (see Everatt, in preparation), consistent with the data on the traditional Stroop effect. Interference from red digits was the only reliable effect by age 12.

   In addition to measuring the level of interference shown by each subject (calculated using the subtraction method of taking the appropriate control condition from each interference condition), we also assessed reading ability via a measure of comprehension involving subjects reading three short (approximately 100-words) age-appropriate passages and answering 10 yes/no questions related to the content of each passage (passages were taken from Taylor *et al.* 1994). Comprehension was based on the number of questions correctly answered out of a maximum of 30. Correlations between reading comprehension and the interference produced by red digits and global letters indicated modest relationships in the youngest children ($r = -0.22$ for digit interference; $r = -0.10$ for letter interference), no relationships in the 8 to 9 year olds ($r = -0.01$ for digit interference; $r = -0.03$ for letter interference), but reliable relationships at age 12 to 13 ($r = -0.40$ for digit interference; $r = -0.42$ for letter interference); the latter correlation suggesting that reduced interference is related to improved reading comprehension in the older subjects. However, as with the data from the previous study, non-linear correlations provided more consistent relationships across ages, varying around 0.2 to 0.4 for all age groups. These findings suggest that there is a modest relationship between interference and reading ability (see also Table 1.1) which increases with age.

Individual differences in reading ability

Although there is evidence for some common development between interference and reading, and for a relationship between increased reading ability and reduced interference (at least, in adolescents), our investigations of the same relationship in adult readers produced correlations which varied from 0 to -0.30. In these studies we gave the numerical Stroop task to four separate groups of subjects (30+ college students in each). Three of the four studies showed significantly

($p < .05$) slower counting times in the digit conditions used (222 or A33A) compared with the non-numerical symbol conditions (XXX or AXXA), consistent with previous research (see the previous sub-section; Hock and Petrasek 1973; Reisberg, Baron and Kemler 1980; Shor 1971; Windes 1968). (The one group who showed non-significant findings were given the basic numerical Stroop version, 222 versus XXX, and indicated a trend in the predicted direction; $p < .15$). Subjects were also given one of two measures of reading comprehension. The first comprehension test involved subjects filling in missing words within two passages; correct answers relied on the subject's comprehension of the text around the missing words (the same task was used by Everatt and Underwood 1994). The second comprehension test involved subjects answering six written questions about each of four 20-word passages of differing complexity, the subject being required to read each passage prior to answering its related questions. None of the studies found evidence for a significant relationship between comprehension and interference. Other studies have found larger correlations between Stroop interference and reading – for example, Toma (1991) found correlations as large as 0.38 between reading comprehension errors and interference errors in a picture-word version of the Stroop effect – but such increases could be explained by the common word processing factor within the tasks used. Our data, and the marginally significant correlations found by Toma (1991), suggest that such interference measures are poor predictors of adult subjects' reading ability.

The small relationship between interference measures and reading ability in adults may be due to the measure of interference used throughout these studies. To assess this possibility, and further investigate the relationship between selective attentional processes and reading, we selected a series of tasks which required the subject to inhibit visual information. Dempster (1991) has identified several cognitive tasks susceptible to interference; successful performance on these requiring the suppression of irrelevant information. These tasks included the Stroop task, priming paradigms and text processing.

In terms of the Stroop task, the inhibition of the irrelevant information (usually a word) would enhance performance, thereby providing one plausible explanation for reductions in Stroop interference with age, particularly given that the size of inhibitory effects varies with age in a manner consistent with the changes found in Stroop interference (see Tipper *et al.* 1989; Tipper 1991).

Evidence for the active inhibition of distractors in priming tasks has been found with a large range of visual stimuli: words, letters, pictures, colours and random shapes (see Houghton and Tipper 1994). The main paradigm used is that of negative priming. For example, Tipper (1985) used a negative priming task in which line drawings of common objects were presented in pairs, the subject's task being to respond to one of the objects and ignore (inhibit) the other. The sequence of presentation was manipulated such that an inhibited item on trial N became an item which has to be responded to on trial $N + 1$. Compared with conditions where there was no relationship between adjacent trials, the effect of inhibition leads to a delay in response time on trial $N + 1$.

In terms of text processing, Gernsbacher *et al.* (1990) used an ambiguous word task to measure how well comprehenders of varying ability suppressed irrelevant meanings of words. Subjects were required to silently read a sentence as it appeared word by word on a computer screen. A target word then appeared after the last word of the sentence, either immediately or following some delay, and the subjects' task was to verify whether the target word matched the meaning of the preceding sentence. Two types of negative response conditions were used. In the first, the last word of the sentence was an ambiguous word (e.g. 'He dug with the spade'), with the target word being consistent with the irrelevant meaning of the ambiguous word (e.g. 'ace'). In the second negative response condition, the last word of the sentence was replaced by a non-ambiguous word (e.g. 'He dug with the shovel'). A comparison between these two types of negative response conditions provided a measure of how able the subject was to inhibit the irrelevant meaning of the ambiguous word.

In the present study, we required 30 adult subjects to perform these three tasks: the traditional Stroop colour-word task (as used in previous studies outlined in this chapter), the negative priming task of Tipper (1985), and the ambiguous word paradigm of Gernsbacher *et al.* (1990). The Stroop and negative priming tasks were presented on sets of cards (one set per condition), whereas the ambiguous word task was computer generated to allow the precise timing between sentences and target words stipulated by Gernsbacher *et al.* (1990). In addition, the subject's reading comprehension ability was assessed using six passages and related questions taken from the same battery (Taylor *et al.* 1994) as used in the studies outlined in the previous sub-section.

The results (see Table 1.2) indicated evidence of Stroop interference, negative priming and ambiguous word effects, consistent with previous findings from the literature. To assess relationships between reading comprehension and inhibitory mechanisms, three derived variables were calculated, each taking the control condition from the experimental condition, producing measures of Stroop

Table 1.2 Average response times (in seconds), and correlations with reading comprehension

	Baseline condition (seconds)	Experimental condition (seconds)	Correlations with reading comprehension
Stroop	14.58 (3.08)	20.54 (4.25)	–0.32
Negative priming	34.65 (9.05)	37.78 (9.43)	0.28
Ambiguous word	0.93 (0.21)	0.98 (0.20)	–0.29

Notes
(i) Stroop, 'baseline' indicating the colour block condition, 'experimental' indicating the incongruous colour-word condition; (ii) negative priming, 'baseline' indicating no relationship between subsequent trials, 'experimental' indicating inhibited items on trial N require responses on trial $N + 1$; and (iii) ambiguous word tasks, 'baseline' indicating condition where the last word of the sentence was not ambiguous, 'experimental' indicating the condition where the last word was ambiguous. (For response times, standard deviations are presented in brackets.)

interference, negative priming, and ambiguous word effects. Table 1.2 also presents the results of correlations between these variables and reading comprehension. In each case, the relationship is consistent with the previous findings outlined in this chapter: higher comprehension scores are related to (i) lower Stroop interference scores, suggesting enhanced inhibition of words, (ii) larger negative priming scores, which suggests enhanced inhibition of the irrelevant object within the visual array; and (iii) lower ambiguous word effects, which may indicate that more able readers can inhibit irrelevant meanings of words better than poorer comprehenders (consistent with Gernsbacher *et al.* 1990). Again, however, these correlations are small and suggest only a marginal relationship between reading and inhibitory mechanisms in adult readers.

An unexpected finding of the present study was that none of the inhibition tasks were related to each other (Stroop interference with negative priming, $r = 0.03$; Stroop interference with the ambiguous word effect, $r = -0.10$; negative priming with the ambiguous word effect, $r = -0.07$). This suggests that further research is necessary to assess exactly what these inhibitory tasks are measuring – are there several independent inhibitory mechanisms, each explaining some level of variance in reading ability?

Reading disabilities

There is, however, evidence that the magnitude of Stroop interference may be different in disabled readers compared with their reading-able peers. Several studies indicate that differentially large Stroop interference is found in individuals classified as dyslexic (Everatt *et al.* 1997), poor readers (Das 1993) or learning disabled (Lazarus, Ludwig and Aberson 1984). The Everatt *et al.* study is worth considering further since it compared Stroop interference in a group of dyslexic children and two groups of control subjects, one matched with the dyslexics' chronological age, the other matched with their reading age. The findings were that the dyslexics showed larger Stroop interference than the chronological age controls, but showed interference roughly equivalent to the reading age controls; the reading disabled individuals showing attentional effects commensurate with their reading ability. However, not only did the disabled subjects show increased interference (compared with normal levels), they also showed slower word and colour naming skills, which presents the problem of comparing performance derived from an underlying measure which itself shows differential performance (see Chapman and Chapman 1978). For example, the Stroop effect is usually simply measured by taking an incongruous condition (a colour-word) and subtracting a baseline condition (a block of colour). However, say the underlying colour naming of one group is 10 seconds, whereas it is 1 second in another group. Now, say these increased to 20 seconds and 2 seconds, respectively, under colour-word Stroop condition. By the subtraction method, we would conclude that the first group shows 10 seconds of interference, whereas the second group shows only 1 second of interference. However, both groups have increased by 100 per cent over their base rate colour naming ability. The subtraction method biases the amount of interference shown by an initially slow responding group. One solution is to divide the incongruous condition by the baseline condition (see Everatt *et al.* 1997), although this method may not entirely solve the problem.

Additionally, there is evidence to indicate that the Stroop interference effect is not inflated within reading disabled children if word processing is removed from the task. For example, Alwitt (1966) used the colour-object interference task in which line drawings of objects were presented in incongruous colours, and found equivalent levels of interference for reading disabled and control subjects. A potential problem with this study, however, is that both colour and object had to be named, making it difficult precisely to interpret the nature of the interference being produced. Another study, by Denney (1974), used a task in which subjects had to name the correct colour of incongruously coloured objects, and found that some poor readers showed longer naming times compared with control subjects, although these differences were inconsistent across ages. A potential confound within Denney's study is the memory aspect of the procedure – recalling the correct colour of an object.

In our own studies, we used the colour-object paradigm which required nothing more than the naming of the presented colour. Comparisons of both young (8 to 10-year-old) and adult dyslexics with chronological-age matched non-dyslexics showed roughly equivalent levels of interference between able and disabled readers (see Table 1.3). However, interpretation of these data is complicated by the fact that neither dyslexic nor non-dyslexic children showed evidence of inter-ference from the line drawings. Although the data suggest that increased

Table 1.3 The time taken by dyslexic (D) and non-dyslexic (C) children and adults to name 24 colours presented in baseline conditions of coloured blocks (colour naming) or neutral black words (word reading) and several interference conditions

	Colour-object Stroop		Colour-object Stroop		Colour-word Stroop		Reverse Stroop	
	Child data			Adult data				
	D	C	D	C	D	C	D	C
	$N = 24$	$N = 24$	$N = 26$	$N = 26$	$N = 20$	$N = 20$	$N = 30$	$N = 30$
Baseline	20.42	15.04	22.71	20.99	24.69	23.65	23.77	23.64
condition	(5.31)	(3.76)	(5.52)	(5.04)	(4.58)	(4.68)	(4.45)	(4.76)
Interference	21.75	15.79	26.97	24.34	32.33	26.68	28.64	23.32
condition	(6.79)	(3.38)	(8.57)	(5.18)	(8.39)	(4.78)	(8.79)	(5.16)

Notes
(i) line drawings of objects whose natural colour is different from the one presented, where the task is to name the colour (colour-object Stroop); (ii) incongruous colour words, where the subject is required to name the colour (the traditional colour-word Stroop); (iii) incongruous colour-words, where the subject is required to read the colour-word (the Reverse Stroop). For the children, items were presented on two large cards, one for each condition, in a four by six array. For the adults, each item was presented on a separate card producing sets of 24 cards (one set per condition). (Standard deviations are presented in brackets.)

interference within reading disabled subjects may be confined to tasks involving word processing, clearly further research is necessary to critically assess this intriguing possibility.

In a related study, we compared college level dyslexics and controls on the colour-word paradigm to investigate possible developmental trends between the groups, and the possibility that Stroop interference reduces to 'normal' levels within reading compensated dyslexics. Subjects were tested on their colour naming, word reading and level of Stroop interference. We also tested the groups on reverse Stroop interference; a reverse Stroop effect being found when an incongruous colour interferes with the reading of a colour-word.

Twenty dyslexics and 30 non-dyslexics comprised the subjects. All of the dyslexic subjects had been diagnosed at college, and most had been diagnosed at school. Dyslexics also performed significantly worse than the non-dyslexics on spelling and pseudoword naming tasks. Comparison of performance on base rate colour naming and word reading indicated little difference between the groups, which is consistent with compensated adult dyslexics showing more normal naming times for well practised stimuli; although they still showed increased naming times with unfamiliar information, such as pseudowords. However, in terms of the interfering effect of an incongruous colour-word on colour naming, dyslexics showed much larger effects, replicating the findings with younger dyslexics (see Table 1.3).

Interestingly, there was also a trend for the dyslexics to show a reverse Stroop effect, although there was no such effect in the control subjects. The reversal of interference effects is rare, being confined to certain manipulations of the word, such as obscuring it in some way (Dyer and Severance 1972), or to extreme levels of practice (MacLeod and Dunbar 1988). Reverse Stroop effects in the more traditional colour-word method are usually confined to young children within the early stages of formal reading tuition (see Everatt, in preparation), or groups of subjects showing severe attentional problems, such as schizophrenics (Abramczyk, Jordan and Hegel 1983). These findings may suggest some form of attentional problem within dyslexics analogous with that found among schizophrenics. Alternatively, it is possible that reading high frequency words is compensated within these dyslexic adults such that naming speed is comparable to non-dyslexics' performance, but that this reading process is still not functioning at normal adult reading levels – the dyslexic may be achieving non-dyslexic levels of speed and accuracy but in qualitatively different ways. Whatever the reason for these effects, the findings indicate that increased interference among dyslexic subjects may not simply be due to differential base-rate performance, since roughly equivalent naming times were found in the colour naming task.

In explaining the increased colour-word Stroop effects with child dyslexics, Everatt *et al.* (1997) proposed that the effect was due to a problem within task-biased control mechanisms. This was based on the parallel distributed processing (PDP) model of Cohen, Dunbar and McClelland (1990), which includes control units that increase activity within processes leading to a particular output. In the Stroop paradigm, two outputs are possible – colour naming or word reading

– the control mechanism biasing the output towards one or the other of these and, in the process, reducing interference. The effect would be analogous to focusing attention on one response. Reduced efficiency within this control mechanism would reduce the effects of this bias, thereby not decreasing interference. Such a mechanism has also been used to explain increased interference among schizophrenic individuals (Cohen and Servan-Schreiber 1992), and findings that both adult dyslexics and schizophrenics present evidence of reverse Stroop effects may add weight to the suggestion of a common underlying deficit (see also Richardson and Stein 1993). The problem with this explanation is that it is not clear how Cohen and Servan-Schreiber's (1992) model would predict reverse Stroop effects. Also, the model predicts reduced performance in basic naming (colour and word), something which the adult dyslexics did not present. This explanation is therefore incomplete.

MacLeod and Dunbar (1988) found reversible interference effects from colours to shapes and from shapes to colours when they gave subjects moderate amounts of practice at naming shapes via colour names. They argued that such interference was produced by the automaticity of colour and shape naming. The present findings could also be explained if we assume word processing does not attain the same level of automaticity within the dyslexic as it does within the able reader. The usual criteria for a process being labelled 'automatic' are that it is fast, obligatory and does not use attentional resources. Given that the Stroop effect occurs within dyslexics, it seems that word processing is obligatory. Also, if words and colours can be processed by the dyslexics at similar speeds to non-dyslexics, it is unlikely that the speed of processing is under-developed. The best candidate would seem to be resource allocation. It is possible that the dyslexic requires more resources for the completion of tasks such as word reading or colour naming, or is less able to control those resources. Such a possibility could be tested by comparing dyslexics' and non-dyslexics' performance under dual task conditions. The resource allocation implications of this should be that the dyslexic possesses fewer resources to share between the two tasks, and so should experience greater difficulty in the dual task condition.

Dual tasks

The dual task methodology requires the subject to perform two tasks simultaneously. It derives from the view that there are limited cognitive resources available to complete some process or behaviour, and utilisation of some resources will produce a deficit for other behaviours. If one task requires more attentional resources than the remaining tasks, there should be a noticeable reduction in performance; for example the second task may be completed only after completion of the first. The main explanation for such dual task effects is presented in terms of attention. Either attention is the cognitive resource which is limited, or attention is necessary to switch resources from one behaviour to another. The dual task paradigm is therefore used to assess the efficiency of attention or, more usually, its requirement within tasks/behaviours; for example, no reduction in performance in a dual task procedure is taken as an indication that one behaviour can be performed with little or no drain on attentional resources – the behaviour may be performed automatically.

Reading development

As with most of the effects within reading development, the effects of resource limitations, as assessed by dual task paradigms, suggest that the role of attention reduces with experience. For example, Horn and Manis (1987) gave first, second, third and fifth grade school children word categorisation and identification tasks and compared their performance with those of college students. The important manipulation was that subjects were also required to perform a noise detection task (usually called a probe task) at varying delays following the word tasks. The results of this indicated that if the probe task occurred soon after a word task, reaction times to the probe were slower than those for probes which occurred some time after the word task. This effect was interpreted as indicating that both tasks require the same limited attentional resources. Since the word task has initial access to those resources the probe task may have to wait for them to become available, and so is delayed. Horn and Manis (1987) also found that there was a developmental trend in this effect. All subjects showed some effect of delayed probe reaction times, even the adult readers, indicating that attentional resources are required for all levels of reading experience. However, the first graders seemed to show the largest effects of reading resource requirements; a sharp fall being apparent in the delay effect from first to second graders. The reduction in the delay effect was not as dramatic from second grade to adulthood, but a reduction was still discernible. These data suggest a major role for attentional resources in beginning readers, a diminished role within readers who have had at least 1 to 2 years reading experience, and an even smaller, but observable, role within adult readers.

Individual differences in reading ability

Such effects of limited resources have also been found within processes as basic as letter identification among adult able readers (Paap and Ogden 1981), though they may be reduced as familiarity or experience with a letter string increases; for example Herdman (1992) found that resource effects were diminished with high frequency compared with low frequency words. This implies that we will not find a level of reading experience which is free from attentional resource requirements, and supports the hypothesis that resource requirements for word processing seem to reduce with experience and/or familiarity. Given such effects, there are sufficient grounds to assume that a relationship exists between attentional resources and reading ability: those with larger resources should be the more able readers. One study presenting some evidence for this is that of Herdman and LeFevre (1992). The attentional resource requirements of word processing were assessed by comparing the time taken to detect probes and name words within single task conditions with the time taken to detect primes and name words within a combined, dual task condition, the difference between single and dual task procedures being used to assess resource requirements for word naming. Large differences indicate larger resource requirements, small differences indicate fewer resource requirements. Herdman and LeFevre (1992) assessed reading ability as the increased use of phonology within word processing and increased reading span. The former task included word/nonword classifications (lexical decisions) of pseudohomophones, such as 'korn' and 'fite'; pseudowords which sound like words. The hypothesis is that able readers would process the sound (phonology) of the letter string more automatically and so would be slower to reject the pseudohomophones. The reading span task involved reading an increasing number of sentences (for a sense/nonsense decision) and then recalling the last word of each sentence. The subject's reading span was assessed as the number of final words correctly recalled in the correct order of presentation – analogous to measures of memory span. The results indicated that the dual versus single task measures of attentional resources were related to pseudohomophone effects and reading span. Although the effect was less obvious with reading span, other researchers have found evidence for a relationship between tests of attention and memory span (DeJong and Das-Smaal 1993). Such data suggest that there may be some range of reading ability that can be predicted by measures of attentional resources.

Two flaws with the Herdman and LeFevre (1992) study preclude the possibility of drawing firm conclusions. First, the view that reading ability is related to the increased use of phonology is a controversial one. Second, even if we accept that phonology usage and reading span are related to increased reading ability, all that the findings of the present study tell us is that measures of attentional resources are related to measures which are themselves less than perfectly related to reading ability. For example, those studies which find a relationship between reading span and reading ability (usually assessed by measures of comprehension) suggest that reading span predicts somewhere between 20 per cent and 30 per cent of the variation in reading ability (see Baddeley *et al.* 1985; Daneman and Carpenter 1983). Attentional resources may be involved only in this small proportion of reading ability, or, worse still, may have in common only those aspects of reading span not involved in reading. This is a much less powerful result than finding a direct relationship between attentional resource implications and reading ability.

Reading disability

Given inconclusive findings for experienced, adult readers, our final quest was for a possible correspondence between measures of dual task performance and reading disability. Probably the best dual task examples of possible attentional resource implications within disabled readers are in the research of Nicolson and Fawcett (1990), since this provides evidence of resource implications within non-reading tasks. Disabled readers were required to balance on a beam, or to do the same task while, for example, counting backwards in threes. Under single task conditions the dyslexics' performance was similar to the non-dyslexics'; however, under dual task conditions, the dyslexics performance was much poorer than that of the controls. Nicolson and Fawcett (1990) explain these findings in terms of a general deficit in automaticity, a process which has been proposed as an important aspect of reading development (see Frederiksen 1981; LaBerge and Samuels 1974; Wolf 1986). The automaticity argument considers that certain subprocesses within reading become automatic with experience. Automatic processes are usually those which are fast, obligatory, not under conscious control, and do not require attentional resources. The latter point is the most important here, since, if a subprocess of reading such as word identification does not require attentional resources, they can be used by other reading subprocesses, so improving the efficiency of that aspect of reading. If we consider that a subprocess of reading, such as text integration, is complex and requires large quantities of resources, removing some of those resources because of a lack of automaticity in word recognition could lead to poorer text integration. LaBerge and Samuels (1974) argue that reading would suffer if subprocesses, such as word recognition, required attentional resources, and the developmental findings referred to above seem to confirm the view that word identification processes require less attention as they become more practised. Nicolson and Fawcett (1990) argue that subprocesses which are automatic within the non-dyslexic may not be within the dyslexic because the dyslexic has an automaticity deficit and so requires attentional resources (referred to as conscious compensation) for the completion of these subprocesses. This will lead to fewer resources being available to other reading subprocesses, and consequently less efficient reading. They also argue that their findings in the dual task paradigm are explained by such a deficit. This is based on the idea that motor balance becomes an automatic skill within the non-dyslexic, leaving resources to accomplish the concurrent counting task. Motor balance in the dyslexic cannot be fully automatised, therefore resources are required for its successful completion. When these same resources are required to accomplish the counting task, one task is consequently less efficient and this, they argue, is the cause of the increased 'clumsiness' score produced by dyslexics in the dual task situation. The 'clumsiness' score was derived by counting the number of wobbles, foot movements and over-balancings.

The problem with the Nicolson and Fawcett (1990) hypothesis is that the concept of automaticity is not clearly defined. For example, the four basic aspects of an automatic process (that it is fast, obligatory, not under conscious control, and resource free) are differentiable: (i) Paap and Ogden (1981) found that some processes can be obligatory while still remaining attention demanding; (ii) Horn and Manis's (1987) data show differential developments in speed and resource requirements; (iii) Tzelgov, Herik and Berger (1992) show that an obligatory process can be modified by conscious expectations; (iv) MacLeod and Dunbar's (1988) findings suggest that whether a task shows obligatory processing or not cannot be differentiated by its relative speed of processing. Similar problems are encountered in studies of dyslexics. First, if the dyslexic's word processing were not obligatory, we would expect to find little or no Stroop interference, as we do with the beginning reader. Yet the level of interference shown by the dyslexic seems larger than the able reading non-dyslexic (see the previous section on interference). Word processing seems to be automatic, at least in terms of it being obligatory. Second, there appears to be little correspondence between speed of processing and the effects of obligatory coding, since increased interference in the compensated adult dyslexic is accompanied by roughly equivalent word and colour processing speed, and dyslexic children show equivalent interference levels but slower word naming times compared with reading-age matched controls. Third, we would expect a general automaticity deficit to be accompanied by slower task performance, since increased speed is a feature of an automatic process, and it is true that dyslexics have been shown to process information more slowly, for example in rapid automatic naming tasks (Denckla and Rudel 1976) – where the subject is expected to name a large number of items (letters, numbers, colours) as quickly as possible. However, the slower response may be task dependent. Nicolson and Fawcett (1994) compared the performance of dyslexic and non-dyslexic subjects in simple versus selective versions of a reaction time (RT) task. In the simple RT task, subjects had only to respond to a stimulus. In the selective RT task they had to respond to one stimulus but not to another. Both tasks involved the same button press, so only the aspect of selectivity varied between the two tasks. The results indicated no difference between the dyslexics and non-dyslexics in terms of the simple RT task, but poorer performance by the dyslexics in the selective RT task. The dyslexic's problems may not be due to simple speed of response, but rather to selecting the correct/appropriate response. Speed may be an aspect of the problem, but it is not the defining characteristic. If it is selection of the appropriate response that provides the dyslexic with problems, then slower performance in rapid automatic naming tasks may be due to recovery after a response or continuous changes in response selection. For example, Pashler's (1994) findings suggest that limited resources may affect serial performance (manual responses to a series of letters) as much as concurrent performance. Wolf (1986) gave dyslexics a naming task which involved rapid switches of attention between classes of items, for example from letters to numbers. This task differentiated the disabled reader (reading age at least 1.5 years behind chronological age at grade 2) from the average reader, even as early as pre-school. This concurs with the idea of the problem being in rapid changes in response selection. Similar problems with switches from one feature of a series of items (shape) to another (colour) are found with schizophrenics (for example on the Wisconsin Card Sorting Task; Weinberger 1988), suggesting some common underlying deficit.

If the dyslexic's problems are not simply at the levels of obligatory processing or speed, what about the other two aspects of automaticity: the lack of conscious control of an automatic process and its freedom from resource requirements? As yet, there is little data with which to locate the cause of these effects. Certainly, the evidence from developing readers indicates that resource requirements within reading reduce as experience increases. If the dyslexic experiences difficulties requiring extra resources to process words, or is unable to devote resources to the reading task (say, in controlling their allocation), or even has fewer resources at the outset, then reading failure would be expected. The first of these possibilities suggests that the resource implications are based on reading problems. We would, therefore, only expect to find resource implications in reading situations. The findings of Nicolson and Fawcett (1990) belie this. It is difficult to envisage balancing and counting backwards as reading related. So, we may pinpoint the problem as due to the allocation of resources, either because there are insufficient resources to enable allocation, or because their allocation is poorly controlled. If this is the basis of the dyslexic's problems, an interesting prediction is that effects associated with reading disabled/dyslexic individuals should be found in reading able/non-dyslexic individuals if the same resource allocation problems are induced experimentally. The dual task paradigm may provide one way to study this possibility further. For example, Everatt, Gwynne and Baker in an un-published study using the sorting version of the Stroop effect described in the previous section on interference effects found that if subjects were required to retain digits in memory for a subsequent ordered recall task, the reduction in Stroop interference found by increasingly separating colour and word is diminished. One explanation of these findings is that the memory span task uses resources which are required to ignore the peripherally placed word. However, if word and colour are combined, as in the traditional Stroop effect where the subject is naming the colour of the ink that a word is written in, there was no increase in Stroop interference. This is the case even if Stroop interference is reduced by practice prior to introducing the dual task condition. Although the dual task may reduce the ability to ignore peripherally presented words, it does not in itself increase interference, and therefore cannot be a full explanation of the differences in interference between dyslexics and non-dyslexics.

One potential complication for any study proposing a relationship between attention and reading is the possibility that attention is not a unitary concept. For example, Posner and Rothbart (1992) present an anatomical description of attention which proposes three separate, but interrelated, systems responsible for attentional processing. The first is analogous to selective spatial attention, and is responsible for orientating towards a position in space. The second is involved in detecting an event or selecting a response, and is posited as being responsible for overcoming Stroop-like conflict situations. The final system is involved in sustained attention. The findings of Everatt, Gwynne and Baker (unpublished) could therefore be explained if we consider that the dual memory span task reduced resources available for selective spatial attention, but not the ability to overcome the conflict conditions of the Stroop. The memory span task may affect one attentional system more than the other. However, one problem with the simple view that attentional focusing requires resources is that beginning readers appear to have the ability to focus attention to a spatial location (i.e. the fixated word), and ignore information around the fixated word, as evidenced by findings for a reduced perceptual span (see section on the perceptual span), yet beginning readers seem to require large amounts of attentional resources to process a word (see the sub-section on reading development in the present section).

If there are several attentional systems, then we may have to consider several possible relationships between attention and reading disability. For example, there may be one relationship with selective spatial attention and another with attending to relevant (or suppressing irrelevant) information to aid the production of an appropriate response. Problems with selective spatial attention may explain findings of abnormal selective attention in severely reading disabled individuals. The development of reading suggests that selective spatial attention is functioning within the beginning reader, and is required to aid the process of identifying and integrating words within a text. If such a process were not available, or deficient in some way, reading could be severely affected, perhaps remaining at beginning reader levels. This suggests that there is little reason to assume that variations in reading ability, beyond the level of reading impairment, would be related to measures of selective spatial attention; consistent with the evidence presented earlier in this chapter. A deficit within this system would also be expected to affect any task that involves the focusing of attention to a position on a page. This would include not only reading, but writing, mathematics, and even spatial reasoning. We would thus expect the individual who had problems within this attentional processor to show disabilities within a number of different tasks – evidence of a general learning disability. More typical, less severe, reading problems (such as among dyslexics) would not necessarily be predicted by a dysfunctioning spatial attention system. Perhaps the best evidence that they may is provided by the research of Brannan and Williams (1987) in which a target was presented to the left or right of fixation, preceded by a valid cue to the same side as the target or an invalid cue to the alternative side. The benefits of a valid cue, and the costs of an invalid cue, were used as a measure of the subject's ability to orientate attention towards one side of the visual field in readiness for the target; i.e. as a measure of selective spatial attention. Brannan and Williams (1987) found that poor readers used the peripherally placed cue less than good readers and adults, suggesting that the ability to orientate attention towards a location in space was less advanced in the poor reader. This is consistent with a deficit within the selective spatial attention system, although it could equally be consistent with a dysfunction in the commands required to orientate attention away from a position. Indeed, there is evidence that the conflict system may play an important role in initiating such commands (Posner *et al.* 1989; although see Pashler, Carrier and Hoffman 1989). Further research into the possibility of all reading disabled individuals showing signs of selective spatial attention abnormalities, and under what conditions these are apparent is, therefore, necessary.

Dysfunctions within the second attentional system (that related to the reduction of conflict situations) may be apparent for most reading disabled individuals, and may also be related to general reading ability (but see Segalowitz, Wagner and Menna 1992, who argue that frontal lobe processes may only be predictive of reading disability, not able reading). Reading ability (as measured by comprehension) seems to be related to the ability to disambiguate an ambiguous word (Gernsbacher *et al.* 1990), to suppress an inappropriate homophone, to inhibit an irrelevant word or picture within a visual episode, and incorrectly recalling that a related item appeared within an array of items (Gernsbacher and Faust 1991). A prediction from these conclusions would be that the disabled reader and dyslexic individual would show even poorer performance within these inhibition tasks. This paradigm would also provide a way of testing the functioning of the attentional system outside a reading environment (e.g. arrays of pictures followed by a target picture). This system would obviously be important within reading where understanding may rely on disambiguating some piece of information, or ignoring a related, but unimportant, concept. As such, it is likely to show a more widespread correspondence with reading abilities – from good to poor – although the size of the relationship is debatable. Deficits within this system may also lead to severe problems of selecting an intended action or context, as in schizophrenia, suggesting some correspondence between effects within this patient group and reading disabled individuals (as suggested in the present chapter); though the deficits expected with reading disabled subjects should be milder.

Summary and conclusions

A large amount of data have been covered in this chapter. The purpose of this final section is to summarise these and to present some form of overview for conclusions.

First, it was argued that the studies of the perceptual span provided evidence for attentional focus in reading, and evidence was sought for changes in the size of the span and its relation to reading ability. It seems that larger spans are related to more experienced, adult reading, but not variations within adult reading ability. The beginning reader is well able to focus attention on the text, and may require increased attentional focus to aid word processing. So problems with focusing attention may be a cause of reading problems. The evidence, however, is inconclusive as some studies found poorer attentional focus within reading disabled subjects, others not. The simplest explanation for these inconsistencies is that qualitatively different groups of reading disabled subjects are being tested, and our own data regarding Stroop interference suggest that increased processing of peripheral information is related to severe reading disability. Explanations based around a magnocellular/transient system deficit concur with findings of increased peripheral processing of form and colour which may not be restricted to severely disabled readers. The possibility that reading disabled individuals present increased peripheral processing therefore requires further research for its complete acceptance or rejection.

Second, it was proposed that abnormal parafoveal/peripheral processing of information may lead to problems with eye movement control, but little evidence was found to allow us to conclude that abnormal eye movement behaviour leads to poor reading ability in children or adults. Variability in eye movement behaviour is more parsimoniously explained as due to word processing problems rather than poor saccadic programming. Possible caveats to this conclusion may relate to the problems experienced by disabled readers. There is some evidence for differences between normal and disabled readers in terms of the optimal viewing position, the coordination of information between the eyes, and the initiation of rapid eye movements. These differences may be related to the orientation of attention or engaging/disengaging attention. Such processes have also been associated with the functions of the magnocellular visual pathway. As such, idiosyncratic peripheral processing and poor eye movement control may be identified as due to the same underlying problem.

Third, evidence was sought for relationships between reading ability and attention using measures of interference or inhibition; the Stroop task was the main example used. Findings indicate increases in interference with initial reading experience, assumed to be due to improved word processing skills, then decreased interference with further reading experience. This latter effect was explained as due to the focusing upon one aspect of the conflict situation, or inhibiting the other. Interference and reading experience/ability seem to co-vary. However, when age is controlled, small to moderate relationships between interference and reading ability are found, and whether this extends beyond word-based environments has yet to be confirmed. An additional problem was the data suggesting that different measures of inhibition were poorly correlated. Either some of the tasks employed were not measuring inhibition, or there are several inhibitory mechanisms, a line of argument which has resonance with the views that consider attention as separable at some level of functioning.

Finally, the chapter argued that Stroop interference effects were probably linked to control processes and/or resources and, to some extent, evidence from dual task paradigms support this view. Variations in the resources required for word processing are related to reading experience and possibly to adult reading ability, although the evidence suggests that the role played by attentional resources within adult reading is minor compared with beginning reading. There is also some correspondence between reading disability and dual task performance, which is often presented as evidence for automaticity deficits within dyslexics. Given problems with the definition of automaticity, such effects may be better theorised as due to problems with the control of an automatic process or the allocation of resources. Posner and Rothbart's (1992) view that the attentional system is composed of several separate processors may help clarify some of these findings. Problems within a selective spatial attention system would lead to unintended/irrelevant information being processed. This would lead to severe reading problems and/or general learning problems, given that this process may be an important part of beginning reading and that some disabled readers seem to show evidence of normal perceptual span. Variations within the attentional processor responsible for resolving conflict situations seem more likely to be related to general reading ability and less severe reading difficulties. Further evidence is required to assess these possibilities, and to account for those findings which are inconsistent with these conclusions.

References

Abramczyk, R.B., Jordan, D.E. and Hegel, M. (1983) 'Reverse Stroop effect in the performance of schizophrenics', *Perceptual and Motor Skills*, 56, 99–106.

Allport, A. (1987) 'Selection for action: Some behavioural and neurophysiological considerations of attention and action', in H. Heuer and A.F. Sanders (eds), *Perspectives
on Perception and Action*. Hillsdale, NJ: LEA.

Alwitt, L.F. (1966) 'Attention in a visual task among non-readers and readers', *Perceptual
and Motor Skills*, 23, 361–362.

Baddeley, A. (1993). 'Working memory or working attention', in A. Baddeley and L.
Weiskrantz (eds), *Attention: Selection, Awareness and Control*. Oxford: Oxford
University Press.

Baddeley, A., Logie, R., Nimmo-Smith, I. and Brereton, N. (1985) 'Components of fluent
reading', *Journal of Memory and Language*, 24, 119–131.

Boder, E. (1971) 'Developmental dyslexia: Prevailing diagnostic concepts and a new
diagnostic approach', in H. Myklebust (ed.), *Progress in Learning Disabilities*. New
York: Grune/Stratton.

Bouma, H. and Legein, Ch.P. (1977) 'Foveal and parafoveal recognition of letters and
words by dyslexics and average readers', *Neuropsychologia*, 15, 69–80.

Brannan, J. and Williams, M. (1987) 'Allocation of visual attention in good and poor
readers', *Perception and Psychophysics*, 41, 23–28.

Breitmeyer, B.G. (1993) 'Sustained (P) and transient (M) channels in vision: A review
and implications for reading', in D.M. Willows, R.S. Kruk and E. Corcos (eds), *Visual
Processes in Reading and Reading Disabilities*. Hillsdale, NJ: Erlbaum.

Brim, B.J. (1968) 'Impact of a reading improvement program', *Journal of Educational
Research*, 62, 177–182.

Brown, R.T. (1982) 'A developmental analysis of visual and auditory sustained attention
and reflection-impulsivity in hyperactive and normal children', *Journal of Learning
Disabilities*, 10, 614–618.

Brysbaert, M. and Meyers, C. (1993) 'The optimal viewing position for children with
normal and with poor reading abilities', in S.F. Wright and R. Groner (eds), *Facets of
Dyslexia and its Remediation*. North Holland: Elsevier.

Burr, D.C., Morrone, M.C. and Ross, J. (1994). 'Selective suppression of the magnocellular visual pathway during saccadic eye movements', *Nature*, 371, 511–513.

Carpenter, P.A. and Just, M.A. (1983) 'What your eyes do while your mind is reading',
in K. Rayner (ed.), *Eye Movements in Reading: Perceptual and Language Processes*.
New York: Academic Press.

Carver, R.P. (1985) 'How good are some of the world's best readers?', *Reading Research
Quarterly*, 20, 389–419.

Chapman, L.J. and Chapman, J.P. (1978) 'The measurement of differential deficit',
Journal of Psychiatric Research, 14, 303–311.

Chase, C.H. (1996) 'A visual deficit model of developmental dyslexia', in C.H. Chase,
G.D. Rosen and G.F. Sherman (eds), *Developmental Dyslexia: Neural, Cognitive and
Genetic Mechanisms*. Baltimore: York Press.

Cohen, J.D., Dunbar, K., and McClelland, J.L. (1990) 'On the control of automatic
processes: A parallel distributed processing account of the Stroop effect', *Psychological Review*, 97, 332–361.

Cohen, J.D. and Servan-Schreiber, D. (1992) 'Context, cortex and dopamine: A
connectionist approach to behavior and biology in schizophrenia', *Psychological
Review*, 99, 45–77.

Comalli, P.E., Wapner, S. and Werner, H. (1962) 'Interference effects of Stroop color-
word test in childhood, adulthood and aging', *Journal of Genetic Psychology*, 100,
47–53.

Conners, C.K. (1990) 'Dyslexia and the neurophysiology of attention', in G. Th. Pavlidis (ed.), *Perspectives on Dyslexia, volume 1*. Chichester: Wiley.

Cornelissen, P., Richardson, A., Mason, A., Fowler, S. and Stein, J. (1995) 'Contrast sensitivity and coherent motion detection measured at photopic luminance levels in dyslexics and controls', *Vision Research*, 35, 1483–1494.

Daneman, M. and Carpenter, P.A. (1983) 'Individual differences in integrating information between and within sentences', *Journal of Experimental Psychology: Learning, Memory and Cognition*, 9, 561–584.

Das, J.P. (1993) 'Differences in cognitive processes of children with reading disabilities and normal readers', *Developmental Disabilities Bulletin*, 21, 46–62.

Dautrich, B.R. (1993) 'Visual perceptual differences in the dyslexic reader: Evidence of greater visual peripheral sensitivity to color and letter stimuli', *Perceptual and Motor Skills*, 76, 755–764.

DeJong, P.F. and Das-Smaal, E.A. (1993) 'Factor structure of standard attention tests for children: A distinction between perceptual speed and working memory', *European Journal of Psychological Assessment*, 9, 94–106.

Dempster, F.N. (1991) 'Inhibitory processes: A neglected dimension of intelligence', *Intelligence*, 15, 157–173.

Denckla, M.B. and Rudel, R. (1976) 'Rapid "automatized" naming (RAN): Dyslexia differentiated from other learning disabilities', *Neuropsychologia*, 14, 471–479.

Denney, D.R. (1974) 'Relationship of three cognitive style dimensions to elementary reading abilities', *Journal of Educational Psychology*, 66, 702–709.

Dulaney, C.L. and Rogers, W.A. (1994) 'Mechanisms underlying reduction in Stroop interference with practice for young and old adults', *Journal of Experimental Psychology: Learning, Memory and Cognition*, 20, 470–484.

Dyer, F.N. and Severance, L.J. (1972) 'Effects of irrelevant colours on reading of colour names: A controlled replication of the "reversed Stroop" effect', *Psychonomic Science*, 28, 336–338.

Dykman, R.A. and Ackerman, P.T. (1991) 'Attention deficit disorders and specific reading disability: Separate but often overlapping disorders', *Journal of Learning Disabilities*, 24, 97–103.

Ehri, L.C. and Wilce, L.S. (1979) 'Does word training increase or decrease interference in a Stroop task?', *Journal of Experimental Child Psychology*, 27, 352–364.

Ellis, N.R., Woodley-Zanthos, P., Dulaney, C.L. and Palmer, R.L. (1989) 'Automatic-effortful processing and cognitive inertia in persons with mental retardation', *American Journal of Mental Retardation*, 93, 412–423.

Evans, B.J.W., Drasdo, N. and Richards, I.L. (1996) 'Dyslexia: The link with visual deficits', *Ophthalmic and Physiological Optics*, 16, 3–10.

Everatt, J. (1997) 'The abilities and disabilities associated with adult developmental dyslexia', *Journal of Research in Reading*, 20, 13–21.

Everatt, J. (in preparation) 'Inhibitory processes and reading ability'.

Everatt, J., Bradshaw, M.B. and Hibbard, P.B. (in press) 'Individual differences in reading and eye movement control', in G. Underwood (ed.), *Eye Guidance in Reading, Driving and Scene Perception*. Oxford: Elsevier.

Everatt, J., Bradshaw, M.B. and Hibbard, P.B. (in press) 'Visual processing and dyslexia', *Perception*.

Everatt, J., Gwynne, C. and Baker, D. (unpublished manuscript) 'Effortful processing in Stroop interference: Attentional aspects of an automatic process'.

Everatt, J. and Underwood, G. (1994) 'Individual differences in reading subprocesses', *Language and Speech*, 37, 283–297.

Everatt, J., Warner, J., Miles, T.R. and Thomson, M.E. (1997) 'The incidence of Stroop interference in dyslexia', *Dyslexia: An International Journal of Research and Practice*, 3, 222–228.

Fergusson, D.M. and Harwood, L.J. (1992) 'Attention deficit and reading achievement', *Journal of Child Psychology and Psychiatry*, 33, 375–385.

Fields, H., Newman, S. and Wright, S.F. (1993) 'Saccadic eye movements in dyslexia, low achievers, and competent readers', in S.F. Wright and R. Groner (eds), *Facets of Dyslexia and its Remediation*. North Holland: Elsevier.

Fischer, B. and Weber, H. (1990) 'Saccadic reaction times of dyslexic and age-matched normal subjects', *Perception*, 19, 805–818.

Flowers, J.H. and Stoup, C.M. (1977) 'Selective attention between words, shapes and colors in speeded classification and vocalization tasks', *Memory and Cognition*, 5, 299–307.

Francolini, C.M. and Egeth, H.E. (1980) 'On the non-automaticity of automatic activation: Evidence of selective seeing', *Perception and Psychophysics*, 27, 331–342.

Frederiksen, J. (1981) 'Sources of process interactions in reading', in A.M. Lesgold and C.A. Perfetti (eds), *Interactive Processes in Reading*. Hillsdale, NJ: Erlbaum.

Gatti, S.V. and Egeth, H.E. (1978) 'Failure of spatial selectivity in vision', *Bulletin of the Psychonomic Society*, 11, 181–184.

Geiger, G. and Lettvin, J.Y. (1987) 'Peripheral vision in persons with dyslexia', *New England Journal of Medicine*, 316, 1238–1243.

Geiger, G. and Lettvin, J.Y. (1989) 'Dyslexia and reading as examples of alternative visual strategies', in C. von Euler, I. Lundberg and G. Lennerstrand (eds), *Brain and Reading*. New York: Stockton Press.

Geiger, G., Lettvin, J.Y. and Zegarra-Moran, O. (1992) 'Task determined strategies of visual process', *Cognitive Brain Research*, 1, 39–52.

Gernsbacher, M.A. and Faust, M.E. (1991) 'The mechanism of suppression: A component of general comprehension skill', *Journal of Experimental Psychology: Learning, Memory and Cognition*, 17, 245–262.

Gernsbacher, M.A., Varner, K.R. and Faust, M.E. (1990) 'Investigating differences in general comprehension skill', *Journal of Experimental Psychology: Learning, Memory and Cognition*, 16, 430–445.

Goolkasian, P. and King, J. (1990) 'Letter identification and lateral masking in dyslexic and average readers', *American Journal of Psychology*, 103, 519–538.

Goulandris, N., McIntyre, A., Snowling, M., Bethel, J.-M. and Lee, J.P. (1998) 'A comparison of dyslexic and normal readers using orthoptic assessment procedures', *Dyslexia: An International Journal of Research and Practice*, 4, 30–48.

Grosser, G.S. and Spafford, C.S. (1989) 'Perceptual evidence for an anomalous distribution of rods and cones in the retinas of dyslexics: A new hypothesis', *Perceptual and Motor Skills*, 68, 683–698.

Hagen, J.W. (1967) 'The effects of distraction on selective attention', *Child Development*, 38, 685–694.

Herdman, C.M. (1992) 'Attentional resource demands of visual word recognition in naming and lexical decision', *Journal of Experimental Psychology: Human Perception and Performance*, 18, 460–470.

Herdman, C.M. and LeFevre, J.-A. (1992) 'Individual differences in the efficiency of word recognition', *Journal of Educational Psychology*, 84, 95–102.

Higgins, A.T. and Turnure, J.E. (1984) 'Distractibility and concentration of attention in children's development', *Child Development*, 55, 1799–1810.

Hill, R. and Lovegrove, W.J. (1993) 'One word at a time: A solution to the visual deficit in SRDs?', in S.F. Groner and R. Groner (eds), *Facets of Dyslexia and its Remediation*. North Holland: Elsevier.

Hock, H. and Petrasek, J. (1973) 'Verbal interference with perceptual classification: The effect of semantic structure', *Perception and Psychophysics*, 13, 116–120.

Hogaboam, T.W. (1983) 'Reading patterns in eye movement data', in K. Rayner (ed.), *Eye Movements in Reading: Perceptual and Language Processes*. New York: Academic Press.

Hogben, J.H. (1997) 'How does a visual transient deficit affect reading?', in C. Hulme and M. Snowling (eds), *Dyslexia: Biology, Cognition and Intervention*. London: Whurr Publishers.

Horn, C.C. and Manis, F.R. (1987) 'Development of automatic and speeded reading of printed words', *Journal of Experimental Child Psychology*, 44, 92–108.

Houghton, G. and Tipper, S.P. (1994) 'A model of inhibitory mechanisms in selective attention', in D. Degenbach and T.H. Carr (eds), *Inhibitory Processes in Attention, Memory and Language*. London: Academic Press.

Hulme, C. (1988) 'The implausibility of low-level visual deficits as a cause of children's reading difficulties', *Cognitive Neuropsychology*, 5, 369–374.

Ishida, T. and Ikeda, M. (1989) 'Temporal properties of information extraction in reading studies by a text-mask replacement techniques', *Journal of the Optical Society of America*, 6, 1624–1632.

Jackson, M. and McClelland, J. (1975) 'Sensory and cognitive determinants of reading speed', *Journal of Verbal Learning and Verbal Behavior*, 14, 565–574.

Jackson, M. and McClelland, J. (1979) 'Processing determinants of reading speed', *Journal of Experimental Psychology: General*, 108, 151–181.

Jeannerod, M. (1997) *The Cognitive Neuroscience of Action*. Oxford: Blackwell.

Just, M.A. and Carpenter, P.A. (1987) *The Psychology of Reading and Language Comprehension*. Boston: Allyn & Bacon.

Kennedy, A. (1987) 'Eye movements, reading skill and the spatial code', in J. Beech and A. Colley (eds), *Cognitive Approaches to Reading*. Chichester: Wiley.

Kingstone, A. and Klein, R.M. (1993) 'What are human express saccades?', *Perception and Psychophysics*, 54, 260–273.

Klein, R., Berry, G., Brians, K., D'Entremont, B. and Farmer, M. (1990) 'Letter identification declines with increasing retinal eccentricity at the same rate for normal and dyslexic readers', *Perception and Psychophysics*, 47, 601–606.

LaBerge, D. and Samuels, S.J. (1974) 'Towards a theory of automatic information processing in reading', *Cognitive Psychology*, 6, 293–323.

Latour, P. (1962) 'Visual threshold during eye movements', *Vision Research*, 2, 261–262.

Lazarus, P.J., Ludwig, R.P. and Aberson, B. (1984) 'Stroop color-word test: A screening measure of selective attention to differentiate LD from non LD children', *Psychology in the Schools*, 21, 53–60.

Levinson, H.N. (1989) 'Abnormal optokinetic and perceptual span parameters in cerebellar-vestibular dysfunction and learning disability or dyslexia', *Perceptual and Motor Skills*, 68, 35–54.

Lovegrove, W.J. (1991) 'Is the question of the role of visual deficits as a cause of reading disability a closed one? Comments on Hulme', *Cognitive Neuropsychology*, 8, 435–441.

Lovegrove, W.J., Martin, F. and Slaghuis, W. (1986) 'A theoretical and experimental case for a visual deficit in specific reading disability', *Cognitive Neuropsychology*, 3, 225–267.

Lovegrove, W.J. and Williams, M.C. (1993) 'Visual temporal processing deficits in specific reading disability', in D.M. Willows, R.S. Kruk and E. Corcos (eds), *Visual Processes in Reading and Reading Disabilities*. Hillsdale, NJ: Erlbaum.

MacLeod, C.M. (1991) 'Half a century of research on the Stroop effect: An integrative review', *Psychological Bulletin*, 109, 163–203.

MacLeod, C.M. and Dunbar, K. (1988) 'Training and Stroop like interference: Evidence for a continuum of automaticity', *Journal of Experimental Psychology: Learning, Memory and Cognition*, 14, 126–135.

Miles, T.R. (1993) *Dyslexia: The Pattern of Difficulties* (second edition). London: Whurr.

Navon, D. (1977) 'Forest before trees: The precedence of global features in visual perception', *Cognitive Psychology*, 9, 353–383.

Nicolson, R.J. and Fawcett, R. (1990) 'Automaticity: A framework for dyslexia research?', *Cognition*, 35, 159–182.

Nicolson, R.J. and Fawcett, R. (1994) 'Reaction-times and dyslexia', *Quarterly Journal of Experimental Psychology*, 47A, 29–48.

Olson, R.K. (1985) 'Disabled reading processes and cognitive profiles', in D. Gray and J. Kavanagh (eds), *Biobehavioral Measures of Dyslexia*. Parkton, MD: York Press.

Olson, R.K. Kliegl, R. and Davidson, B.J. (1983) 'Dyslexic and normal readers' eye movements', *Journal of Experimental Psychology: Human Perception and Performance*, 9, 816–825.

O'Regan, J.K. and Jacobs, A.M. (1992) 'Optimal viewing position effect in word recognition: A challenge to current theory', *Journal of Experimental Psychology: Human Perception and Performance*, 18, 185–197.

O'Regan, J.K. and Levy-Schoen, A. (1987) 'Eye-movement strategy and tactics in word recognition and reading', in M. Coltheart (ed.), *Attention and Performance XII: The Psychology of Reading*. Hove: LEA.

Paap, K.R. and Ogden, W.C. (1981) 'Letter encoding is an obligatory but capacity-demanding operation', *Journal of Experimental Psychology: Human Perception and Performance*, 7, 518–527.

Pashler, H. (1994) 'Overlapping mental operations in serial performance with preview', *Quarterly Journal of Experimental Psychology*, 47A, 161–191.

Pashler, H., Carrier, M. and Hoffman, J. (1993) 'Saccadic eye movements and dual-task interference', *Quarterly Journal of Experimental Psychology*, 46A, 51–82.

Patberg, J.P. and Yonas, A. (1978) 'The effect of the reader's skill and the difficulty of the text on the perceptual span in reading', *Journal of Experimental Psychology: Human Perception and Performance*, 4, 545–552.

Pavlidis, G.Th. (1981) 'Sequencing, eye movements and the early objective diagnosis of dyslexia', in G.Th. Pavlidis and T.R. Miles (eds), *Dyslexia Research and its Applications to Education*. London: Wiley.

Pennington, B.F., Groisse, D. and Welsh, M.C. (1993) 'Contrasting cognitive deficits in attention deficit hyperactivity disorder versus reading disability', *Developmental Psychology*, 29, 511–523.

Perry, A.R., Dember, W.N., Warm, J.S. and Sacks, J.G. (1989) 'Letter identification in normal and dyslexic children: A verification', *Bulletin of the Psychonomic Society*, 27, 445–448.

Posner, M.I. (1980) 'Orienting of attention', *Quarterly Journal of Experimental Psychology*, 32, 3–25.

Posner, M.I. and Rothbart, M.K. (1992) 'Attentional mechanisms and conscious experience', in A.D. Milner and M.D. Rugg (eds), *The Neuropsychology of Consciousness*. London: Academic Press.

Posner, M.I., Sandson, J., Dhawan, M. and Shulman, G.L. (1989) 'Is word recognition automatic? A cognitive anatomical approach', *Journal of Cognitive Neuroscience*, 1, 50–60.

Raymond, J. (1994) Talk given to the Department of Psychology, University of Wales, Bangor.

Raymond, J.E., Shapiro, K.L. and Arnell, K.M. (1992) 'Temporary suppression of visual processing in an RSVP task: An attentional blink?', *Journal of Experimental Psychology: Human Perception and Performance*, 18, 849–860.

Rayner, K. (1979) 'Eye guidance in reading: Fixation locations within words', *Perception*, 8, 21–30.

Rayner, K. (1986) 'Eye movements and the perceptual span: Evidence for dyslexic topology', in G.Th. Pavlidis and D.F. Fisher (eds), *Dyslexia: Its Neuropsychology and Treatment*. New York: Wiley.

Rayner, K. and Bertera, J.H. (1979) 'Reading without a fovea', *Science*, 206, 468–469.

Rayner, K. and Pollatsek, A. (1981) 'Eye movement control during reading: Evidence for direct control', *Quarterly Journal of Experimental Psychology*, 33A, 351–373.

Rayner, K. and Pollatsek, A. (1987) 'Eye movement control during reading', in M. Coltheart (ed.), *Attention and Performance XII: The Psychology of Reading*. Hove: LEA.

Rayner, K. and Pollatsek, A. (1989) *The Psychology of Reading*. Englewood Cliffs, NJ: Prentice-Hall.

Rayner, K., Murphy, L.A., Henderson, J.M. and Pollatsek, A. (1989) 'Selective attentional dyslexia', *Cognitive Neuropsychology*, 6, 357–378.

Reisberg, D., Baron, J. and Kemler, D.G. (1980) 'Overcoming Stroop interference: The effects of practice on distractor potency', *Journal of Experimental Psychology: Human Perception and Performance*, 6, 140–150.

Richardson, A.J. and Stein, J.F. (1993) 'Personality characteristics of adult dyslexics', in S.F. Wright and R. Groner (eds), *Facets of Dyslexia and Remediation*. North Holland: Elsevier Science Publishers.

Richey, D.D. and McKinney, J.D. (1978) 'Classroom behavioral styles of learning disabled boys', *Journal of Learning Disabilities*, 11, 297–302.

Ross, S.M. and Ross, L.E. (1987) 'Children's and adults' predictive saccades to square-wave targets', *Vision Research*, 27, 2177–2180.

Satz, P. and Morris, R. (1981) 'Learning disability subtypes: A review', in F.J. Pirozzolo and M.C. Wittrock (eds), *Neuropsychological and Cognitive Processes in Reading*. New York: Academic Press.

Schiller, P.H. (1966) 'Developmental study of color-word interference', *Journal of Experimental Psychology*, 72, 105–108.

Segalowitz, S.J., Wagner, W.J. and Menna, R. (1992) 'Lateral versus frontal ERP predictors of reading skill', *Brain and Cognition*, 20, 85–103.

Shaywitz, B.A., Fletcher, J.M. and Shaywitz, S.E. (1994) 'Interrelationships between reading disability and attention deficit-hyperactivity disorder', in A.J. Capute, P.J. Accardo and B.K. Shapiro (eds), *Learning Disabilities Spectrum: ADD, ADHD and LD*. Baltimore: York Press.

Shea, S.L. (1992) 'Eye movements: Developmental aspects', in E. Chekaluk and K.R. Llewellyn (eds), *The Role of Eye Movements in Perceptual Processes*. North Holland: Elsevier Scientific Publishers.

Shor, R.E. (1971) 'Symbol processing speed differences and symbol interference effects in a variety of concept domains', *Journal of General Psychology*, 85, 187–205.

Sinclair, E., Guthrie, D. and Forness, S.R. (1984) 'Establishing a connection between severity of learning disabilities and classroom attention problems', *Journal of Educational Research*, 78, 18–21.

Slaghuis, W.L. and Pinkus, S.Z. (1993) 'Visual backward masking in central and peripheral vision in late-adolescent dyslexics', *Clinical Vision Science*, 8, 187–199.

Snodgrass, J.G. and Vanderwart, M. (1980) 'A standardized set of 260 pictures: Norms for name agreement, image agreement, familiarity, and visual complexity', *Journal of Experimental Psychology: Human Learning and Memory*, 6, 174–215.

Solman, R.T. and May, J.G. (1990) 'Spatial localization discrepancies: A visual deficiency in poor readers', *American Journal of Psychology*, 103, 243–263.

Stanley, G., Smith, G.A. and Howell, E.A. (1983) 'Eye-movements and sequential tracking in dyslexic and control children', *British Journal of Psychology*, 74, 181–187.

Stein, J. (1993) 'Visuospatial perception in disabled readers', in D.M. Willows, R.S. Kruk and E. Corcos (eds), *Visual Processes in Reading and Reading Disabilities*. Hillsdale, NJ: Erlbaum.

Stein, J. (1996) 'Visual system and reading', in C.H. Chase, G.D. Rosen and G.F. Sherman (eds), *Developmental Dyslexia: Neural, Cognitive and Genetic Mechanisms*. Baltimore: York Press.

Stein, J. and Walsh, V. (1997) 'To see but not to read: The magnocellular theory of dyslexia', *Trends in Neuroscience*, 20, 147–152.

Stroop, J.R. (1935) 'Studies of interference in serial verbal reactions', *Journal of Experimental Psychology*, 18, 643–662.

Taylor, S.E., Morris, H.F. and White, C.E. (1994) *Ober2 Visagraph Test Booklet*. New York: Taylor Associates.

Tipper, S.P. (1985) 'The negative priming effect: Inhibitory priming by ignored objects', *Quarterly Journal of Experimental Psychology*, 37A, 571–590.

Tipper, S.P. (1991) 'Less attentional selectivity as a result of declining inhibition in older adults', *Bulletin of the Psychonomic Society*, 29, 45–47.

Tipper, S.P., Bourque, T., Anderson, S. and Brehaut, J.C. (1989) 'Mechanisms of attention: A developmental study', *Journal of Experimental Child Psychology*, 48, 353–378.

Toma, R.J. (1991) 'Correlates of modified Stroop tasks, reading ability and mental ability among college students', *Perceptual and Motor Skills*, 72, 961–962.

Turnure, J.E. (1970) 'Childrens' reactions to distractions in a learning situation', *Developmental Psychology*, 2, 115–122.

Tzelgov, J., Henik, A. and Berger, J. (1992) 'Controlling Stroop effects by manipulating expectations for color words', *Memory and Cognition*, 20, 727–735.

Underwood, G. and Everatt, J. (1992) 'The role of eye movements in reading', in E. Chekaluk and K.R. Llewellyn (eds), *The Role of Eye Movements in Perceptual Processes*. North Holland: Elsevier Scientific Publishers.

Underwood, G., Hyönä, J. and Niemi, P. (1987) 'Scanning patterns on individual words during the comprehension of sentences', in J.K. O'Regan and A. Levy-Schoen (eds), *Eye-movements: From Physiology to Cognition*. Amsterdam: North-Holland.

Underwood, N.R. and Zola, D. (1986) 'The span of letter recognition of good and poor readers', *Reading Research Quarterly*, 21, 6–19.

van der Leij, A. (1993) 'The development of the autonomous lexicon of reading disabled students', in S.F. Wright and R. Groner (eds), *Facets of Dyslexia and its Remediation*. North Holland: Elsevier.

Vrana, F. (1980) 'Selective attention deficit in learning disabled children: A cognitive interpretation', *Journal of Learning Disabilities*, 7, 387–391.

Watson, B.U., Goldgar, D.E. and Ryschon, K.L. (1983) 'Subtypes of reading disability', *Journal of Clinical Neuropsychology*, 5, 377–399.

Weinberger, D.R. (1988) 'Schizophrenia and the frontal lobes', *Trends in Neuroscience*, 11, 367–370.

Whyte, J. (1994) 'Attentional processes and dyslexia', *Cognitive Neuropsychology*, 11, 99–116.

Windes, J.D. (1968) 'Reaction time for coding and naming of numerals', *Journal of Experimental Psychology*, 78, 318–322.

Wolf, M. (1986) 'Rapid alternating stimulus naming in the developmental dyslexias', *Brain and Language*, 27, 360–379.

2   The effects of different types of text presentation on children with a specific reading disability

Karen Pepper and William Lovegrove

Introduction

A significant minority of children experience difficulties in learning to read in spite of having normal intelligence, normal educational opportunities, no brain damage, and no gross behavioural problems. Children like these who read at a standard which is at least 2 years behind the level expected for their age and intelligence are regarded as having a specific reading disability (SRD). The research to be described investigates whether SRD children benefit from certain types of text presentation. The rationale for these different text presentations is derived from research showing that many SRDs have a subtle visual problem that does not show up in standard optometric tests.

For some years the commonly accepted view within the reading disability literature has been that normal and specifically disabled readers (SRDs) do not differ systematically in terms of visual processing (Benton 1962; Vellutino 1979a, 1979b). Extensive work over the last 10 years in a number of laboratories, however, has clearly demonstrated that the two groups do differ in terms of visual processing. Much of this work has been conducted within a transient/sustained visual subsystems framework.

The transient and sustained subsystems in vision

The properties of these two subsystems within the visual system have been identified and are shown in Table 2.1. An extensive discussion of the properties of these systems and how they are identified can be found in Breitmeyer (1988). Breitmeyer also discusses the evidence indicating the physiological basis of these two systems. (It should be noted that the literature in this area sometimes uses the terms 'magnocellular pathway' and 'parvocellular pathway' in reference to the transient and sustained subsystems respectively.)

The transient system is predominantly a flicker or motion detecting system transmitting information about stimulus change and general shape. The spatial information it transmits is coarse and thus well suited for transmitting peripheral information in reading. The sustained system is predominantly a detailed pattern detecting system transmitting information about stationary stimuli. In reading, the

Table 2.1 Properties of the sustained and transient visual systems

Sustained system	Transient system
Most sensitive to high spatial frequencies.	Most sensitive to low spatial frequencies.
Most sensitive to low temporal frequencies, (e.g. stationary stimuli).	*Most sensitive to high temporal frequencies, (e.g. moving or flickering stimuli).*
Less sensitive to contrast.	Sensitive even to low contrasts.
Able to distinguish between colours.	*Effectively 'colour-blind', but may be enhanced by blue light, and inhibited by red light.*
Slow transmission times.	Fast transmission times.
Responds throughout stimulus presentation.	*Responds at stimulus onset and offset.*
Predominates in central vision.	Predominates in peripheral vision.
Has relatively small receptive fields.	*Has relatively large receptive fields.*
May inhibit transient system.	May inhibit sustained system.

sustained system should be most important in extracting detailed information during fixations and the transient system in extracting general information from the periphery. Below we shall see that the two systems also interact in important ways.

There is evidence, both physiological (Singer and Bedworth 1973) and psychophysical that the two systems may inhibit each other (Breitmeyer and Ganz 1976). In particular, if the sustained system is responding when the transient system is stimulated, the transient system will terminate the sustained activity. This is believed to be part of the basis of saccadic suppression, which is important to the reading process.

Transient and sustained subsystems and reading

When reading, the eyes move through a series of rapid eye movements called saccades separated by fixation intervals when the eyes are stationary. Saccadic eye movements function to bring unidentified regions of text into foveal vision for detailed analysis during fixations.

The role of transient and sustained subsystems in reading has been considered by Breitmeyer (Breitmeyer 1980, 1983, 1988; Breitmeyer and Ganz 1976). He argued that clear vision on each fixation results from transient-on-sustained inhibition. Consequently, transient-sustained channel interaction seems to be important in facilitating normal reading. Any problem in either the transient or the sustained system or in the way they interact may have harmful consequences for reading. Specifically, any weakness in the transient system may lead to problems in either integrating information from successive fixations, or integrating peripheral and central information, or both.

Transient and sustained processing in SRDs and controls

The possibility of a visual deficit in SRDs has recently been investigated within the framework outlined above. Much of this research has been directed at the functioning of the transient and sustained systems in normal and specifically disabled readers.

On measures of visible persistence it has been shown that SRDs aged from 8 to 15 years have a significantly smaller increase in persistence duration with increasing spatial frequency than do controls (Badcock and Lovegrove 1981; Lovegrove, Heddle and Slaghuis 1980b; Slaghuis and Lovegrove 1985). When visible persistence is measured in both groups under conditions which reduce transient system activity (using a uniform field flicker mask), persistence differences between the groups essentially disappear (Slaghuis and Lovegrove 1984). This finding suggests that SRDs may differ from controls mainly in the functioning of their transient systems.

The two groups have also been compared on a task which measures the minimum contrast required to see a pattern. It has been shown that SRDs are less sensitive than controls at low (1.0 to 4 c/deg) spatial frequencies (Lovegrove *et al.* 1980; Lovegrove *et al.* 1982; Martin and Lovegrove 1984). In some studies the two groups do not differ in contrast sensitivity at higher (12 to 16 c/deg) spatial frequencies (Lovegrove *et al.* 1980a) and in others SRDs are slightly more sensitive than controls in that range at low luminance levels (Lovegrove *et al.* 1982; Martin and Lovegrove 1984). At high luminances SRDs have been found to be less sensitive than controls at high spatial frequencies. Once again inhibition of the transient system by uniform-field masking influenced the SRDs less than controls (Martin and Lovegrove 1988) thus providing further support for a difference between the groups in transient system function.

Similarly, in a number of experiments SRDs have been shown to be less sensitive than controls to counterphase flicker (Brannan and Williams 1988b; Martin and Lovegrove 1987, 1988). This is regarded as a direct measure of transient system processing. Additional support for differences between the groups in transient but not sustained system processing has been found in a number of recent visual evoked potential studies (Lehmkuhle *et al.* 1993; Livingstone *et al.* 1991; May *et al.* 1991b; May, Dunlap and Lovegrove 1991a)

There is, therefore, considerable evidence to support the existence of a transient system difference in many dyslexics.[1] What is of interest, of course, is whether such differences may influence the reading process. As argued above, a transient system deficit would predict difficulties for SRDs in integrating information across fixations or with integrating peripheral and central information. (Even though these two situations may differ, they are often the same.) Hill and Lovegrove (1992) argued that this should be apparent in SRDs if the load on the transient system was varied by manipulating the amount of information in the periphery to be integrated. This prediction led to the hypothesis that many SRDs may benefit from having text presented *one word at a time*.

The 'one word at a time' advantage

Over the years there have been anecdotal reports from parents and teachers that SRDs read more easily if text is presented one word at a time. Typically, this is achieved by the reader laying a piece of card with a small window cut out of it over the text to be read. The card is moved along the line of text as it is read, exposing only the word currently being read and covering the surrounding text. This reported phenomenon suggests that the presence of text around the fixated word may somehow interfere with the perception of that word, although the nature of this interference was not immediately clear.

A number of recent experimental studies have also found that many SRDs perform best when text is presented one word at a time rather than a whole line at a time (Hill and Lovegrove 1992; Lovegrove and Macfarlane 1990; Williams, LeCluyse and Faucheux, reported in Williams and Lovegrove 1990). These experiments have used computers to achieve more controlled *whole line* and *one word at a time* text presentations. Interestingly, these experiments have also sometimes found that normal readers perform somewhat worse with *one word at a time* text than with *whole line* text.

Williams *et al.* (reported in Williams and Lovegrove 1990) compared the performance of SRDs and normal readers in reading stories with three different types of computer-based text presentation. The first type involved presenting text one word at a time in the centre of the computer screen. The second condition was also one word at a time, but with the words printed left to right across the screen in sequence, as in a moving window display. The third condition presented a whole line of text at a time. Using comprehension as the measure of reading performance, these experimenters found that the SRDs performed significantly worse with the *whole line* presentation compared with the two *one word* conditions. The normal readers performed about equally in all three conditions.

These experimenters investigated the possible role of a transient visual subsystem deficit in the SRDs' results by modifying the text stimuli in ways that should favour transient subsystem functioning. Such modifications may compensate for any weakness in the transient subsystems of the SRDs. They found that by blurring the text (which makes the low spatial frequency components of the stimulus more prominent) or by using blue coloured text they could produce significant improvements in the SRDs' performance in the *whole line* condition. In fact the SRDs' results in the *whole line* condition with these modified stimuli compared favourably with their results in the *one word* conditions with un-modified stimuli, and with the results of normal readers in the *whole line* condition with unmodified stimuli. On the other hand, they found that stimuli that did not favour the transient subsystem, such as unblurred white or red text, produced relatively poor reading performances in the SRDs (Williams *et al.*, reported in Williams & Lovegrove 1990). Since stimulus blurring, blue coloured text, and *one word at a time* text presentation produce similar reading improvements in SRDs, it seems reasonable to suspect that *one word* presentation works well for SRDs because it somehow compensates for deficiencies in their transient subsystems.

The study by Williams *et al.* (reported in Williams and Lovegrove 1990) used comprehension as the measure of reading ability. In related studies looking at the effects of different types of text presentation, Lovegrove and Macfarlane (1990) found that SRDs also made fewer reading errors and read at a faster rate with *one word at a time* presentation compared with *whole line* presentation; and Hill and Lovegrove (1992) also found that SRDs made their fewest number of reading errors in *one word* conditions.

Hill and Lovegrove (1992) also attempted to demonstrate a connection between the *one word* advantage for SRDs and a possible transient subsystem deficit. In experiment 1 of their study, using flicker contrast sensitivity as a measure of transient subsystem functioning, they found that SRDs were indeed less sensitive to flicker than normal readers. Furthermore, they found a small negative correlation between flicker sensitivity and the *one word* advantage for their sample, suggesting that there is some relationship between the *one word* advantage and a deficient transient subsystem.

Attempts have also been made to use *one word* text presentations as an aid to the remediation of SRDs (Geiger and Lettvin 1987; Geiger, Lettvin and Fahle 1994). These studies involved having adult and child SRD subjects practise reading by moving a card with a small window cut out of it along the lines of printed text, as well as practising a range of tasks intended to improve hand–eye coordination. These researchers found that their subjects achieved significant improvements in their reading after 3 months of this training regimen.

The first purpose of the present study is to corroborate the findings of these previous studies; namely, that poor readers have a transient subsystem deficit, and that poor readers perform best with *one word at a time* text presentations. The possible causes of the latter effect will be investigated by examining the types of errors that good and poor readers make under different text presentation conditions. The second purpose of this study is to test whether giving reading training to SRDs using *one word at a time* text presentation produces greater improvements in their reading than training with *whole line* text.

The study consists of three stages. In the first stage a group of SRDs and a reading-age-matched group of normal readers are compared on a series of reading, intelligence and visual measures. In the second stage the SRDs are divided into two training groups, and receive either *whole line* or *one word at a time* reading training sessions. In the third stage the SRDs' reading standard is re-tested, and the results of the two training groups compared to see whether the different types of text presentation produce differing amounts of improvement.

Experiment stage 1: pre-training comparisons between SRDs and normal readers

Method

Subjects

There were 12 SRDs, recommended as poor readers by their teachers, and more than 1 year behind the average reading standard expected for their age as measured by the accuracy score on the Neale Analysis of Reading Ability. Six normal readers were also selected, recommended as normal readers by their teachers, and at or above the average reading standard expected for their age, as measured by the accuracy score on the Neale Analysis of Reading Ability. All subjects were of at least average intelligence, as measured by WISC-R subtests. The SRD and normal reader groups were all of primary school age, and were matched in reading age as measured by the Neale Analysis of Reading Ability accuracy score. This means that the normal reader group was, on average, somewhat younger than the SRD group. (See Table 2.2 for details of the two groups.)

Apparatus and procedure

General intelligence test. Four subtests of the Wechsler Intelligence Scale for Children – Revised (WISC-R) (Wechsler 1974) were completed by each child. These were Vocabulary and Digit Span (verbal subtests), and Block Design and Coding (non-verbal Performance subtests). The scaled scores were calculated for each of these subtests, and an estimated full scale IQ score was calculated by the deviation quotient method described by Tellegen and Briggs (1967).

Reading tests. The Neale Analysis of Reading Ability – Revised (NARA-R), Form 1 (Neale 1988) was used to measure oral reading accuracy, comprehension and reading speed.

Castles and Coltheart's lists (Castles and Coltheart 1993) were used to measure oral reading of regularly and irregularly spelled words, and nonsense words.

The Processing Power Program (Taylor, White and Reilly 1983) was used to measure the subjects' performance with different types of text presentation. This computer software presents stories on Apple IIe (and compatible) personal computers. The stories are graded in difficulty from Kindergarten to grade 6 standard, and may be presented at set speeds (from 30 words per minute). Each story includes 20 multiple choice comprehension questions presented at intervals during the story. Stories may be presented using one of three formats:

 (i) whole line at a time;
(ii) one word at a time, across the screen;
(iii) one word at a time, in the centre of the screen.

Each subject was given a practice story presentation (one word at a time, across screen), to familiarise them with the procedure and to determine the appropriate

Table 2.2 Means, standard deviations and *t*-test results for pre-training tests, comparing SRD and normal-reader control groups

Test		SRDs	Controls	t
		(n = 12)	(n = 6)	
Age (in months)	Mean	121.3	87.8	4.89[c]
	SD	12.6	15.7	
WISC-R subtests:				
Vocabulary		8.4	12.0	3.01[b]
		2.4	2.3	
Digit Span		7.0	10.8	2.74[a]
		3.0	2.1	
Block Design		10.9	13.5	1.92
		3.0	1.8	
Coding		7.8	9.0	0.89
		2.9	3.4	
Neale Analysis of Reading Ability:				
Accuracy (in months)		93.0	100.8	1.16
		13.6	13.3	
Comprehension (months)		100.3	97.7	0.29
		18.5	15.6	
Rate (in months)		96.5	98.7	0.14
		30.4	29.0	

Notes
[a] $p < 0.05$
[b] $p < 0.01$
[c] $p < 0.001$

reading speed (guided by the Neale Reading Rate result). Every subject then read aloud three stories suitable for their current reading level, using each of the three text presentation types set at the same pre-determined reading speed. The order of presentation of the three text presentation types was randomised across subjects. The following results were recorded for each story:

(i) Reading errors (total).
(ii) Reading error types. These were the same as the NARA-R test error classifications (Neale 1988).
(iii) Comprehension (number correct).
(iv) Reading speed (in words per minute).

Vision test (flicker contrast sensitivity). Stimuli were generated by personal computer (President AT-PC) and the Innisfree Picasso CRT Image Generator on a Tektronix X-Y display monitor. In front of the display screen was a white occluding screen containing a centrally placed circular aperture, which had a diameter of 8.5° of visual angle. The occluding screen was lit so that its luminance matched that of the stimulus displays. Space average luminance of stimulus displays was measured using a Tektronix J6523 1° narrow-angle luminance probe. Correct viewing distance (57 cm) was maintained by the use of a fixed chin rest.

This test is designed to measure the subjects' ability to detect high (12 Hz) and low (2 Hz) temporal frequency stimuli. The stimulus displays were of two types: one stimulus was a blank uniform field; the other was a vertical sine-wave grating with a spatial frequency of 1 cyc/deg, and a temporal frequency (i.e. flicker rate) of either 12 Hz or 2 Hz. The space average luminance of the stimuli were 10 cd/m^2, and the initial contrasts of the gratings were 0.03 for both flicker conditions.

Subjects viewed the stimuli through the circular aperture in the occluding screen. For each trial, the computer sounded 3 tones, each 50 ms apart. The computer presented the blank field and the grating, in random order, after the first and second tones. The third tone signalled the end of the displays. The subject then indicated whether the grating appeared after the first or the second tone by pressing one of two buttons ('1' or '2').

The dependent variable was the contrast of the grating, which was varied using a randomised double-staircase Wetherill-Levitt (1965) procedure with six reversals. The contrast threshold was determined by calculating the mean of the contrast values for the last four reversals.

This procedure was performed once with gratings flickering at a rate of 12 Hz, and once with gratings flickering at a rate of 2 Hz. The order of presentation of these two conditions was counterbalanced across subjects, and each was preceded by a separate set of practice trials to familiarise the subject with the stimuli and procedure.

Results

General intelligence tests. The results of the four WISC-R subtests (Wechsler 1974) for the SRDs and normal readers are shown in Table 2.2, together with the results of independent groups *t*-tests between the two reading ability groups. These showed that there was no significant difference between the two groups on the performance subtests (block design and coding), indicating that the two groups do not differ on non-verbal intellectual skills. On the other hand, the SRDs were significantly worse than the normal readers at the verbal subtests (vocabulary and digit span). The SRDs' relatively poor vocabulary subtest score is perhaps no surprise, because their reading difficulties must place some limits on their exposure to new and unusual words. Of more interest is the relatively poor digit span subtest result for the SRDs. Digit span is a test of verbal short-term memory.

Reading tests. The difference between chronological and reading age for each subject was calculated by subtracting the Neale Analysis of Reading Ability

(NARA-R) reading accuracy age from chronological age. This showed that the SRD group were, on average, 28.3 months behind the normal reading accuracy standard for their age, and 21 months behind in comprehension. The mean NARA-R scores of the normal readers were slightly above the average for their age. Independent groups *t*-tests between the results of SRD and normal reader groups for each NARA-R measure confirmed that the two groups were well matched on reading accuracy, comprehension and rate (Table 2.2).

The Castles and Coltheart (1993) lists also tested the subjects' ability to deal with real and nonsense words. The number of items correct for each subject was calculated for each of the three lists (Figure 2.1), and a two-way ANOVA was performed on these results, with list type as a within-subjects factor and reading ability group as a between-subjects factor. There was a significant main effect for reading ability group, with normal readers performing better than SRDs, $F_{(1,16)} =$ 7.53, $p < .05$; and a significant main effect for list type, $F_{(2,32)} = 28.18$, $p < .001$. Once again, there was no interaction between these two factors, $F_{(2,32)} = 0.79$, $p > .05$, indicating that the SRDs were equally deficient at dealing with both real and nonsense words when compared with the normal readers.

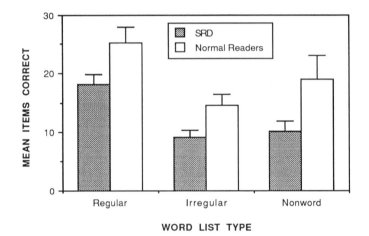

Figure 2.1 Mean items correct for Castles and Coltheart regular, irregular and nonsense word lists, comparing SRDs and normal readers before reading training.

The numbers of reading errors, including total errors and subtotals for each error type, were calculated for each of the three different types of text presentation of the Processing Power Program (Taylor *et al.* 1983) for each subject. (See Figure 2.2.)

For the reading error results a 3-way ANOVA was performed with reading ability group as a between-subjects factor, and text presentation type and reading error type as within-subjects factors. There was a significant main effect for reading ability group, with normal readers generally performing better than SRDs, $F_{(1,16)} = 7.20$, $p < .05$; and a significant main effect for text presentation

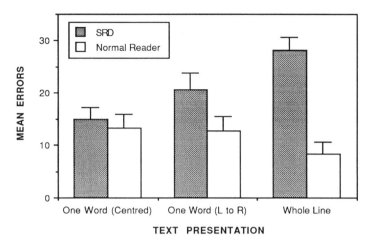

Figure 2.2 Mean reading errors for *one word (centred), one word (left-to-right)* and *whole line* computer-controlled text presentations, comparing SRDs and normal readers before reading training.

type, $F_{(2,32)} = 3.42, p < .05$. There was also a significant interaction between these two factors, $F_{(2,32)} = 16.19, p > .001$, indicating that there were different patterns of errors across the three text presentation types for the SRDs and normal readers. As predicted, the SRDs seemed to perform best with the *one word at a time* text presentations (see Figure 2.2). In fact, Figure 2.2 indicates that there was virtually no difference in the performance of SRDs and normal readers when text was presented *one word at a time (centred)*. These effects were tested using Tukey HSD pairwise comparisons. It was confirmed that the SRDs performed significantly worse with the *whole line* presentation than with either of the *one word at a time* presentations, and that they performed significantly better with the *one word (centred)* presentation than *one word (left-to-right)*. On the other hand, there was no significant difference in performance across the three text presentation types for the normal readers. The normal readers performed significantly better than the SRDs for the *whole line* and *one word (left-to-right)* conditions, but there was no significant difference between the two groups for the *one word (centred)* condition (familywise error rate for comparisons, $p < .05$).

These results tell us only about patterns of total errors. An examination of the patterns of error *types* for each of the text presentations may help us understand the source of the differences in total errors between SRDs and normal readers. The same 3-way ANOVA mentioned above also showed a significant main effect of error type, $F_{(5,80)} = 22.23, p < .01$, indicating that some error types were generally more common than others. There were also significant two-way interactions between error type and reading ability group, $F_{(5,80)} = 6.30, p < .01$; between error type and text presentation type, $F_{(10,160)} < .05$; and a significant three-way interaction between error type, text presentation type and reading group, $F_{(10,160)} = 18.08, p < .01$. These interactions reflect the different patterns of errors found

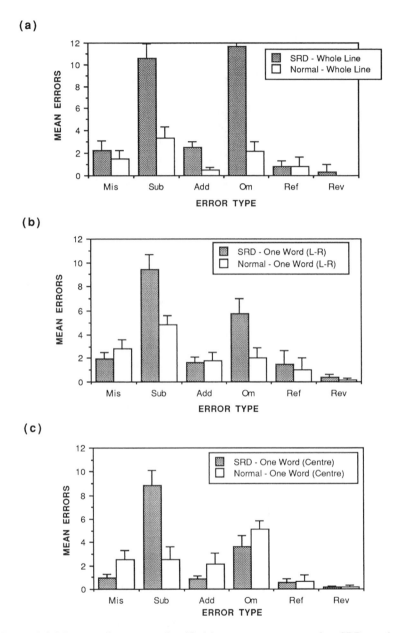

Figure 2.3 Mean reading errors classified by error type, comparing SRDs and normal readers before reading training. Panels show results for each type of computer-controlled text presentation: (a) *whole line*, (b) *one word (left-to-right)*, and (c) *one word (centred)*.

between the two reading ability groups and across the three text presentation types. These patterns of error types are shown in Figure 2.3.

Figure 2.2 indicated that the *whole line* text presentation produced the greatest amount of difference in total errors between SRDs and normal readers, and Figure 2.3(a) suggests that this difference stems from the greater propensity of SRDs to make word substitutions, omissions and (to a lesser extent) additions in their reading under this condition. There were very few differences between the SRDs and normal readers in terms of mispronunciation, word reversals or refusals to attempt a word. For the *one word at a time (left-to-right)* presentation the gap between the SRDs and normal readers began to close (Figure 2.3(b)). The SRDs were still making many more substitutions, but their average number of word omissions had halved. There now appeared to be no difference in the number of word additions between the two groups, mostly because of an increase in addition errors by the normal readers. The normal readers also showed slight increases in mispronunciation and substitution errors. The *one word at a time (centred)* presentation showed a continuation of these trends (Figure 2.3(c)). The SRDs were still making many substitutions under this condition, but they were now actually making slightly fewer additions, omissions or mispronunciations than the normal readers.

In summary, it seems that *one word at a time* presentations reduce the relative number of omission and addition errors made by SRDs, but they have little effect on substitution errors.

Vision test (flicker contrast sensitivity). The contrast sensitivity score for each stimulus condition (2 Hz and 12 Hz flicker) was determined for each subject by calculating the reciprocal of the mean contrast threshold. It appeared that normal readers performed better on these tests of transient subsystem functioning than the SRDs, and that both groups performed better with the faster flicker rate (12 Hz) (Figure 2.4.)

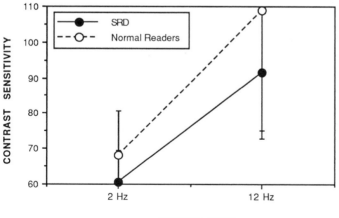

Figure 2.4 Vision test results. Flicker contrast sensitivity as a function of flicker rate, comparing SRDs and normal readers before reading training.

It should be recalled that the two reading ability groups in this study were matched for reading age, not chronological age. This means that the normal-reader group was, on average, almost 3 years younger than the SRD group. Furthermore, there was a chronological age range of 3 years for the subjects within each of the two groups. Previous research has shown that child subjects become more sensitive to flicker as they grow older (Brannan and Williams 1988b), so the analysis of the present data must take these age differences into account. For this reason a two-way analysis of covariance was performed on the contrast sensitivity results, with flicker rate as a within-subjects factor, reading ability group as a between-subjects factor and chronological age as the covariate. This revealed that there were significant main effects for reading ability group, $F_{(1,15)} = 5.35$, $p < .05$; and for flicker rate, $F_{(1,16)} = 7.29$, $p < .05$. However, there was no interaction between these two factors, $F_{(1,16)} = 0.14$, $p > .05$, indicating that the normal readers were equally superior to the SRDs across the two flicker rates.

Discussion (stage 1)

The results of the flicker contrast sensitivity test showed that the SRDs were less sensitive to flickering stimuli than normal readers, indicating that the SRDs have relatively weak transient visual subsystems. This finding corroborates those of previous studies (Brannan and Williams 1988b; Hill and Lovegrove 1992; Martin and Lovegrove 1987, 1988). The result of the present test is particularly notable in that our SRDs were shown to be less sensitive to flicker than a significantly younger group of normal readers. Previous research has found that older children are generally *more* sensitive to flicker than younger children (Brannan and Williams 1988b).

The results obtained from the computer-generated text presentation trials also confirmed previous findings that SRDs perform significantly better with *one word at a time* presentations compared with *whole line* presentations (Hill and Lovegrove 1992; Lovegrove and Macfarlane 1990; Williams *et al.*, reported in Williams and Lovegrove 1990). It was further shown that the performance of SRDs was comparable to that of the normal readers for text presented *one word at a time*, although the normal readers had been far superior to the SRDs for *whole line* presentations. The results of these tests also revealed that the improvement connected with *one word* presentations for the SRDs was attributable to relative drops in addition and, especially, omission errors. On the other hand, the different types of text presentation had no effect on the number of substitution errors made by the SRDs.

The previous studies mentioned above have suggested that the *one word* advantage in SRDs may be connected to a transient visual subsystem deficit. If this is so, then this visual deficit may have been causing at least some of the excess omission, addition and substitution errors that occurred for the present sample of SRDs when text was presented a whole line at a time. Specifically, a visual deficit was most likely to be causing the omission and addition errors, as these were decreased by altering only the visual characteristics of the text. The linguistic difficulty of the texts was held constant across the three text presentation conditions, as was the speed of presentation, so these factors were unlikely to be behind the changes in the omission and addition errors. On the other hand, the substitution errors were less likely to be linked to visual deficits because changing the appearance of the text had no significant effect on the frequency of this type of error. It is possible that the excess substitution errors of the SRDs were caused by other factors, such as language difficulties.

However, the exact nature of the connection between a transient subsystem deficit and reading disability in general is not clear. One theory that has been put forward to explain this connection suggests that SRDs suffer from excessive visible persistence (Breitmeyer 1980; Lovegrove, Martin and Slaghuis 1986). This theory proposes that the sustained visual subsystem is activated when a reader fixates on a word, and that the transient subsystem is activated when the reader makes an eye movement (saccade) to the next word. This transient subsystem activation is hypothesised to suppress any continuing sustained subsystem response to the previous fixation (i.e. visible persistence). If the transient subsystem is deficient, however, the reader may suffer from continuing visible persistence from one fixation to the next, which may interfere with the clear perception of the print at the new fixation. However, this theory would appear to be contradicted by our evidence that SRDs perform best with *one word at a time (centred)* text presentation. In this type of presentation the subject makes no eye movements at all because the words are all presented sequentially at a central fixation point. Such a situation should produce strong visible persistence in the subject due to the lack of saccadic suppression between fixations, yet this certainly did not have a deleterious effect on the SRDs' performance in the present case.

A more likely explanation of the connection between a transient subsystem deficit and reading disability lies in the capacity of SRDs to integrate visual information from central and peripheral visual fields. It is now well established by this and other studies that SRDs perform better with *one word at a time* text presentations compared with *whole line* text. The most obvious visual difference between the two types of text presentation is that the *whole line* presentation has more peripheral visual information around the fixated word than the *one word* conditions. The *whole line* presentation shows words to the left and right of the currently fixated word, while the *one word (left-to-right)* presentation shows only words to the left of the fixated word, and the *one word (centred)* presentation shows the fixated word alone. The results of the present study demonstrated that the SRDs made the most errors with *whole line* presentations and the least errors with *one word* presentations, especially the *one word (centred)* presentation. This suggests that reading may be made less difficult for SRDs if unfixated text is wholly or partially removed from the periphery of their visual field.

It has already been mentioned that the sustained subsystem usually predominates in central vision, while the transient subsystem is predominant in peripheral vision (Table 2.1). There is considerable evidence that the transient subsystem deficit in SRDs manifests itself as abnormalities in peripheral vision, which may in turn affect foveal vision as well. In an experiment looking at the masking of pattern by light, Williams, LeCluyse and Bologna (1990) found that SRDs experienced masking at longer target/mask delay intervals than normal readers when stimuli were presented foveally. On the other hand, SRDs experienced enhancement of target detection when stimuli were presented in peripheral vision, while the normal readers experienced masking of the target. Williams *et al.* interpreted these findings as indicating that SRDs suffer from longer-than-normal integration times and/or visible persistence due to slow transient subsystem response in central vision, and that the SRDs show an enhancement of sustained subsystem activity in peripheral vision due to a lack of transient-on-sustained inhibition. A related experiment by Williams, Molinet and LeCluyse (1989) similarly found that SRDs experienced sluggish metacontrast masking for foveal stimuli, and no metacontrast masking at all for peripheral stimuli. These experiments used diagonal line segments as target stimuli, but a series of experiments by Geiger and Lettvin (1987) used letters and letter strings as target stimuli. They found that SRDs were poorer than normal readers at identifying letters presented close to the fixation point. However, the SRDs were better than normal readers at identifying single letters presented in the periphery and were also less affected by lateral masking with letter strings when these targets were presented peripherally.

Taken together, this evidence suggests that SRDs may suffer from excessive masking of visual stimuli in central vision and inadequate masking of stimuli in peripheral vision, especially for tasks such as reading where rapid temporal integration of visual information is needed. Such a situation is likely to make it relatively difficult to identify a word being fixated within a line or page of text, not only because of the masking of foveally-presented stimuli but also due to interference or confusion caused by inadequately suppressed peripheral information. In particular, an SRD subject in this situation will probably omit or add words or parts of words as they read. The removal of peripheral material is, therefore, likely to alleviate the visual difficulties encountered by SRDs, and thereby reduce the number of omission and addition errors made by them.

Experiment stage 2: reading training for SRDs

The aims of Stage 2 are to determine whether reading training using *one word at a time* presentation produces more improvement in the SRDs' reading ability than *whole line* presentation, and to determine whether *one word* and/or *whole word* training produce changes in the types of reading errors.

Method

Subjects

The 12 SRDs were divided into 2 groups matched on the Neale accuracy score, and each group was randomly assigned to either *one word at a time* or *whole word*

Table 2.3 Means, standard deviations and *t*-test results for pre-training tests, comparing the *one word at a time* and *whole line* training groups

Test		One word	Whole line	*t*[a]
		(*n* = 6)	(*n* = 6)	
Age (in months)	Mean	118.5	124.0	0.74
	SD	13.0	12.8	
WISC-R subtests:				
Vocabulary		8.2	8.7	0.34
		2.8	2.3	
Digit span		6.3	7.7	0.74
		3.7	2.3	
Block design		9.3	12.5	2.06
		3.3	1.9	
Coding		8.0	7.5	0.29
		3.3	2.7	
Neale Analysis of Reading Ability:				
Accuracy (in months)		90.8	95.2	0.53
		10.8	16.7	
Comprehension (months)		96.3	104.2	0.72
		14.6	22.5	
Rate (in months)		102.3	90.7	0.65
		35.7	26.0	
Castles and Coltheart lists:				
Regular words		17.7	18.5	0.23
		6.8	5.5	
Irregular words		8.8	9.3	0.18
		4.8	4.7	
Nonsense words		10.0	10.3	0.09
		6.1	6.2	

Note
[a] None of these *t*-tests were statistically significant.

reading training. (Examination of the results of independent groups *t*-tests between other stage 1 measures for these two groups shows that they were well matched on other abilities as well. See Table 2.3.)

Apparatus and procedures

Each subject was trained by reading aloud one story per session from the Processing Power Package (Taylor *et al.* 1983) and answering the comprehension questions, as in stage 1. Each subject began with stories at their current reading level and speed (determined in the stage 1 tests). Each training trial took approximately 35 minutes. Training trials took place twice a week for 5 weeks. Subjects assigned to the *one word at a time* training group were always given the *one word at a time (left-to-right)* text presentation, and the *whole line* group were always given the *whole line* presentation. (Both 'left-to-right' and 'centred' *one word* presentations produced fewer errors than the *whole line* presentation for SRDs in the pre-training tests. The *one word* group were trained using the 'left-to-right' presentation rather than the 'centred' presentation because the 'left-to-right' format is more similar to normal printed text, and may therefore be expected to produce reading improvements that will transfer to normal text.) Reading errors, error types, comprehension and speed were recorded for each session by the examiner. The reading speed for an individual subject was increased by 5 words per minute for the present reading session if they had maintained a record of at least 80 per cent comprehension accuracy and no more than 10 reading errors for the past two reading sessions.

Results

The mean of total errors, and types of errors for each training trial were calculated. Separate two-way within-subjects ANOVAs were performed on the each of these reading measures, with reading training group and training trial as the within-subjects factors.

The mean total errors across training trials for the two training groups are shown in Figure 2.5(a). The ANOVA on these results shows that there is a significant main effect for training group, with the *one word* group performing better than the *whole line* group, $F_{(1,5)} = 44.26$, $p < .01$. The main effect of training trial was not significant, indicating there was no overall change in performance over training trials, $F_{(8,39)} = 1.16$, $p > .05$. There was also no significant interaction between the two factors, indicating that there was no difference in the pattern of results over trials between the two groups, $F_{(8,38)} = 2.0$, $p > 0.05$. It seems that the *one word* group performed consistently better than the *whole line* group throughout the training period.

The pattern of results across trials for each error type was also examined. Only the word omission results showed clear differences between the two training trials (Figure 2.5(b)). The ANOVA on omission results demonstrated a significant main effect of training group, with the *one word* training group performing better than the *whole line* group, $F_{(1,5)} = 11.99$, $p < .05$. There was no significant main effect of training trial, $F_{(8,39)} = 1.58$, $p > .05$, but there was a significant interaction between training group and training trial, $F_{(8,38)} = 4.84$, $p < .001$. This latter result reflected the growing gap between the results of the two training groups as the trials progressed. The *whole line* training group made more errors as they moved on to more difficult stories, but the *one word* group maintained a consistently low number of errors.

(a)   Total   Errors

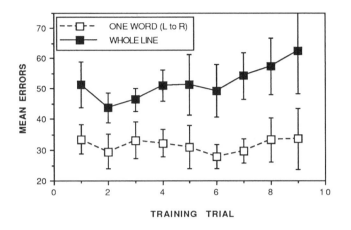

(b)   Omission   errors

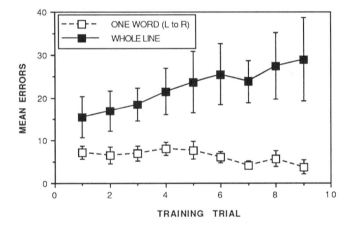

Figure 2.5 Mean total reading errors across reading training trials, comparing the *one word (left-to-right)* and *whole line* training groups. Panels show (a) total reading errors, and (b) omission-type reading errors.

The total error results, discussed above, also showed a trend towards this pattern, although it was not statistically significant. (See Figure 2.5(a).)

Experiment stage 3: post-training tests

The aim of stage 3 is to re-test the 2 groups of SRDs using normal printed text after the completion of their computer training to determine if using *one word at a time* training produces greater reading improvements than *whole line* training.

Method

Subjects

All SRDs who had completed the training trials ($n = 12$).

Apparatus and procedure

The subjects' new reading standard was measured immediately after completing the 5 weeks of training trials. This was done using the alternative form of the Neale Analysis of Reading Ability – Revised, Form 2, (Neale 1988); and by repeating Castles and Coltheart's word lists (Castles and Coltheart 1993). These were blind tests, in that the examiner was not aware which training group each subject had been in during stage 2 (note, however, that this examiner had performed the testing for stage 1).

Results

The results of these tests were compared with the results obtained by the subjects in the pre-training tests. The relative improvements of the two training groups for each of the Neale Analysis of Reading Ability (1988) measures were compared using separate two-way within-subjects ANOVAs for each of the measures. The results for pre-training and post-training NARA-R tests are shown in Figure 2.6. They show that the NARA-R comprehension performance of the SRDs in both training groups improved by the equivalent of almost 10 months after only 5 weeks of reading training (Figure 2.6(b)). The ANOVA for comprehension scores showed that this main effect of test time was significant for a one-tailed test, $F_{(1,5)} = 5.19$, $p < .05$. However, there was no significant main effect of training group, $F_{(1,5)} = 0.93$, $p > .05$, nor was there a significant interaction of test time with training group, $F_{(1,5)} = 0.01$, $p > .05$, indicating that there was no difference in comprehension performance between the training groups before or after the training stage. Similar ANOVAs on NARA-R reading accuracy and reading speed scores indicated that neither training group showed significant improvements in accuracy or speed after training (all main effects and interactions, $p > .05$).

Improvements on the Castles and Coltheart (1993) lists are shown in Figure 2.7, and were also analysed using a three-way within-subjects ANOVA. There was a general difference in performance between the three list types (main effect of list type, $F_{(2,10)} = 27.02$, $p < .001$), and there was an overall improvement in performance on the set of lists after training (main effect of test time, $F_{(1,5)} = 19.39$, $p < .01$). Moreover, performance on some list types improved more after training than others (interaction of list type with test time, $F_{(2,10)} = 6.62$, $p < .05$). However, there were no differences in performance between the two training groups in respect of list type, nor were there differences between the groups in improvement after training (main effect of training group, $F_{(1,5)} = 0.17$, $p > .05$; interaction of training group with list type, $F_{(2,10)} = 0.07$, $p > .05$; interaction of

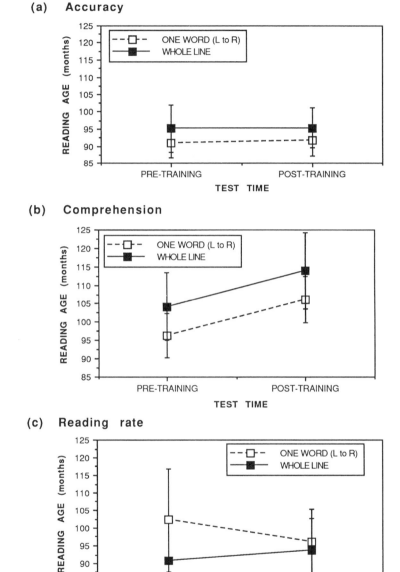

Figure 2.6 Mean Neale Analysis of Reading Ability subtest results, comparing the *one word (left-to-right)* and *whole line* training groups before and after reading training. Panels show results for (a) accuracy, (b) comprehension, and (c) reading rate.

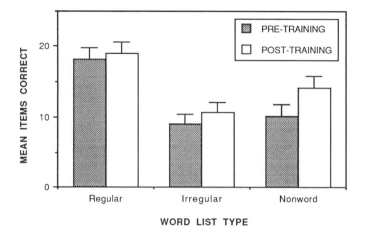

Figure 2.7 Mean items correct for the Castles and Coltheart regular, irregular and non-sense word lists, comparing the results for all SRDs before and after reading training.

training group with test time, $F_{(2,10)} = 6.62$, $p > .05$; interaction of training group with list type and test time, $F_{(2,10)} = 0.29$, $p > .05$).

Discussion (stage 2 and stage 3)

This test of the relative efficacy of *one word* text presentation as a remediation method proved equivocal. As expected, the SRDs in the *one word* training group consistently made fewer reading errors than those in the *whole line* group during the training sessions, and this was chiefly due to the difference in the number of omission errors between the conditions. Furthermore, this gap between the two groups widened as the training period progressed, so it seemed that *one word* text presentation not only made it easier for SRDs to read in the immediate term, but also allowed them to improve their reading performance over time compared with those who were trained with *whole line* presentations only.

However, when the subjects returned to normal whole pages of text in the post-training tests, there appeared to be no differences in the amount of improvement shown by the two training groups. Both showed equal and significant improvements in comprehension, and no significant improvement in reading accuracy and speed. It seems that the relative improvement shown by the SRDs in the *one word* group during training sessions did not transfer to the reading of text presented in whole pages. The overall improvement in comprehension for all SRDs can probably be attributed to the fact that any kind of one-on-one reading training is likely to produce improvements in reading. It should be noted, however, that the training period in this study was relatively short (5 weeks). Previous studies that claimed that *one word* text and similar sorts of training can improve reading (e.g. Geiger and Lettvin 1987; Geiger *et al.* 1994) usually involved training over several months.

General conclusions

This study has confirmed previous findings that SRDs read better when text is presented *one word at a time* rather than a *whole line at a time*, while normal readers are only minimally affected by changes in text presentation type. It was found that the advantage in reading performance shown by the SRDs with *one word at a time* presentations is attributable mainly to a reduction in omissions and additions. This study also replicated previous findings that SRDs suffer from weaker flicker contrast sensitivity than normal readers, indicating that SRDs have some deficiency of the transient visual subsystem. The results of this and other similar studies would seem to indicate that this transient subsystem deficit is likely to interfere with the ability of SRDs to integrate information from peripheral and central vision, especially when performing tasks such as reading that demand rapid processing of such information.

It should be noted that although the present study concentrates on the role of visual deficits in SRDs, we do not deny the role of language and other deficits in reading difficulties. In fact, there is even some evidence of a connection between visual and language deficits in SRDs (Lovegrove *et al.* 1989). The results of the Castles and Coltheart word lists in stage 1 of the present study showed that SRDs were poorer than normal readers at reading both real words and nonsense words. This implies that the SRDs had trouble both with identifying real words by sight (i.e. visual recognition), and with sounding out nonsense words (i.e. phonological analysis). In addition, the changing of text presentation types had no significant effect on the high number of word substitution errors made by the SRDs, so this type of error most likely reflects a language deficit rather than a visual deficit. Finally, the relatively poor performance of the SRD group on the digit span subtest of the WISC-R suggests that the SRDs suffer from inadequate verbal short-term memory. This study suggests that reading training with *one word at a time* presentation may be useful, but longer training studies with larger numbers of subjects are necessary to fully evaluate this possibility.

Note

1   It should be noted that not all recent studies have produced such results (e.g. Gross-Glenn *et al.* 1995; Ruddock 1991). It is not clear what accounts for these discrepancies but they probably relate to differences in methodology and sampling procedures. Borsting *et al.* (1996), for example, have demonstrated transient/magnocellular differences in Boder's (1973) dysphoneidetic dyslexics but not with her dyseidetic dyslexics.

References

Badcock, D. and Lovegrove, W. (1981) 'The effect of contrast, stimulus duration and spatial frequency on visible persistence in normal and specifically disabled readers', *Journal of Experimental Psychology: Human Perception and Performance*, 7, 495–505.

Benton, A. (1962) 'Dyslexia in relation to form perception and directional sense', in J. Money (ed.), *Reading Disability: Progress and Research Needs in Dyslexia*. Baltimore: Johns Hopkins Press.

Boder, E. (1973) 'Developmental dyslexia: A diagnostic approach based on three atypical reading patterns', *Dev. Med. Child Neurol.*, 15, 663–687.

Borsting, E., Ridder, W.H., Dudeck, K., Kelley, C. *et al.* (1996) 'The presence of a magnocellular defect depends on the type of dyslexia', *Vision Research*, 36, 1047–1053.

Brannan, J. and Williams, M. (1988a) 'Developmental versus sensory deficit effects on perceptual processing in the reading disabled', *Perception and Psychophysics*, 44, 437–444.

Brannan, J. and Williams, M. (1988b) 'The effects of age and reading ability on flicker thresholds', *Clinical Vision Sciences*, 3, 137–142.

Breitmeyer, B. (1980) 'Unmasking visual masking: A look at the "why" behind the veil of the "how"', *Psychological Review*, 87, 52–69.

Breitmeyer, B.G. (1983) 'Sensory masking, persistence and enhancement in visual exploration and reading', in K. Rayner (ed.), *Eye Movements in Reading: Perceptual and Language Processes*. New York: Academic Press.

Breitmeyer, B.G. (1988) 'Reality and relevance of sustained and transient channels in reading and reading disability', paper presented to the 24th International Congress of Psychology, Sydney, Australia.

Breitmeyer, B. and Ganz, L. (1976) 'Implications of sustained and transient channels for theories of visual pattern masking, saccadic supression, and information processing', *Psychological Review*, 83, 1–36.

Castles, A. and Coltheart, M. (1993) 'Varieties of developmental dyslexia', *Cognition*, 47, 149–180.

Geiger, G. and Lettvin, J. (1987) 'Peripheral vision in persons with dyslexia', *New England Journal of Medicine*, 316, 1238–1243.

Geiger, G., Lettvin, J. and Fahle, M. (1994) 'Dyslexic children learn a new visual strategy for reading: A controlled experiment', *Vision Research*, 34, 1223–1233.

Gross-Glenn, K., Skottun, B.C., Glenn, W., Kushch, A., Lingua, R., Dunbar, M., Jallad, B., Lubs, H.A., Levin, B., Rabin, M., Parke, L.A. and Duara, R. (1995) 'Contrast sensitivity in dyslexia', *Visual Neuroscience*, 12, 153–163.

Hill, R. and Lovegrove, W. (1992) 'One word at a time: the solution to visual problems of dyslexia?', in R. Groner and S. Wright (eds), *Facets of Dyslexia and its Remediation*. Amsterdam: North-Holland.

Lehmkuhle, S., Garzia, R.P., Turner, L. and Hash, T. (1993) 'A defective visual pathway in reading disabled children', *New England Journal of Medicine*, 328, 989–996.

Livingstone, M.S., Rosen, G.D., Drislane, F.W. and Galaburda, A.M. (1991) 'Physiological and anatomical evidence for a magnocellular defect in developmental dyslexia', *Proceedings of the National Academy of Sciences USA*, 88, 7943–7947.

Lovegrove, W., Bowling, A., Badcock. D. and Blackwood, M. (1980a) 'Specific reading disability: Differences in contrast sensitivity as a function of spatial frequency', *Science*, 210, 439–440.

Lovegrove, W., Heddle, M. and Slaghuis, W. (1980b) 'Reading disability: Spatial frequency specific deficits in visual information store', *Neuropsychologia*, 18, 111–115.

Lovegrove, W. and Macfarlane, T. (1990) 'The effect of text presentation on reading in dyslexic and normal readers', *Perception*, 19, A46.

Lovegrove, W., Martin, F., Bowling, A., Badcock, D. and Paxton, S. (1982) 'Contrast sensitivity functions and specific reading disability', *Neuropsychologia*, 20, 309–315.

Lovegrove, W., Martin, F. and Slaghuis, W. (1986) 'A theoretical and experimental case for a visual deficit in specific reading disability', *Cognitive Neuropsychology*, 3, 225–267.

Lovegrove, W., Pepper, K., Martin, F., Mackenzie, B. and McNicol, D. (1989) 'Phonological recoding, memory processing and visual deficits in specific reading disability', in D. Vickers and P.L. Smith (eds), *Human Information Processing: Measures, Mechanisms, and Models*. North Holland: Elsevier Science Publishers.

Martin, F. and Lovegrove, W. (1984) 'The effects of field size and luminance on contrast sensitivity differences between specifically reading disabled and normal children', *Neuropsychologia*, 22, 73–77.

Martin, F. and Lovegrove, W. (1987) 'Flicker contrast sensitivity in normal and specifically disabled readers', *Perception*, 16, 215–221.

Martin, F. and Lovegrove, W. (1988) 'Uniform field flicker in control and specifically-disabled readers', *Perception*, 17, 203–214.

May, J., Dunlap, W. and Lovegrove, W. (1991a) 'Visual evoked potentials latency factor scores differentiate good and poor readers', *Clinical Vision Sciences*, 67, 67–70.

May, J., Lovegrove, W., Martin, F. and Nelson, W. (1991b) 'Pattern-elicited visual evoked potentials in good or poor readers', *Clinical Vision Sciences*, 2, 131–136.

Neale, M. (1988) *Neale Analysis of Reading Ability – Revised*. Hawthorn, Vic: ACER Ltd.

Ruddock, K. (1991) 'Visual search in dyslexia', in J. Stein (ed.), *Vision and Visual Dyslexia*. London: Macmillan.

Singer, W. and Bedworth, N. (1973) 'Inhibitory interaction between X and Y units in the cat lateral geniculate nucleus', *Brain Research*, 49, 291–307.

Slaghuis, W. and Lovegrove, W. (1984) 'Flicker masking of spatial-frequency dependent visible persistence and specific reading disability', *Perception*, 13, 527–534.

Slaghuis, W. and Lovegrove, W. (1985) 'Spatial-frequency mediated visible persistence and specific reading disability', *Brain and Cognition*, 4, 219–240.

Taylor, S.E., White, C.E. and Reilly, P. (1983) *Processing Power Program*. New York: Instructional/Communications Technology, Inc.

Tellegen, A. and Briggs, P.B. (1967) 'Old wine in new skins: Grouping Wechsler subtests into new scales', *Journal of Consulting Psychology*, 31, 499–506.

Vellutino, F.R. (1979a) 'The validity of perceptual deficit explanations of reading disability: A reply to Fletcher and Satz', *Journal of Learning Disabilities*, 12, 160–167.

Vellutino, F.R. (1979b) *Dyslexia: Theory and Research*. London: MIT Press.

Wechsler, D. (1974) *Wechsler Intelligence Scale for Children – Revised*. New York: The Psychological Corporation.

Wetherill, G.B. and Levitt, H. (1965) 'Sequential estimation of points on a psychometric function', *British Journal of Mathematical and Statistical Psychology*, 18, 1–10.

Williams, M., LeCluyse, K. and Bologna, N. (1990) 'Masking by light as a measure of visual integration time and persistence in normal and disabled readers', *Clinical Vision Sciences*, 5, 335–343

Williams, M. and Lovegrove, W. (1990) 'Sensory and perceptual processing in reading disability', in J. Brannan (ed.), *Applications of Parallel Processing in Vision*. North Holland: Elsevier Science Publishers.

Williams, M., Molinet, K. and LeCluyse, K. (1989) 'Visual masking as a measure of temporal processing in normal and disabled readers', *Clinical Vision Sciences*, 4, 137–144.

3 How dyslexics see and learn to read well

Gadi Geiger and Jerome Lettvin

Introduction

In doing a visually guided task we are aware of seeing more distinctly things that are immediately involved with the task, less distinctly things that are not. The former define foreground, the latter are background. We note in ourselves that the clarity of foreground is wilfully had by 'visual attention'. Things in the foreground have forms and are spatially well ordered; things in the background are neither so well-defined nor so unambiguously arrayed. It is natural to assume that some directed refining process on the material in the foreground accounts for the difference.

We propose instead that wherever attention plays it degrades clarity everywhere else except in the region attended; i.e. inattention is an active process. This process does not involve the optically described properties of the image (resolution acuity, spatial frequency limits, contrast threshold and the like). Rather it weakens the coherent organisation of perceptual attributes into distinctly perceived forms. The background, in short, is actively de-emphasised by the process called 'lateral masking' which, as we demonstrate, reduces an arrangement of visual forms to a less definite aggregate of attributes, a visual texture. By this description, the content of perception is not changed by lateral masking, but rather the clarity of its form.

At first glance it may seem a matter of indifference whether foreground is actively clarified or background actively declarified; the distinction between foreground and background stays the same. But we will argue later that experiments on 'demasking' (Geiger and Lettvin 1986) favour the latter view.

We show evidence that the distribution of lateral masking is learned by practising the performance of visually guided tasks. Further, this distribution, being task-dependent, is different for different tasks. Each kind of visually-guided task calls for its own dedicated visual strategy in which the characteristic states and state-sequences of the distributions of lateral masking play an important role. As with other kinds of expert task performance, a learned strategy improper to the task interferes with the development of a proper strategy.

Our goal in this chapter is to show how dyslexics and ordinary readers differ in visual strategies. First we describe visual strategy and sketch how lateral masking relates to it. Then we explain why we view dyslexia as the symptom of an inappropriate strategy. Next we compare dyslexics and ordinary readers by a non-reading measure which shows the difference between them in terms of the distribution of lateral masking. Finally, by showing how dyslexics learn a new visual strategy for reading as the result of a particular regimen of practice, and by following their progress both by performance and by our non-reading measure, we justify our approach to the problem.

Task-determined visual strategies and lateral masking

If the goal is not a simple end-state, rather a method of efficient task performance in real time (e.g. figure-skating, piano-playing or reading), different strategies of task performance are separately optimised. Good performance in real time for a large variety of such different visually-guided tasks calls for a menu of task-related processes (strategies of perception as much as action) separately established but of easy access. Expert performance involves not only training of action but training of what to attend in perception, and so the strategy involves what to see as much as what to do.

Practically speaking, what is meant by this? In driving a car you are aware of at least two distinct attention states. Suppose you are in fast dense traffic. You must keep your eyes on the car ahead of you. But while this limits your gaze you can switch attention between the surrounding traffic and the car you are following, without much movement of your eyes. When you attend the traffic, the details of the car in front are not clear; when you attend the car, the details of traffic are not clear. The experience is familiar enough. In either case what is attended is salient and has form, what is unattended has only texture, a distribution of attributes without distinct form. For the two tasks, observation of traffic or of the car ahead, you switch between two states, masking in the centre of the field for viewing the traffic or masking in the periphery for viewing the car ahead. In this instance you pay for a clarity in the peripheral field by a lesser impression of the central field and vice versa. The attention switch is more efficient than searching about in the periphery and is common experience in the expert performance of daily tasks.

A visual strategy is defined in part by the distribution of what is not salient. Since, as we suggest, lateral masking reduces an ensemble of well-defined forms to a textured array as mentioned above, this distribution of what is not salient suggests a distribution of lateral masking. Of course the complete visual strategy is a complex of many cooperative processes (like accommodation, vergence, colour identification, motion identification, etc.) which are all set for optimising task performance; but the spatial distribution of lateral masking is one of them. The idea of a strategy is to optimise planned action. In that sense it calls for a running prediction of what actions will provide what perceptions. The optimisation is gained not only by refining action but by anticipating the change of perception that attends the action. In short, you have to know what to look for in order to see it in the progress of carrying out a task. In tasks with a relatively

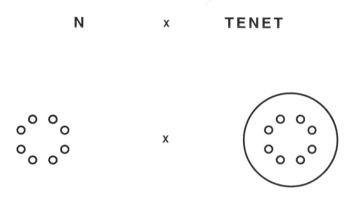

Figure 3.1 A demonstration of lateral masking.

static field such as given for reading, the measurement of the distribution of lateral masking becomes possible.

A demonstration of lateral masking is given in Figure 3.1. Fix your gaze on the upper x in Figure 3.1 and keep it fixed. Now consider what you see to either side. There are Ns on both sides equidistant from the x. The one on the left is clear and distinct, not so clear as if you looked directly at it, but still easily recognised. The one on the right, in the centre of the letter string, is not recognisable for most of you. The question is not whether you know ahead of time that there is an N on the right, but whether you see it while your gaze is fixed on the x. Whatever is there on the right has some vaguely appreciated details, but exactly where in the string the details reside is not clear.

There are some who will see the N on the right while fixing the x. In our experience two groups have this ability, namely those who are dyslexic, and some of those who have learned speed reading. The point is important and will be illuminated by later discussion.

Now fix your gaze on the lower x in Figure 3.1. You will note that on the left the circular array of the circles is not as clear as the circles themselves. However there is still a feeling of some kind of order in the array, such as that it surrounds a blank space. On the right the small circles are individually clear but they seem best qualified as having no distinct order among them even though on direct inspection the large circle seems to enhance the circularity of the array. Thus spatial arrangement is ambiguated by lateral masking due to the large ring.

The phenomenon of lateral masking is crudely demonstrated here. How is the process to be described? Since by no act of will is the lateral masking on the right relieved, we might initially suppose it to be a fixed property of interactions in peripheral vision as has been assumed by the vast body of research on lateral masking (e.g. Bouma 1970, Mackworth 1965; Townsend, Taylor and Brown

1971; Wolford and Chambers 1983). We hold instead that lateral masking is actively imposed. In an earlier paper (Geiger and Lettvin 1986) we showed that if a letter of the same font, sign and orientation as one in a peripheral letter string is flashed at the fixation point simultaneously with the letter string, that letter in the string, which is normally masked, is identified as if it was not masked, and at the same time the other letters around it are also more easily identified. This 'demasking' does not work unless the two identical letters are congruent by translation alone. There is little language cognition involved – a lower case letter does not significantly demask the same letter in upper case (which has a different appearance), nor does the same letter in a distinctly different font, size or orientation. The same holds true for icons that are not letters.

Such a criterion for demasking is the reason that we suppose lateral masking to be an active process. For, were the masked letter in the peripheral string not identifiable pre-cognitively, how should it be demasked? Further, how should the adjacent letters also be better identified? We suggested in that paper, that the information in what is masked is retrievable and not degenerated by early processing, otherwise demasking is not possible. An important point to add is that regional masking is relieved by demasking, not simply the specific masking of a single letter.

As to the mechanism of lateral masking there may be some physiological ground. The receptive field size for single neurons of a certain class in the tectum of a frog were observed to change size, seemingly spontaneously, but without changing the description of those visual attributes that excite the response (Lettvin *et al.* 1961). Changes in receptive field sizes are also seen in the cortex of mammals, for example as the result of a scotoma (Pettet and Gilbert 1992). Such a process preserves detail of the objects that excite it. In an ensemble of receptive fields that change size, the exciting features remain the same but their spatial order is made uncertain if the receptive fields enlarge. (We discuss this notion at length in an earlier paper (Geiger, Lettvin and Zegarra-Moran 1992).) If receptive fields are observed to change size without changing the qualities or details that are reported, whatever influences the change makes the distribution of lateral masking controllable. Note that the content of details in the image, as reported in receptive fields, is not changed but only the degree of overlap of receptive fields. Thus a directed controlling action of this sort on the representation of the image does not change the content but only the definiteness of spatial organisation of the content. In this way there can be an efferent task-controlled action on the fine spatial organisation of visual perceptions.

What we suggest is that in the acquisition of expert performance of a task, this control becomes learned in task-specific operation, very like the control in expert motor performance, and accounts for a task-specific visual strategy. Such strategies become well-formed when the tasks are practised, and fast switching between strategies becomes possible. This is the idea exemplified in the changes of visual strategy that we show in dyslexics when they learn a new way of reading.

Dyslexia as a symptom

By all measures of intelligence and of clinical optics, and by the results of neuro-logical screening, the dyslexic should be able to read efficiently but doesn't, and seems unable to learn the skill. The symptom of dyslexia raises three questions. What is its cause? How is it explained? Can it be remedied?

As to physical cause, some organic pathologies have been proposed (e.g. Denckla 1977; Galaburda and Kemper 1979; Galaburda *et al*. 1985; Geschwind and Behan 1982; Livingstone *et al*. 1991). But their diversity and the absence of strong correlations suggest that, at best, they may be only contributory factors.

With regard to explanation, dyslexia is currently thought to be mainly a problem of language ability, especially phonemic awareness (e.g. Liberman 1971, 1982; Liberman *et al*. 1974; Lundberg 1982, 1989; Olson *et al*. 1989; Zurif and Carson 1970). This view is adopted by the Orton Dyslexia Society in its definition of dyslexia (Shaywitz, Fletcher and Shaywitz 1995). But other studies have shown consistent differences in visual perception between dyslexics and ordinary readers (e.g. Di Lollo, Hanson and McIntyre 1983; Fowler, Riddell and Stein 1990; Lovegrove, Martin and Slaghuis 1986; Stein and Fowler 1981; Williams, LeCluyse and Bologna 1990). Those differences are not attributed to early visual processes. The one common ground for all proposed explanations is that a higher order process is involved. Such processes are notoriously hard to qualify.

However the symptom is definite enough. Common to all dyslexics is the specific weakness of the ability to read in spite of dedicated tutoring. Our approach to the problem has been to address the symptom directly. There should be some measure, aside from scoring a test for reading ability, that suggests a physiology for the expression of the symptom, whatever the remote causes. The difficulty, considered naively, seems to us to be at a level where the objects of perception are either given definite forms and spatial order or else are treated as collections of impressions combined in a texture, which is to say, an aggregate characterised statistically rather than by detailed order. There is no reason to disbelieve the experience reported by dyslexics: that the letters or words in texts 'are all over the place'. This signifies a lack of coherence in the seen parts when those parts are letters. Thus our working definition of dyslexia excludes any references to causes and only describes the symptom. Dyslexia is an unexplained retardation of reading skill in spite of dedicated tutoring and in the absence of any recognisable aberration in visual resolution or neurological findings or intellectual status. We will show that dyslexia as a symptom can be remediated.

How dyslexics and ordinary readers differ in visual perception of letters

Measuring the form-resolving field (FRF)

We measure perception/recognition ability across the visual field. Icons are tachistoscopically presented away from the centre of gaze singly or in strings together with an icon coincidentally given at the centre of gaze. We use a projected optical image for reasons discussed below.

In our studies of dyslexia the icons are letters, and the measurements are made only along the horizontal axis because that is how we read western languages. Although we have used letter strings in a few studies, the aim of our effort here has been to get the most discriminating measure while fatiguing the subject least (many of our subjects are children). Preliminary observations led us to a standard measure which we call the FRF (form-resolving field).

In setting up the measure, two observations are most important. First is that in peripheral vision, letters of complex shape such as E or X are self-masking for all viewers; i.e. the parts of the letters mask each other. A simple bar such as 'I' is not self-masking (Geiger *et al.* 1992). Second is that in or near the centre of gaze adjacent letters tend to mask each other for dyslexics (Bouma and Legein 1977; Atkinson *et al.* 1988).

We measure the FRF with pairs of unlike letters back-projected tachisto-scopically on a diffusing screen. The screen is 69 cm from the subject's eyes, and at that distance is 39° wide and 26° high. The arrangement uses three projectors adjusted to equal luminance. They are equipped with fast shutters, electronically driven, and timed in opening and closing so that luminance stays constant on the screen as we switch between projectors. The first projector carries a slide with a fixation point on it at the centre and is otherwise blank. The second projector carries the stimulus slide with two unlike letters on it. The third projector carries a blank slide. The sequence is this: (1) the subject holds gaze on the fixation point; (2) following a verbal warning the stimulus slide is presented for 2–35 ms duration (individually adjusted to the subject as will be explained shortly); (3) the stimulus slide is immediately followed by the blank slide for 2.5 s, after which the fixation point slide returns and remains until the next stimulus.

Each stimulus slide has one letter located at the fixation point, the other at one of five eccentricities (2.5°, 5°, 7.5°, 10°, 12.5°) to the right or left. The two letters are always different from each other. These letters are taken from a group of 10 upper case letters (Helvetica medium), and are seen on the screen with 90 per cent contrast and subtended to angular height of 35 minutes of arc. There are 10 different slides for each eccentricity on the right and 10 for each eccentricity on the left: a total of 100 slides. (In some studies we used the same set twice over to have 200 presentations.) Each letter appears with equal frequency at all eccen-tricities. The stimulus slides are randomised for right and left eccentricities. After each stimulus display the subject reports verbally the letters seen, and the response to both letters is recorded. The plot of correct recognition score of the peripheral letters as a function of their eccentricity is the FRF. The scores of correct central letter recognition are usually given numerically.

Throughout the measurement the duration of stimulus presentations is constant, but the determination of stimulus duration is made individually for each subject. Before the actual measurement a few stimulus durations are probed at various eccentricities to find which duration will result in recognition of the peripheral letter of just below 100 per cent. We call this normalisation auto-scaling.

As the FRF is a measure of recognition acuity only, the procedure prevents saturation effect, yet allows a full range of recognition for each subject. It also allows comparison between subjects.

The FRF not only measures the recognition of letters as a function of eccentricity, but also measures the perceptual interactions between the letter in the periphery and the letter at the centre. In addition the tachistoscopic nature of this measurement relates it to a dynamic process like reading. Although the stimulus durations are much shorter than the usual fixation durations (200–400 ms, O'Reagan 1990), we argue that since only two letters are involved the timing adjustment is appropriate.

The FRFs of adult severe dyslexics and adult ordinary readers

The FRFs of 10 adult English-native severe dyslexics (2 females and 8 males, 18 to 58 years of age) were compared with the FRFs of 10 adult English-native ordinary readers (3 females and 7 males, 18 to 45 years of age). The severe dyslexics came from the general population and had been diagnosed as dyslexic by their neurologists or psychologists prior to calling on us. Their reading skills were much below the expected level for their ages and other skills in spite of ample tutoring. Their intelligence was average or above and they had received no special remediation for at least 3 years before they came to us. The ordinary readers came from the general university-level student population. All the subjects had normal vision or had been corrected to normal vision and had no obvious visual or neurological pathologies. Two average FRF plots are shown in Figure 3.2. One plot is the average of the 10 adult ordinary readers and the other of the 10 adult severe dyslexics.

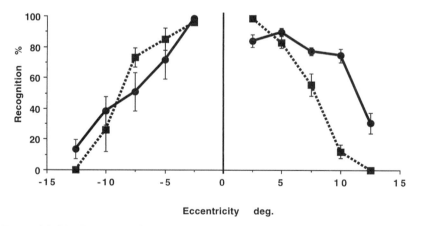

Figure 3.2 The FRF plots for adult English-native subjects: average for 10 ordinary readers (dashed line) and average for 10 severe dyslexics (solid line).

Notes

The measure is of correct recognition (in %) of the peripheral letters of the letter pairs, at different eccentricities. The vertical bars denote the standard deviation.

The average FRFs of the two groups are significantly different. Ordinary readers recognise letter pairs best when the peripheral letters are closest to the centre of gaze. Recognition of the peripheral letter diminishes rapidly with eccentricity. That is, the FRFs of ordinary readers are narrow, symmetric to the left and right of the centre of gaze and fall off monotonically as is suggested by a version of the Aubert–Foerster law (1857). The FRFs of the severe English-native dyslexics are significantly different on the right side from those of ordinary readers but on the left side are similar to those of ordinary readers. On the right side, adult severe dyslexics recognise letter pairs best when the peripheral letters are at 5° or 7.5° eccentricity, while recognition of the letter pairs is significantly lower nearer to the centre of gaze at 2.5° eccentricity. The adult severe dyslexics also recognise letters significantly better than ordinary readers further in the periphery on the right side. Thus the FRFs of adult severe dyslexics are significantly wider than those of ordinary readers, do not fall off monotonically with eccentricity, and are distinctly asymmetric. For the letter pairs, the letters appearing at the centre of gaze are recognised above 93 per cent by both groups for all eccentricities of the peripheral letter (Geiger and Lettvin 1989; Geiger *et al.* 1992). When we say 'significant' we mean as given by the ANOVA and the *t*-test, to the level of confidence of at least $p < 0.05$.

The FRFs of adult dyslexics and ordinary readers native to languages read from left to right

The FRF graph shown in Figure 3.2 is that for the adult severe dyslexics whose reading retardations were most severe and who had had no remediation procedure for at least 3 years before we tested them. Before measuring the severe dyslexics we reported on a study of adult 'residual' dyslexics who were receiving active remedial training for reading at the period we were testing them and whose reading retardations were not as severe (Geiger and Lettvin 1987). There were only minor differences between the FRFs of severe dyslexics and those of residual dyslexics. We have tested many more adult dyslexics since, and had similar results. In order to demonstrate the generality of the approach, Figure 3.3 shows separately the average FRFs of 29 adult dyslexics, native to English, German and Italian and of 34 adult ordinary readers native to the same languages. None were selected by us. Most of the dyslexics had been diagnosed as such by their respective neurologists and psychologists. All had severe retardation of reading skills and average or above average intelligence. We did not measure their IQ (although some subjects had it measured elsewhere) as it is under dispute (e.g. Siegel 1989), but we gauged intelligence during the interview and there were no noticeable deficiencies.

The characteristic differences in the FRFs are the same as shown in Figure 3.2. A symmetric, monotonic and rapidly diminishing recognition of the peripheral letters with increase of eccentricity characterises the adult ordinary readers. For adult dyslexics the FRF is significantly asymmetric, being wider in the right periphery than for ordinary readers. At 2.5° to the right of the centre of gaze letter

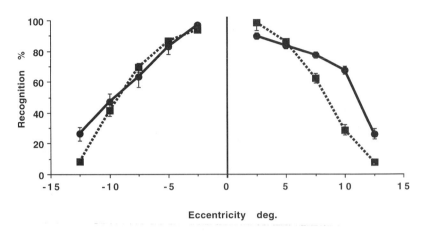

Figure 3.3 The FRF plots for adult English, Italian and German-native subjects: average for 34 ordinary readers (dashed line) and average for 29 dyslexics (solid line).

recognition is significantly lower than that of ordinary readers. At 10° and 12.5° to the right recognition by the dyslexics of the peripheral letters is at least 2.4 times better than that of ordinary readers. Average recognition of the letters at the centre of gaze is at least 93 per cent for all the eccentricities of the peripheral letter.

In all the cases we measured, an adult person who was dyslexic by the accepted criteria of reading deficit with respect to developmental level (as also mentioned in the introduction), had an FRF similar to that of dyslexics in Figure 3.3 and distinctly different from that of ordinary readers. There was no ordinary reader among those we measured who had an FRF similar to that of the dyslexics. In short, there was no overlap. Adult speed readers also had a wide recognition on the right, but the overall shape of their FRF was distinctly different from that of dyslexics (Zegarra-Moran and Geiger 1993).

The average stimulus exposure duration (due to auto-scaling) for adult ordinary readers was 5.57 ms (SD=3.6) and for adult dyslexics 8.62 ms (SD=9.5). These differences are not statistically significant and do not account for the differences in the FRFs, as will be seen in the later section on learning.

The FRFs of dyslexics depend on the direction of reading

The FRF measurements described above were performed with subjects who were native to languages which are read from left to right (English, Italian and German). The FRFs of dyslexics who were native to these languages, were distinctly asymmetric with wide letter recognition to the right which is the direction of reading these languages. To investigate the relation between the direction of reading the language and the asymmetry of the dyslexic FRF we measured the FRFs of subjects native to a language read from right to left. Other factors like hemispheric specialisation or handedness could be the reason for the asymmetry, but we thought that reading direction was most obvious and should be tried first. Hebrew is a language which is read from right to left and therefore Hebrew-natives were the natural choice for subjects to be tested since one of us (GG) is native to this language.

All the subjects measured in this experiment were Hebrew-native adults who had been exposed primarily to Hebrew through the first 10 years of their life and had been taught to read only Hebrew during the first 3 years at school. All of them had learned English from the 4th year at school. The FRFs were measured with Hebrew letters to ensure competence in the report comparable to that of English-natives with roman letters. These letters were closely matched to the font and size used with the roman letters. Five subjects were dyslexic males (17–28 years of age). They had been diagnosed as dyslexics by their respective neurologists and/or psychologists, and were not under remedial training at the time of testing but had received such training within 3 years prior to testing. Their reading was profoundly impaired; those still at school had deficits of at least two grade/age levels below their expected level. But their comprehension of heard texts was normal. Another five subjects (2 females and 3 males 20–31 years old), who were ordinary readers, were measured for comparison. All subjects came from a background similar to that of the English-native subjects described previously.

As seen from Figure 3.4 the average FRF of adult Hebrew-native ordinary readers is symmetric, narrow and falls off monotonically with best recognition of letter pairs in and near the centre of gaze, similar to that of English-native ordinary readers. On the other hand, the average FRF of adult Hebrew-native dyslexics is significantly different from that of ordinary readers. Recognition of the peripheral letters by Hebrew-native dyslexics extends significantly further to the periphery in the left visual field but not on the right (except at 12.5°), a mirror image of what English-native adult dyslexics show. However, recognition of the letter pairs by Hebrew-native dyslexics near the centre at 2.5° eccentricity to the

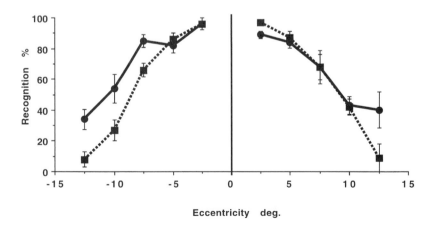

Figure 3.4 The plots for the FRF of adult Hebrew-native subjects: average for 5 ordinary readers (dashed line) and average for 5 dyslexics (solid line).

right is significantly lower than that of ordinary readers and is similar to that of English-native dyslexics (Geiger *et al.* 1992).

We conclude that the FRFs of all adult dyslexics are asymmetric and are significantly different from those of ordinary readers. The FRFs of dyslexics extend far in the direction of reading, to the right for English-native and to the left for Hebrew-native subjects, and do not relate to any other attributes known to us.

The FRFs of 'conditional dyslexics'

If the difference in direction of reading affects the measure of dyslexics by the FRF, there are other variations to be considered. We describe here a person we labelled a 'conditional' dyslexic. He alternates between two states in the same day, being either an ordinary reader or a dyslexic depending on how 'tired' he is.

The subject is a man 28 years old whose profession is in the graphic arts. When he is 'fresh' in the morning, he reads easily and well but his artistic skill is not at its best. By early afternoon he feels 'tired' and he reads with great difficulty, only skimming the text and making many word errors. At the same time his graphic skill improves and it is the best time for pursuing his artistic work. As shown in Figure 3.5, the FRF, measured in the morning when reading was easy, is like that of ordinary readers. In the afternoon, when reading was difficult, the FRF is like that of dyslexics. The FRF is narrow with rapid fall-off of recognition in the morning and it is shallow and wide in the right visual field in the afternoon when reading is impaired. Stimulus duration was the same for both measurements which were repeated on three successive days with similar results.

After we were alerted to the condition by this subject we found three others who showed similar alternation between the two states: proficient reading and

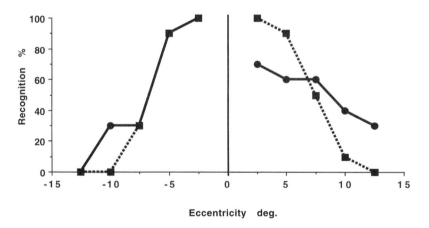

Figure 3.5 The plots for the FRF of the same person at two different 'phases': when alert in the morning (dashed line) and 6 hours later, when tired (solid line).

Note

Correct recognition of the letter at the centre for all peripheral letter eccentricities was above 90%.

dyslexic. They too had the corresponding FRF measures. Such a finding demonstrates two points. First, there is an immediate correlation between reading skill and the shape of the FRF, i.e. the distribution of letter recognition. Second, the symptom of dyslexia can be a plastic (changing) state rather than a 'hard wired' constant state.

The FRFs of children

Once we established a measure for the differences in perception between adult dyslexics and adult ordinary readers, we went on to measure perceptual differences in children, using the FRF. All the children were 8–13 years old (3rd–7th grade) and were English, German and Italian natives. We compared the FRFs of 11 children who were ordinary readers (average age of 9.1 (SD = 1.7) years) whose reading levels were on average 0.3 (SD = 0.5) grade level above their respective expected levels, with the FRFs of 30 dyslexic children (average age of 10.9 (SD = 2.5) years) whose average reading retardation was 2.2 (SD = 0.9) grades below their respective expected grade levels (and 2.3 years below their expected age level). Each individual dyslexic child was at least 2 grade/year levels below expected grade and/or age level. The average FRFs for the dyslexics and ordinary readers among these children are shown in Figure 3.6.

The differences between the dyslexics and ordinary readers are significant. Recognition of the peripheral letters by the dyslexic children is significantly better at larger eccentricities than that of ordinary readers, not only on the right side as with adults, but also on the left side. Recognition by dyslexics of letters at eccentricities of 10° and 12° is at least twice as good as that of ordinary readers. Therefore the FRFs of dyslexic children are significantly wider than those of children who are ordinary readers.

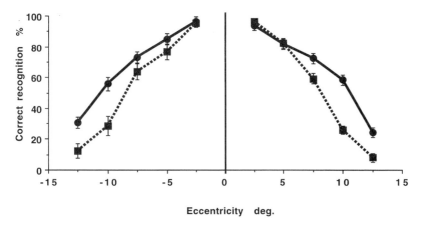

Figure 3.6 The plots for the FRF of German, Italian and English-native children: average for 11 ordinary readers (dashed line) and average for 30 dyslexics (solid line).

Note

Correct recognition of the letter at the centre for all peripheral letter eccentricities was above 94%.

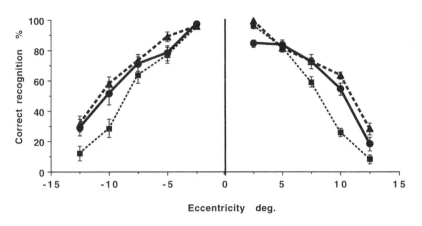

Figure 3.7 The plots for the FRF of German, Italian and English-native dyslexic children: average for 11 children who showed reduced recognition near the centre of gaze (solid line) and average for 19 dyslexic children who did not have that reduction (dashed line).

Note

The dotted line is the FRF of 11 children who are ordinary readers, shown for reference.

There are differences between the FRFs of dyslexic children and dyslexic adults. The FRFs of dyslexic children are not significantly asymmetric as are those of adult dyslexics. And the average FRF of dyslexic children does not show the reduced recognition at 2.5° to the right of the centre of gaze as the FRF of the adult dyslexic shows. On closer scrutiny the FRF average of the dyslexic children is actually an average of two sub-groups, those who do not have reduced recognition to the right at 2.5° (sub-group A, $N = 19$) and those who had reduced recognition there (sub-group B, $N = 11$). The average FRFs of the two sub-groups are shown in Figure 3.7; they are similar except at 2.5° eccentricity. These two sub-groups were of a similar age (average 11.4 (SD = 1.37) years of age for sub-group A and 10.1 (SD = 1.52) for sub-group B). They had similar reading retardations (2.51 (SD = 0.94) grade levels for sub-group A and 2.09 (SD = 0.4) grade levels for sub-group B), and were similar in male–female composition as well as in handedness.

Note that the average FRF of children who are ordinary readers is almost identical to that of adults who are ordinary readers (see also Zegarra-Moran and Geiger 1993).

The average stimulus exposure durations for children were much the same for the dyslexics (9.1 SD = 3.4 ms) and ordinary readers (9.2 SD = 4.9 ms) and so could not be the cause of the difference seen in the FRFs.

The differences between the FRFs of adult and children dyslexics might be related to differences of age. But we found that the remedial procedure given at school to some of the children (before our experiment) was to use a finger as marker while reading. As this was correlated with the children who did not show reduction of recognition at 2.5°, we suspect, also on other observational grounds, that this regimen is conducive to the particular visual strategy as qualified by the FRF.

What do the differences in the FRFs mean?

Ordinary readers and dyslexics, whether children or adults, differ significantly and consistently in their FRFs. The difference is shown in the Figures. This non-reading measure, systematically distinguishing the two groups, becomes diagnostic.

Our approach was to regard dyslexia as a symptom, whatever its cause, and to search out a measure that correlates with it. All the dyslexics we have measured, after developing the method, markedly differ in their FRF plots from ordinary readers. There were no ambiguous plots. We have measured 59 dyslexics, none of whom were chosen by us. Among them were different 'types' of dyslexia (as described by Boder (1973) or by Bakker (1972)), yet all had similar FRFs (Geiger and Lettvin 1993).

After we reported the differences in FRFs between dyslexics and ordinary readers, several other investigators attempted to reproduce our results directly or by modifications. Those studies that used projective optical displays, as we did, verified our findings (Perry *et al.* 1989; Dautrich 1993). Those that used CRT displays (Bjaalid, Hoien and Lundberg 1993; Goolkasian and King 1990; Klein *et al.* 1990; Slaghuis, Lovegrove and Freestun 1992) mostly did not. We had found earlier, but did not publish, that CRTs were unsatisfactory. Some of the reasons are given by Zegarra-Moran and Geiger (1993). Among them is the flicker of screen renewal which many dyslexics seem to see in the central field.

A second point was the auto-scaling of the stimulus duration. We found that the stimulus durations chosen by this criterion did not differ significantly between ordinary readers and dyslexics. Especially with children, the FRFs of dyslexics were significantly wider than those of ordinary readers although stimulus durations were the same. Furthermore, Perry *et al.* (1989) showed that by choosing a common stimulus duration carefully, so that recognition was below 100 per cent at all eccentricities, they obtained results similar to ours. As mentioned, auto-scaling as a normalising procedure simply avoids saturation and allows longitudinal comparison on the same subject and cross-comparisons between subjects.

A third point shows the nature of what the FRF measures. Bouma and Legein (1977) had reported that dyslexics are significantly worse than ordinary readers in recognising letters in strings presented in the central field while recognising single letters equally as well as ordinary readers. Therefore, both groups seemed to have equivalent measures of optical resolution acuity. (We should add that in a later paper Bouma and Legein (1980) attributed the differences in recognition to response latencies for single letters and therefore faulted the decoding process.) It is important to note again that since the FRF does not measure visual resolution acuity but rather visual recognition, the difference between dyslexics and ordinary readers must be sought at a higher processing level and not in early processing.

Fourth, we have attributed the differences in shape of the FRF between dyslexics and ordinary readers to differences in the distribution of lateral masking. Initially (Geiger and Lettvin 1987) we showed this tachistoscopically by using three-letter strings in the right periphery at different eccentricities along with a single letter in the centre field. Lateral masking within the string increased rapidly and mono-tonically with eccentricity for ordinary readers as shown by Bouma (1970). But the dyslexics showed marked lateral masking near the centre where ordinary readers showed little. And at greater eccentricities the dyslexics showed signifi-cantly less masking than ordinary readers, a pattern of the distribution of lateral masking similar to that given by the FRF (Geiger and Lettvin 1987, 1989; Geiger *et al.* 1992). Given the notion of self-masking for complex letters as described earlier, single letters rather than strings in the periphery are less arduous in measuring the distribution of lateral masking in the visual field.

That the FRFs of ordinary readers are narrow around the centre of gaze and fall off sharply with eccentricity argues that readers see clearly words they gaze at while the surrounding text is unclear. In this way the reader, by shifting gaze, progresses from one word fixation to another. But for dyslexics, words as letter strings are laterally masked where they gaze; while at 5°–10° in the direction of reading and beyond, a large part of the text is much less laterally masked. That is, letter strings or words which are gazed at are perceived as a swarm of letters while at the same time the letter strings in the periphery are perceived clearly. However, because the FRF in the periphery is wide, words are not perceived in isolation. As a result the dyslexics have great trouble in picking out one word from another in the welter of them, all seen at once, and so cannot read any word in isolation as in ordinary reading. This crude account tallies with what dyslexics report to us. They say that they 'see the whole page' at once, that they 'cannot see what is first and second', that 'the letters fly all over the page', that 'the text is moving'.

There is a tacit assumption in the literature since Aubert and Foerster (1857) that given a fixed luminance and a fixed contrast, font and angular size of icons, the angular distance into the periphery over which an icon can be identified is constant. They used themselves as subjects; we assume that they were readers. But what we have found is that in dyslexics the angular distance for recognition in the direction of reading is significantly larger than in ordinary readers, and recognition is significantly worse at a small angular distance from the centre of gaze. In the other direction there are no such differences, i.e. the distribution of lateral masking is correlated with the task of reading. That suggests that such distribution is a spatial delimiting of a task-determined visual strategy rather than a fixed characteristic in the visual field.

Several questions are raised by what has been given so far. We have hypo-thesised visual strategies as if they are task-conformed, operational states to be switched in as needed. Is this view of task-determined states of vision supported by observations other than those we have shown? Do these differences reflect different task-dependent strategies (operational states) of vision? Can such new strategies be learned and how can they be taught?

1   Held and his co-workers (Held and Gottlieb 1958; Held and Hein 1958) worked with hand–eye coordination in visually guided tasks. When a lateral displacement of the seen world was introduced by prismatic spectacles the hand performed as if in a displaced world. Cognitive knowledge of the displacement given passively resulted in little correction of the displacement. That is, the subject knew the correction to be made but could not always make it. However if the subject practised moving the hand by actively controlling it in the displaced visual field, the correction was made most efficiently. This shows that the relation of perception to action in task performance cannot generally be improved simply by knowing what is wrong, but can be corrected most efficiently by actively working towards what is proper by practice. Yet, although suggestive, this is not enough to attribute improvement in task performance to a change in perceptual state.

Kohler's work (1962, 1964), however, drives the point home. His subjects wore inverting spectacles or half-prism spectacles (among other types of spectacles which changed the seen world dramatically) continually for prolonged durations. In the case of the inverting spectacles he reports that at first the world appeared right side up sporadically for short durations. When hand-reach movements were made or any other directed movements were made the world was seen right side up. By the end of the experiments the changes due to the spectacles had been 'corrected' in visual perception and behaviour was 'normal'. Another important point is that after removal of the spectacles, right side up or upside down images of the world sporadically appeared to the subjects but the shifts were not directly influenced by the will. In the case of the inverting spectacles, learning to adjust to the inversion by seeing the world 'right side up', occurred only after actively moving and acting, and there were only two states of the perceived image, right side up or inverted.

2   The FRF, a non-reading procedure, gives measures that differ significantly and consistently between dyslexics and ordinary readers. The differences accompany subjective differences – the adult dyslexics cannot read words at the centre of vision, the reader can. But in other non-reading tasks guided by central vision, and in tests of visual resolution acuity there is no difference in performance between dyslexics and readers as there is with reading.

The point is not that measures other than the FRF do not show such difference but that this measure does, and shows the difference to be task-dependent by our choice of stimulus objects. The cases of the conditional dyslexics in particular show that in the same subject two different states, reading and dyslexic, are switchable.

3   Based on the observation of conditional dyslexics, on the demonstration of reversed asymmetry of the FRFs between Hebrew-native dyslexics and English-native dyslexics and on the difference in the FRFs between ordinary readers and dyslexics, we concluded that dyslexia is a learned symptom.

Learning of new visual strategies

We ended the previous section by suggesting that a visual strategy is learned. A critical test is to show that dyslexic persons can learn a new visual strategy which provides a marked improvement of reading skills, and that at the same time the distribution of lateral masking changes and comes to resemble that of ordinary readers.

We first describe how a few adults dyslexics learned a new visual strategy, then recount a controlled experiment with dyslexic children.

Adults

A 25-year-old male severe dyslexic whose reading level was at about 3rd grade of school, had no obvious pathologies and showed average or above average intelligence. After assessment of his reading deficit and the measurement of the FRF, which is shown in Figure 3.8, we suggested to the subject a regimen of practice which consisted of two complementary parts. One was to devote 2 hours a day to novel small-scale hand–eye coordination activities like painting, drawing, clay modelling, etc. For the other part we asked the subject to use a specially designed mask to be laid on a text. The mask was a blank sheet with a rectangular window, cut to be somewhat larger than a long word in the text. His best letter recognition was at 5° to the right, so we put a fixation mark 5° to the left of the window. He placed this mask on the text to be read, fixed his gaze on the mark, and was to read the word which appeared in the window to the right. He was to shift the mask along the text and read word by word. This gave him the possibility of recognising words in isolation at that eccentricity where letter strings were

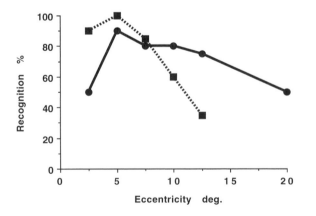

Figure 3.8 The right side plots for the FRF of an adult severe dyslexic. The solid line is the plot of the initial test and the dashed line 4 months later after practising the regimen.

Note

Correct recognition of the letter at the centre for all peripheral letter eccentricities, except for 2.5° of the first plot, was above 90%. The score of the centre letter (before the practice) for 2.5° eccentricity of the peripheral letter was 70%; after the practice of the regimen it was 90%.

best recognised. He followed this two-part regimen for the next 4 months, unsupervised but with occasional phone calls from us for encouragement.

Four months after the start of practice we tested him again. His reading had improved markedly to the level equivalent to 10th grade of school and his FRF had changed as shown in Figure 3.8. As seen from that Figure, the FRF had narrowed; there was a marked reduction of correct recognition in the periphery and increased recognition in and near the centre. In a second test we presented a string of three letters in place of the peripheral letter of the pair. This was to give a direct measure of lateral masking as a function of eccentricity. The results of this experiment show that, after practice, lateral masking in and near the centre of gaze was markedly reduced, while lateral masking in the periphery increased (Geiger and Lettvin 1987, 1989).

We tested the same regimen of practice on another three severe dyslexics. Within 12 to 20 weeks after the initial testing and starting practice of the regimen, we noted marked improvements in reading skills for all subjects, and at the same time changes of the FRF toward that of ordinary readers. This demonstrates that learning a new visual strategy for reading is possible. It also shows that rapid improvement in reading is accompanied by change of the distribution of lateral masking toward that of ordinary readers.

Interestingly, the learning of the new visual strategy produced other changes which are of a more general nature. Before practice of the regimen the subjects were very good at doing things simultaneously, like listening to or attending several unrelated sources at a time, perceiving at a glance complex gestalts or structures, sculptures or diagrams. However, after practice of the regimen their ability to perceive simultaneous spatial arrangements was compromised while their ability to perceive sequential things was sharpened. This is a vague description which might be made clearer by an example. Before practice of the regimen one of the subjects was able to listen to the radio, look at TV, speak on the phone and interact with a visiting friend all at the same time. After the practice and marked improvement in reading he was able to attend only one of these sequences at a time.

Three of the dyslexics who practised the regimen felt that the new strategy for reading had 'robbed' them of important skills and they preferred the old modus vivendi. According to our experience, adults retain the new visual strategy and the advanced level of reading conditional on continuing practice for a prolonged period. The only one of the adults who chose to continue was a college student. We suggested to the others who insisted on having the old strategies back, that they stop the practice of the regimen, which they did. After a few months their reading skills returned to the initial state with which they came to us; at the same time their FRFs returned to the original shape. This establishes a relation between the distribution of lateral masking and the strategy for reading.

Dyslexic children learn a new visual strategy for reading

The experiences with adult dyslexics on learning a new visual strategy for reading were important in showing the way but were essentially anecdotal. Therefore we performed a controlled experiment with dyslexic children to check the validity of our approach and to show that it also applies to children. The general idea was to divide the dyslexic children into two groups of similar composition. One group, the 'experimental dyslexics', would be given our new regimen of practice while the other group, the 'control dyslexics', was to continue the remedial programme given by the schools. After 3 to 4 months, the two groups would be compared for reading skills and for their FRFs. Then the regimen would be given also to the control dyslexics. After a few more months the measurements would be repeated on all the children. In this way we could judge the effectiveness of the regimen by comparing two groups with two different practice regimens over the same period of time and measure the achievement of each child before and after practice of the regimen. The results would test the validity of our approach in a measurable way.

The subjects in this study were 15 children (3rd–6th grade) who were considered as dyslexics and 6 children who were ordinary readers. All came from the public school system in Tübingen, Germany. The results of this study were published in 1994 (Geiger, Lettvin and Fahle 1994). We give here only the important points.

The initial session of tests for all subjects included an ophthalmological examination, a standardised reading test (Züricher Lesetest (ZLT)), a handedness preference test (Briggs and Nebes 1975) and an interview. The subjects were confirmed to be either dyslexics or ordinary readers on the basis of these tests

Table 3.1 Average age, grade and reading retardation taken at the initial testing of the Tübingen children

Group	Subjects no.	Age years (SD)	At school grade (SD)	Reading test (ZLT)
				grades behind (SD)
Experimental dyslexics	9	11.23 (1.46)	4.89 (1.27)	2.67 (0.87)
Control dyslexics	6	10.79 (0.97)	4.5 (0.55)	2.25 (0.42)
All dyslexics together	15	11.05 (1.27)	4.73 (1.03)	2.50 (0.73)
				grades in advance
Ordinary reading	6	10.45 (0.72)	4.17 (0.98)	0.33 (0.52)

Note
SD stands for standard deviation

together with the assessment of their intelligence. Then the FRF test was given to all. The results of the initial session of testing are shown in Table 3.1 which gives the average age, grade and reading retardation of the subjects. It distinguishes the dyslexics and establishes the difference in reading skills between them and the ordinary readers. The FRF plots are incorporated in the averages shown by Figure 3.6, where the FRF plot is significantly wider for dyslexics than for ordinary readers.

At the end of the session the dyslexic children were divided into two groups; experimental dyslexics (9) and control dyslexics (6). The two dyslexic groups were matched for age, reading level and reading retardation as also seen in Table 3.1. The average FRF plots of both groups were also similar as seen in Figure 3.9. At the end of the session the regimen of practice was given to the experimental dyslexics while the control dyslexics continued their remedial practices at school.

The regimen of practice is similar to the one described for adults in the previous experiment and has two complementary parts. One part consists of novel, small-scale hand–eye coordination tasks like drawing, painting, modelling, etc. It was important that the activity be novel to the child and preferably enjoyable. All kinds of art work and small-scale mechanical constructions (and disassembly) were suggested as tasks. Each dyslexic was asked to engage for about an hour daily in these activities which were to be performed in a private and unsupervised manner, not in a structured lesson. It was important that the child initiated and chose the activities and enjoyed doing them. This gave strong motivation.

The second part of the regimen was to read (recognise) words in isolation. To this end we asked the children to use a specially designed mask sheet for reading. The mask is the same as described in the previous section but it was not always made of a blank sheet. At times it was made of a coloured transparent sheet. For the subjects who had lateral masking in or near the centre, as shown in their FRFs,

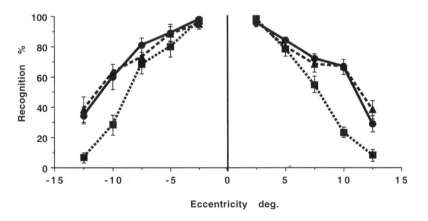

Figure 3.9 The FRF plots for children: the average for the experimental dyslexic group (solid line), the average for the control dyslexic group (dashed line) and the average for ordinary readers group (dotted line).

a fixation point was marked left of the window. The others used a window centrally located. The distance of the fixation point was determined individually, and was given by the measure of the FRF for best recognition. The subject was to fixate the point and read the word in the window to the right.

Three months after the initial testing the second testing was conducted. It included reading assessment with the same standardised test, and measurement of the FRF. Every subject who was included in the experimental group had practised for at least half an hour per day (on average) hand–eye coordination tasks (mostly art work) in addition to similar work given in school. These subjects also did at least half an hour per day of reading with the mask sheet. During this period the control dyslexics continued the remedial procedure given by the school. It included additional reading and writing assignments with syllable awareness training and the use of a finger as a pointer in reading.

Figure 3.10 shows the improvement in reading after 3 months for each individual of both groups and the average improvement of each group. On average the experimental dyslexics improved by 1.22 (SD = 0.36) grade level, while the average improvement for the control dyslexics was 0.17 (SD = 0.26) grade level. Every child in the experimental group had improved reading by at least 1 grade level, at the same time the highest improvement rate reached by any control dyslexic was 0.5 grade level. The FRFs of the experimental dyslexics taken before practice and after 3 months practice are shown in Figure 3.11. As can be seen, the FRFs of the experimental dyslexics narrowed significantly on the right side while remaining the same on the left side. The FRFs of the experimental dyslexics after practice were not significantly different from those of the ordinary readers on the right but were significantly wider on the left. The FRFs of the control dyslexics, taken in the second testing session, were significantly wider

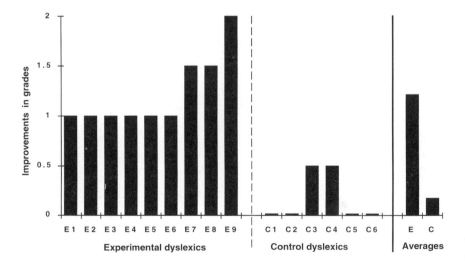

Figure 3.10 Improvements in reading for all the dyslexic individuals and the averages for each group: E = experimental dyslexics, C = control dyslexics.

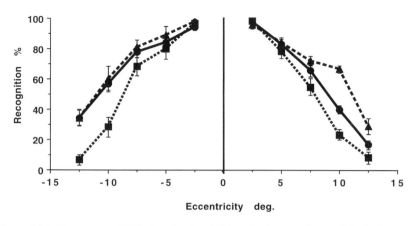

Figure 3.11 The average FRF plots for the children in the experimental dyslexics group before practising the regimen (dashed line) and after practice (solid line).

Note

The FRF narrowed significantly on the right-hand side after practice. The plots for the FRF of the ordinary readers (dotted line) are from Figure 3.9 and are given for reference.

than those of the experimental dyslexics taken in the same session, and had not changed since the initial testing.

At the end of this second session our regimen of practice was then given also to the control dyslexics. Five months later (8 months from the start of the study), reading levels and the FRF were measured again. From the 15 dyslexics, 9 practised the regimen for 8 months and 2 control dyslexics practised for 5 months (3 of the control dyslexics failed to take the third session of testing and 1 did not practise). The initial reading deficit of all the dyslexics who practised the regimen was 2.5 (SD = 0.73) grade levels. After 8 months of practice the deficit was on average only 0.75 (SD = 0.76) grade levels, i.e an average improvement in reading of 1.75 grade levels, a rate of improvement faster than that of ordinary reading subjects. At the end of 8 months, of the 11 dyslexics who practised the regimen 9 had reading retardation equal to or below 1 grade level, one child had retardation of 1.2 grade levels and only one child was still 2.5 grade levels behind the expected.

Discussion

As shown in these experiments, dyslexic adults and children are able to learn a new visual strategy which dramatically improves their reading skills. This learning is a result of practising the regimen we suggested. New results by Fahle and Luberichs (1995) show that 54 children with reading and/or spelling problems, improved their reading at a rate larger than ordinary readers after practising a regimen similar to ours. Although the results were not as specific as the ones given here, the group of children in that study included some dyslexics but more children with problems related mainly to spelling.

This regimen of practice resembles components of an earlier developmental type of motor skill training (Frostig and Horn 1964; Lewis 1968). Ours, however, is task-specific and is based on the formation of a new visual strategy operationally defined by the task in a manner suggested by Held and his colleagues (Held and Gottlieb 1958; Held and Hein 1958) and by Kohler (1964) as remarked earlier.

The empirics are straightforward enough. We have developed a non-reading measure, the FRF, that reliably distinguishes ordinary readers and dyslexics. The FRF measures the distribution of lateral masking along the horizontal axis in the visual field. The differences in distribution provide the diagnostic distinction. The differences in distribution of lateral masking signify different modes or strategic states of vision with respect to the specific task of reading. We argue that the distribution which characterises dyslexics explains their reading difficulties. Finally we show that when dyslexics learn a new visual strategy for reading, the distribution of lateral masking changes to resemble that of ordinary readers.

An important point for discussion here is the unsupervised, simple and inexpensive two-part regimen we give to dyslexics. The juvenile (age 8–13) ordinary readers and the adult ordinary readers (age > 16) have the same narrow symmetrical field of least lateral masking in the central part of the visual field. The juvenile dyslexics have a broad field of reduced lateral masking centred at the fixation point, but some have lateral masking in and near the centre. In the direction of reading, the adult dyslexics have a broad eccentric field of relatively low lateral masking, but have increased lateral masking in and near the centre of gaze. In the juvenile and adult dyslexics, the broad unmasked field of a seen text, however elementary that text may be, does not allow them to identify which arrangement of letters they can see is to be associated with a spoken word. In some of the juvenile dyslexics and in the adult dyslexics, strings of letters are laterally masked in the centre of gaze and of the words seen in the broad peripheral field, the ones that can be associated with a spoken word are not obvious in the plethora. Accordingly the second part of the regimen is the isolation of one or two words by a window in a sheet overlaying the text. The window is placed wherever the subject identifies letters best according to the FRF measure. That masks the surrounding text which is not relevant at that moment, and thereby reinforces the recognition of the form of a word as associated with the sound of the word.

The unsupervised novel hand–eye coordination activities of play and art work, bring the subject into a mode of trying new strategies to optimise performance. This activity results in narrowing the distribution of lateral masking and in reducing the lateral masking in the centre for those who have it. As soon as subjects come to recognise words, they know what to look for with central vision. This process of combined activities resulted in fast improvement in reading and in an FRF that resembled that of ordinary readers.

It is hard to formalise the concept of play which is essential to the development of expert performance in all animals, and is a major topic in the study of cubs in mammalian species. It is also remarked in the published introspections of great discoverers in science, great inventors and great artists. We suspect that too stringent an attention to remediate dyslexia may be counterproductive. The rapid success of our method with adult dyslexics who had seemed refractory to any approach, appears to confirm the efficiency of unsupervised play even in adults.

Under our concept of the process involved there are many reasons why a child, having a broad central field, may not initially learn the strategy of ordinary reading, but we are rather more sure about how the symptom gets reinforced into a full-blown and stubborn disorder. Similarly, the successful regimen developed under our concept does not preclude other variants of treatment. But we are certain that any relief of dyslexia by any other method will be attended by the same characteristic change in the FRF.

We suggest that such a description of the differences in and learning of the distributions of lateral masking may have comparable analogies in other modes of perception such as the temporal ordering of heard information (e.g. Tallal and Katz 1989; Taub, Fine and Cherry 1994).

References

Atkinson, J., Anker, S., Evans, C., Hall, R. and Pimm-Smith, E. (1988) 'Visual acuity testing of young children with the Cambridge crowding cards at 3 and 6 m', *Acta Ophthalmol* (Copenh), 66, 505–508.

Aubert, H. and Foerster, (1857) 'Beitraege zur Kenntniss des indirecten Sehens', *Graefes Archiv Ophthalmol*, 3, 1–47.

Bakker, D.J. (1972) *Temporal Order in Disturbed Reading*. Rotterdam: University Press.

Bjaalid, I.-K., Hoien, T. and Lundberg, I. (1993) 'Letter identification and lateral masking in dyslexics and normal readers', *Scan J Ed Res*, 37, 151–161.

Boder, E. (1973) 'Developmental dyslexia: A diagnostic approach based on three atypical reading patterns', *Dev Med Child Neurol*, 15, 663–687.

Bouma H. (1970) 'Interaction effects in parafoveal letter recognition', *Nature*, 226, 177–178.

Bouma, H. and Legein, Ch.P. (1977) 'Foveal and parafoveal recognition of letters and words by dyslexics and by average readers', *Neuropsychologia*, 15, 69–80.

Bouma, H. and Legein, Ch.P. (1980) 'Dyslexia: a specific decoding deficit? An analysis of response latencies for letters and words in dyslexics and in average readers', *Neuropsychologia*, 18, 285–298.

Briggs, C.G. and Nebes, R.D. (1975) 'Patterns of hand preference in a student population', *Cortex*, 11, 230–238.

Dautrich, B. (1993) 'Visual perceptual differences in the dyslexic reader: Evidence of greater visual peripheral sensitivity to color and letter stimuli', *Percept Mot Skill*, 76, 755–764.

Denckla, M. (1977) 'Minimal brain dysfunction and dyslexia: Beyond diagnosis by exclusion', in M. Blaw, J. Rapin and M. Kinsbourne (eds), *Child Neurology*. NY: Spectrum.

Di Lollo, V., Hanson, D. and McIntyre, J.S. (1983) 'Initial stages of visual information processing in dyslexia', *Journal of Experimental Psychology: Human Perception and Performance*, 9, 923–935.

Fahle, M. and Luberichs, J. (1995) 'Extension of a recent therapy for dyslexia', *German J Ophthalmol*, 4, 350–354.

Fowler, M.S., Riddell, P.M. and Stein, J.F. (1990) 'Vergence eye movement control and spatial discrimination in normal and dyslexic children', in G.Th. Pavlidis (ed.), *Perspectives on Dyslexia, Vol. 1* (pp. 253–273). Chichester: John Wiley & Sons.

Frostig, M. and Horne, D. (1964) *The Frostig Program for the Development of Visual Perception*. Chicago: Follett Publishing Co.

Galaburda, A.M. and Kemper, T.L. (1979) 'Cytoarchitectonic abnormalities in developmental dyslexia: A case study', *Ann Neurol*, 6, 94–100.

Galaburda, A.M., Sherman, G.F., Rosen, G.D., Aboitiz, F. and Geschwind, N. (1985) 'Developmental dyslexia: Four consecutive patients with cortical anomalies', *Ann Neurol*, 18, 222–233.

Geiger, G. and Lettvin, J.Y. (1986) 'Enhancing the perception of form in peripheral vision', *Perception*, 15, 119–130.

Geiger, G, and Lettvin J.Y. (1987) 'Peripheral vision in persons with dyslexia', *N Engl J Med*, 316, 1238–1243.

Geiger, G. and Lettvin J.Y. (1989) 'Dyslexia and reading as examples of alternative visual strategies', in C. von Euler, I. Lundberg and G. Lennerstrand G. (eds), *Brain and Reading* (pp. 331–343). London: Macmillan Press Ltd.

Geiger, G. and Lettvin, J.Y. (1993) 'Manifesto on dyslexia', in S.F. Wright and R. Groner (eds), *Facets of Dyslexia and Its Remediation* (pp. 51–63). North Holland: Elsevier.

Geiger, G., Lettvin, J.Y and Fahle, M. (1994) 'Dyslexic children learn a new visual strategy for reading: a controlled experiment', *Vision Res*, 34, 1223–1233.

Geiger, G., Lettvin, J.Y. and Zegarra-Moran, O. (1992) 'Task-determined strategies of visual process', *Cog Brain Res*, 1, 39–52.

Geschwind, N. and Behan, P.O. (1982) 'Left handedness: Association with immune disease, migraine and developmental learning disorder', *Proc Natl Acad Sci USA*, 79, 5097–5100.

Goolkasian, P. and King, J. (1990) 'Letter identification and lateral masking in dyslexic and average readers', *American Journal of Psychology*, 103, 519–538.

Held, R. and Gottlieb, N. (1958) 'Technique for studying adaptation of disarranged hand–eye coordination', *Percept Mot Skills*, 8, 83–86.

Held, R. and Hein, A.V. (1958) 'Adaptation of disarranged hand–eye coordination contingent upon re-afferent stimulation', *Percept Mot Skills*, 8, 87–90.

Klein, R., Berry, G., Briand, K., D'Entremont, B. and Farmer, M. (1990) 'Letter identification declines with increasing retinal eccentricity at the same rate for normal and dyslexic readers', *Perception & Psychophysics*, 47, 601–606.

Kohler, I. (1962) 'Experiments with goggles', *Sci Am*, 206, 62–72.

Kohler, I. (1964) 'The formation and transformation of the perceptual world', *Psychological Issues*, 3(4) monograph 12, 1–174.

Lettvin, J.Y., Maturana, H.R., Pitts, W.H. and McCulloch, W.S. (1961) 'Two remarks on the visual system of the frog', in W.A. Rosenblith (ed.), *Sensory Communications* (pp. 757–776). New York: John Wiley & Sons.

Lewis, J.N. (1968) 'The improvement of reading ability through a developmental program in visual perception', *Journal of Learning Disabilities*, 1, 652–653.

Liberman, I.Y. (1971) 'Basic research in speech and lateralization of language: some implications for reading disability', *Bull Orton Soc*, 21, 71–87.

Liberman, I.Y. (1982) 'A language oriented view of reading and its disabilities', in H. Myklebust (ed.), *Progress in Learning Disabilities*. New York: Grune & Stratton.

Liberman, I.Y., Shankweiler, D., Fischer, F.W. and Carter, B. (1974) 'Explicit syllable and phoneme segmentation in the young child', *Journal of Experimental Child Psychology*, 18, 201–212.

Livingstone, M.S., Rosen, G.D., Drislane, F.W. and Galaburda, A.M. (1991) 'Physiological and anatomical evidence for a magnocellular defect in developmental dyslexia', *Proc Natl Acad Sci USA*, 88, 7943–7947.

Lovegrove, W.J., Martin, F. and Slaghuis, W. (1986) 'A theoretical and experimental case for a residual deficit in specific reading disability', *Cognitive Neuropsychology*, 3, 225–267.

Lundberg, I. (1982) 'Linguistic awareness as related to dyslexia', in Y. Zotterman (ed.), *Dyslexia: Neuronal, Cognitive and Linguistic Aspects*. Oxford: Pergamon Press.

Lundberg, I. (1989) 'Lack of phonological awareness – a critical factor in dyslexia', in C. von Euler, I. Lundberg and G. Lennerstrand (eds), *Brain and Reading* (pp. 221–231). London: Macmillan.

Mackworth, N.H. (1965) 'Visual noise causes tunnel vision', *Psychonomic Science*, 3, 67–68.

Olson, R.K., Wise, B., Conners, F.A. and Rack, J.P. (1989) 'Deficits in disabled readers' phonological and orthographic coding: ethiology and remediation', in C. von Euler, I. Lundberg and G. Lennerstrand (eds), *Brain and Reading* (pp. 233–242). London: Macmillan.

O'Reagan, J.K. (1990) 'Eye movements and reading', in E. Kowler (ed.), *Eye Movements and Their Role in Visual and Cognitive Processes*. North Holland: Elsevier Science Publishers.

Perry, A.R., Dember, W.N., Warm, J.S. and Sacks, J.G. (1989) 'Letter identification in normal and dyslexic readers: a verification', *Bull Psychon Soc*, 27, 445–448.

Pettet, M.W. and Gilbert, C.D. (1992) 'Dynamic changes in receptive-field size in cat primary cortex', *Proc Natl Acad Sci USA*, 89, 8366–8370.

Shaywitz, B.A., Fletcher, J.M. and Shaywitz, S.E. (1995) 'Defining and classifying learning disabilities and attention-deficit/hyperactivity disorder', *J Child Neurol*, 10 (Suppl 1), s50–s57.

Siegel, L.S. (1989) 'IQ is irrelevant to the definition of learning disabilities', *Journal of Learning Disabilities*, 22, 469–486.

Slaghuis, W.L., Lovegrove, W.J. and Freestun, J. (1992) 'Letter recognition in peripheral vision and metacontrast masking in dyslexics and normal readers', *Clin Vision Sci*, 7, 53–65.

Stein, J.F. and Fowler, M.S. (1981) 'Visual dyslexia', *TINS*, 4, 77–80.

Tallal, P. and Katz, W. (1989) 'Neuropsychological and neuroanatomical studies of developmental language/reading disorder: recent advances', in C. von Euler, I. Lundberg and G. Lennerstrand (eds), *Brain and Reading* (pp. 183–196). London: Macmillan.

Taub, C.F., Fine, E. and Cherry, R.S. (1994) 'Finding a link between selective auditory attention and reading problems in young children: a preliminary investigation', *Percept Mot Skills*, 78, 1153–1154.

Townsend, J.T., Taylor, S.G. and Brown, D.R. (1971) 'Lateral masking for letters with unlimited viewing time', *Perception and Psychophysics*, 10, 375–378.

Williams, M.C., LeCluyse, K. and Bologna, N. (1990) 'Masking by light as a measure of visual integration time in normal and disabled readers', *Clin Vision Sci*, 5, 335–343.

Wolford, G. and Chambers, L. (1983) 'Lateral masking as a function of spacing', *Perception and Psychophysics*, 33, 129–138.

Zegarra-Moran, O. and Geiger, G. (1993) 'Visual recognition in the peripheral field: letters vs. symbols and adults vs. children', *Perception*, 22, 77–90.
Zurif, E. and Carson, G. (1970) 'Dyslexia in relation to cerebral dominance and temporal analysis', *Neuropsychologia*, 8, 351–361.

4 Saccadic eye movements in dyslexia

Burkhart Fischer and Monica Biscaldi

Introduction

This chapter considers the principal aspects of saccade generation, fixation, attention, decision, as the elements of the optomotor cycle serving in vision, visual cognition, and in reading. Periods of no saccades (fixations) last between 100 and 250 ms. Three to five saccades occur every second and they last between 20 and 40 ms. Therefore, 90 per cent of the time the eyes are in rest. Given saccadic reaction times of 180 to 250 ms it looks as if the duration of a fixation is just enough time to prepare the next saccade. On the other hand saccadic reaction times under certain conditions can be as short as 80 to 100 ms (express saccades). This extremely short reaction time still contains some central processing time as well. Considering the different aspects of saccade generation and the corresponding modulation of reaction time distributions it will be possible to construct the basic optomotor cycle and to understand the variations of time consumed within it.

In the second part of the chapter we will begin with a brief review of the recent literature on the controversial issue of saccadic eye movement abnormalities in dyslexic subjects. Finally, the findings of different saccadic reaction time patterns and abnormalities in accuracy in dyslexic as compared to control subjects will be discussed in relation to the different aspects of the normal optomotor cycle.

Components of the normal optomotor cycle

The first part of this chapter considers the neurophysiological and psychophysical evidence for the existence of different components contributing to saccade generation (fixation period). We will review the results of single-cell recordings and lesion studies in monkeys as well as reaction time studies in human subjects.

Saccade

Anatomy and physiology

Using the modern tracing technique one can find the anatomical pathways that connect the retina with the oculomotor centres in the brain stem. The pattern of these connections is rather complicated: there are many ways by which the signals originating in the afferent visual system as a consequence of retinal stimulation can arrive at the efferent structures which activate the extraocular muscles. From a functional point of view it appears that one should consider three main routes, or loops (Fischer and Weber 1993). One route includes the lateral geniculate nucleus, the primary visual cortex, and the tectum (superior colliculus) before it enters the brain stem. The second route includes the frontal eye fields which receive input from the visual cortex and project directly (and indirectly) to the oculomotor centres (Schiller, True and Conway 1979). A third route uses the parietal cortex, which controls saccadic eye movements indirectly by regulating attentional factors. The three routes do not act independently from each other: even though a monkey can make saccades with his superior colliculus deactivated he cannot make saccades with fast latencies (express saccades) using his frontal system alone (Schiller, Sandell and Maunsell 1987). The control of the tectal route by the frontal route probably uses the basal ganglia, which have an inhibitory action on the saccade related cells in the superior colliculus (Hikosaka and Wurtz 1983a).

The coexistence of visual and saccade related activity in single cells has been known for a long time. However, detailed analysis of the modulation of cell discharge in relation to the exact behavioural context has been necessary to see that different groups of cells carry different functional aspects in their impulse activity. It seems suitable to differentiate three groups of saccade-related cells (reviewed by Fischer and Boch 1991): one group is activated in close relation to the occurrence of the saccade itself, irrespective of the context under which the eye movement is made. These oculomotor cells are found in the deep layers of the superior colliculus (and of course in the brain stem). A second group of cells raise their visual activity only in relation to behaviourally relevant saccades, not in relation to spontaneous saccades made in the dark. Cells of this category are found mainly in the frontal eye fields, but also in the superior colliculus. A third group of cells also raise their activity prior to saccades, but when the animal, for some reason, suppresses the eye movement the modulation of the activity occurs as well. Cells of this type are present in the parietal cortex and in the prestriate cortex and have been related to attentional mechanisms rather than to saccade generation (Robinson, Goldberg and Stanton 1978). Besides attention, one should also consider fixation as a functional aspect of vision and eye movements: for example the sustained visual activity of cells in the prestriate cortex (visual area V4) can be modulated up and down by switching the fixation point off and on while the animal suppresses saccades to the peripheral stimulus (Fischer and Boch 1985).

Reaction time of primary saccades

To access the subprocesses involved in saccade generation reaction time, studies have been used quite successfully during the past 10 or 15 years. The idea is that any extra process involved in the preparation of a given saccade will take extra time, adding to the saccadic reaction time (SRT). Here we will consider the reaction time of the first saccade after target onset, called the primary saccade, irrespective of whether it will hit the target at once or will be followed by a corrective saccade, called the secondary saccade.

If one presents a visual target for a saccade a few degrees from the fovea, the human saccadic reaction time can vary from about 80 ms to 250 ms depending on the parameters of visual stimulation and the behavioural task-dependent conditions (monkeys have somewhat shorter SRTs than humans, part of the difference being due to shorter conduction times). In the last 10 years it became clear that the distributions of the SRTs exhibit often two or three peaks (modes). The basic observation in this direction was made in the monkey: the animals produced saccades with extremely short latencies which formed a separate peak in a bimodal distribution (Fischer and Boch 1983). This bimodality was most readily obtained in a condition in which the fixation point was switched off some time (the gap duration) before the target was presented. Later, the gap experiment was repeated with human subjects and yielded the same kind of bimodality (Fischer and Ramsperger 1984). The saccades contributing to the first peak were called express saccades (ES), those contributing to the second peak were called fast regular saccades. The peak of ES was more or less evident in naive human subjects (Fischer *et al.* 1993c) but it could be enhanced by daily practice (Fischer, Boch and Ramsperger 1984).

When the fixation point was left visible SRTs were much longer. They often formed a bimodal distribution as in the gap paradigm, but with the first peak occurring at about the same position as the second peak was located in the gap condition. The other peak was centred at about 200 ms or later. Saccades contributing to this late peak were called slow regular saccades. While the latency reduction effect of the introduction of the gap on SRTs had been known for a long time (Saslow 1967), the interpretation of the gap effect became clearer only after the finding of a separate population of ES in a multimodal distribution (Fischer 1987). Some authors have questioned the existence of a separate population of ES (Wenban-Smith and Findlay 1991; Reuter-Lorenz, Hughes and Fendrich 1991), but the phenomenon has been replicated in humans by several independent research groups (Fischer *et al.* 1993c; Jüttner and Wolf 1994; Nothdurft and Parlitz 1993; Tam and Stelmach 1993).

The exact conditions under which one or the other mode was enhanced or attenuated gave insight into the different functional aspects of saccade generation and the basic optomotor cycle. Details of these sets of experiments have been reviewed elsewhere (Fischer and Weber 1993). Basically, the observation was that with the overlap task the express mode is largely absent in most subjects. By daily practice, however, human subjects and monkeys can learn to make ES when the fixation point remains visible (Fischer and Ramsperger 1986; Boch and Fischer 1986). Yet, in human subjects the training in this case was mostly restricted to one side. Moreover, depending on the instruction to attend to the fixation point or not during overlap trials, the SRT distribution may contain only a small number of fast regular saccades, and many slow regular saccades, or the fast regular mode is favoured. This shows that fixation plays an important role in the control of saccades and in particular in the suppression of ES.

Secondary saccades

When subjects are required to make a saccade to a single target, often two saccades are necessary to reach the target. The correction time – intersaccadic interval between the primary and the secondary saccade – is normally in the order of 130–150 ms or more. Corrective saccades occur also when the subject makes the first saccade in the wrong direction. The analysis of the time when the direction errors were corrected yielded the existence of secondary ES (Fischer, Weber and Biscaldi 1993a): the second saccade is made at about 100 ms after target presentation (not after the end of the primary saccade) and the intersaccadic interval can be close to zero. If the primary saccade was made in the correct direction and landed close to the target, the correction times increased depending on the size of the error: large errors were corrected faster and the asymptotic value of the correction time turned out to be in the order of 100 ms. These findings were related to the observation that ES tend to be blocked by a foveal stimulus (Weber *et al.* 1992): when the secondary saccade corrects a large error, the foveal region is not stimulated at the end of the primary saccade. This observation suggests that a stimulus entering the region of the fovea will tend to arrest saccades for some time.

Fixation

Basically, the evidence for the existence of a fixation system controlling the generation of saccades comes from stimulation experiments in the monkey. Microstimulation of small cell groups in the parietal cortex, the frontal eye fields, and the superior colliculus leads to saccades. However, the threshold for eliciting these responses is increased when the animal is required to actively fixate (Shibutani, Sakata and Hyvarinen 1984; Goldberg, Bushnell and Bruce 1986). In these brain regions there are cells that are active during attentive fixation and inactive during saccades, while other cells behave in the opposite manner. Cells in the rostral part of the superior colliculus seem to belong to the fixation system (Munoz and Wurtz 1992). When this cell group was chemically deactivated, the animals were largely unable to maintain fixation. They made large numbers of unwanted saccades and most of these saccades were of the express type (Munoz and Wurtz 1993). This observation shows that there exists a mechanism that keeps the saccade system from reacting in a reflex-like (express) manner. Since the fixation related cells have small receptive fields including the fovea, one predicts that saccade targets presented close to the fovea would activate the fixation cells which in turn inhibit the saccade cells leading to an abolishment of ES for decreasing saccade size. Indeed, a 'dead zone' for ES has been found around the fovea, in monkeys as well as in man (Weber *et al.* 1992). The 'dead zone' is also responsible for the absence of fast corrections of small errors (see above).

When monkeys freely scan permanently presented stimuli and suddenly an additional stimulus is switched on, they can look at the new stimulus by ES (Sommer 1994). This rather interesting observation indicates that in this scanning situation the fixation system of the animal remains inactive or 'disengaged'.

From these data one arrives at a notion of two reflex-like mechanisms: one serves for a more or less automatic arrest of saccades – a stop reflex – the other serves to automatically trigger a new saccade – a go reflex. The two reflexes therefore need to work alternately and they must be under at least one control mechanism depending on what the subject sees and on what the subject decides to look at.

Attention

The most straightforward control mechanism for saccade generation is that of visual attention. The general idea is: what catches our attention will be foveated. This notion implies that attention is allocated to the target or to the target location before the saccade is executed and the next conclusion is that allocated attention is necessary for the generation of the saccade. This hypothesis has been tested in tasks where attention allocation is achieved before the command for the saccade is given, for example by presenting a valid cue (Posner, 1980). It has been shown that manual RTs are facilitated for (i.e. attention is allocated to) positions within the hemifield toward which a saccade has been prepared (Posner 1980; Shepherd, Findlay and Hockey 1986; Chelazzi *et al.* 1995). Other authors found no experimental support for the hypothesis that a saccade to a target must necessarily be preceded by an attentional shift to that position (Klein and Pontefract 1994). Recently, however, it has been shown that discrimination performance improves selectively for a location that will be foveated just before the saccade is executed (Kowler *et al.* 1995; Deubel and Schneider 1995). This has been interpreted as a demonstration for a 'selective and obligatory coupling of attention allocation and saccade programming' (Deubel and Schneider 1995).

The concept that allocated attention is necessary for saccade generation, however, raises some difficulties. The first is that attention allocated to a foveal stimulus would result in a never ending fixation period unless one introduces another mechanism which releases central attention allocation and shifts the attentional focus to another position. In this case the problem of how the eye gets to the next location is postponed to the problem of how attention is shifted. The second is that one has to assume that attention allocation works in a space-centred coordinate system, because if attention allocation is in retinal coordinates and precedes the saccade then, just after the saccade, attention would be allocated to the past and now 'unwanted' location. In this moment, attention must be shifted back to the fovea, i.e. in a direction opposite to that of the just preceding saccade. For the next saccade attention must be disallocated and allocated again. While space-centred systems may exist, e.g. in the parietal cortex, many cortical areas related to attentional effects are retinotopically organised. The third difficulty comes from an experiment in which subjects were instructed to permanently attend to a certain peripheral location before a target was presented at either this attended location or at the opposite side. The result was a decrease in the number of ES to the permanently attended location as compared to the control situation with no attentional instruction (Mayfrank *et al.* 1986). From this latter observation one could conclude that allocated attention delays saccade generation, thus arriving at a notion contrary to the more classical one mentioned above. One has to keep in mind, though, that the classical idea is based on experiments in which saccade latencies were in the range of regular saccades.

Investigations on attentional shift without saccades have shown that a covert shift of attention is preceded by a disengagement of attention (Posner *et al.* 1984), which must be reached before the saccade can be made. If one introduces two states of attention (disengaged and engaged), part of the problems mentioned above is solved.

Another solution of the contradictory experimental results is suggested by the dissociation between a transient automatic attention allocation mediated by visual stimuli and sustained voluntary components of attention (Nakayama and Mackebe 1989).

sustained	voluntary	bottom up	endogenous (by central cues or instructions)
transient	not voluntary (automatic)	top down	exogenous (by peripheral cues)

Sustained attention

In a situation where the subject keeps his or her direction of gaze straight ahead (without a foveal stimulus), paying attention to a permanently visible peripheral target, the percentage of ES is reduced as compared to the control case with the attention target being located at the fovea (Weber and Fischer 1995). It is important to mention here that in both cases the attention target was extinguished 200 ms before the saccade target was presented. Moreover, this reduction of ES is spatially selective: it is strong if attention and saccade target are presented at the same location. For some subjects the suppression occurs also for saccades directed to the mirror image position in the field contralateral to the attention target, but not for other positions at the same or the other hemifield (Weber and Fischer 1995). These new findings extend the earlier observation of an ES reduction due to the instruction to attend to a peripheral location without the onset of a visible attention target at that position (Mayfrank *et al.* 1986).

Transient attention

If one uses short cues to indicate to the subject where the next target will appear (valid trials) the effect of the cue depends strongly on the cue lead time. Given 100 ms cue lead time and using the gap paradigm, ES occur with high probability to targets presented at the cued location. However, in these experiments the cue makes the saccade size and direction predictable, given a 100 per cent validity of the cue. Mixing valid and invalid trials (e.g. 75/25) indicates a loss of ES for invalid cues, while for valid cues ES are still obtained and their number is increased (Cavegn 1994).

In conclusion, it seems that attention can have opposite effects on the occurrence of ES depending on how and when the allocation is achieved. The question may even be asked whether all these effects should be accounted for by only one control mechanism called 'attention'. Perhaps most of the apparent contradictory interpretations of the experimental results could be avoided if one would assume a visual – stimulus driven – selection process, which works automatically on the basis of retinal information and is closely related to saccades (bottom up) and a mental selection process which works on the basis of the result of perception (top down) and which is under voluntary conscious control. If the visual selection process precedes and facilitates saccades and the mental attention process arrests saccades (increases reaction time) one could explain most of the experimental data. For example the express shifts of 'attention' would belong to the automatic system activated by exogeneous peripheral cues (Mackeben and Nakayama 1993). The state of fixation would be a state in which voluntary sustained attention is allocated to a foveal stimulus.

In reading, the optomotor behaviour is highly automised. In normally developed subjects, the basic optomotor cycle will be perfectly controlled by its bottom up components and it will be also perfectly controlled by top down mechanisms. It is possible that disturbances within the optomotor cycle may lead to difficulties in the reading process.

Decision

Since a normal subject can suppress saccades or can make saccades in the direction opposite to the target or to a cue, the decision process is the next important aspect of saccade generation.

Antisaccades

The strongest test of the ability to overcome a reflex-like response to a suddenly appearing stimulus is to ask the subject to look to the side opposite to where the target is presented (antisaccade task). In this situation the subject not only has to suppress saccades to the target but also has to generate a saccade to a position where no visual stimulus is seen. Using the gap paradigm, it was shown that in general antisaccades cannot be of the express type. They are delayed by about 30 ms even after extensive training and even if the saccade direction and size are predictable (Fischer and Weber 1992). The usually small number of errors (unwanted saccades to the stimulus; i.e. prosaccades), on the other hand, often form bimodal distributions with the first peak at about 100 ms. This observation emphasises once more the reflex character of the ES and proves that a normal subject can usually control the reflex by suppressing it in favour of a movement to the opposite side. That the delay of the antisaccades could not be attributed to interhemispheric transfer times was demonstrated by an experiment where saccades had to be made in the same hemifield but not to the stimulus.

The problem of decision making in saccade generation has been studied also by introducing catch trials in a gap task where trained subjects made many ES in bimodal distributions (Jüttner and Wolf 1994). Increasing the probability of catch trials decreased the overall number of ES. Specifically, the chances for an ES in a given trial were systematically smaller if in the preceding one no target had been presented. In another experiment the command for making a pro- or an antisaccade was given by the form of visual fixation stimuli (cues) trial by trial. The detailed analysis of the many errors occurring in a gap condition with no cue-lead time showed that, in a given trial, subjects tend to follow the instructions of the preceding trial (Weber 1995)

Saccades across structured backgrounds

Under natural viewing conditions saccades occur in sequences across structured pattterns without external commands. 'Onsets' are produced in this case by each saccade shifting the retinal image such that previous contrast borders are suddenly replaced by others at any given retinal region. A question was whether ES could be obtained across structured backgrounds. The answer is that they can when, in the presence of a permanent texture background, a local target for a saccade is suddenly presented (Weber and Fischer 1994). If a structured background or single stimuli (distractors) are presented simultaneously with the target, the express mode is reduced or disappears altogether (Nothdurft and Parlitz 1993; Weber and Fischer 1994). This implies that a popout stimulus where all stimuli – the target and the distractors – are presented at the same time cannot be foveated by ES. Therefore, the assumption that preattentive processes inhibit ES is not necessary. Rather the distractor effects, which occur at relatively low levels, can explain these results.

The optomotor cycle

Our present knowledge suggests that at least three processes are involved in saccade generation: sustained attentive fixational engagement and its disengagement (permitting saccades), decision processes, and the computational process. To explain the multimodal reaction time data a corresponding three-loop model has been developed on the basis of artificial neurons grouped together in three different modules (Fischer, Gezeck and Huber 1995). Figure 4.1 shows schematically the structure of the model and how it may be used to simulate the optomotor cycle. Each saccade acts as a visual transient stimulus by shifting the retinal image rapidly. The visuomotor (bottom up) mechanisms will be activated and initiate a cycle which, when operating 'undisturbed', will result in the next saccade, and so on. If, however, cognitive processes activate the attentional system and produce an engagement of attention, the cycle length can be

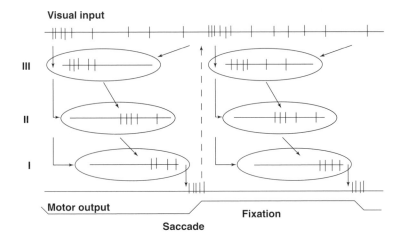

Figure 4.1 Schematic drawing of the three components of the optomotor cycle.

Note

Each saccade activates a new cycle as indicated by the vertical broken line in the middle.

increased: the next saccade will be delayed. If, on the other hand, the optomotor system stays in the disengaged state, only decision and computation processes must be completed within the cycle: the next saccade occurs earlier. Under certain circumstances even decision processes may be skipped and the next saccade can occur after the shortest time, i.e. after about 100 ms.

If one tries to understand the patterns of eye movement performance in reading by normal and dyslexic subjects and their relationship to cognitive processes one should look first of all at very simple eye movement tasks to see to what extent these subjects can produce normal saccades, normal fixations, and normal sequences of optomotor cycles when no cognitive effort is required.

Saccade generation in dyslexia

Review

The eye movements of dyslexic and control subjects have been studied both during reading and during non-cognitive eye movement tasks. During reading dyslexics have longer fixation durations and shorter saccades than age-matched controls (for a review see Rayner 1985). It has been discussed, however, whether this eye movement behaviour is specific for dyslexia or instead reflects either reading and comprehension problems (Olson, Conners and Rack 1991) or visuo-spatial problems of the dyslexics (Pirozzolo and Rayner 1988). The observation of 'reverse staircase' or regressive eye movements during reading was considered as more specific for dyslexia (Zangwill and Blakemore 1972; Adler-Grinberg and Stark 1978; Rubino and Minden 1973), but other studies suggested that such unusual eye movement patterns can be observed in young children as well and occasionally even in skilled readers during reading of a difficult text (Stark, Giveen and Terdiman 1991). It was also claimed that when the reading eye movement behaviour of dyslexic subjects is compared with that of younger control children reading a text of similar difficulty, no differences at all are detected (Olson *et al.* 1991; Hyönä and Olson 1995; Fields, Newman and Wright 1993). This result would suggest that the eye movement pattern reflects the reading ability of the subject.

Pavlidis claimed that saccadic abnormalities can be observed also during sequential tracking of simple light stimuli (Pavlidis 1981; Martos and Vila 1990; Jerabek and Krejcova 1991). He put forward the idea that an oculomotor dysfunction could be the key to dyslexia. Other researchers, however, failed to find any difference in the tracking ability of dyslexics as compared with control subjects (Brown *et al.* 1983; Black *et al.* 1984; Stanley, Smith and Howell 1983; see also Fields *et al.* 1993). Since the experimental procedures were not consistent among the studies, Olson attempted to replicate Pavlidis's method in all details but analysed separately saccades with amplitudes larger and smaller than 2.5° (Olson, Kliegl and Davidson 1983). Since the targets appeared 5° apart, the hypothesis was that saccades smaller than 2.5° had been corrective ones. In neither the number of large saccades nor the number of small saccades was a significant difference found between the dyslexic and the control subjects. He concluded that regressive saccades are not a marker for dyslexia. A clearer solution to the problem, however, would be given by taking into account the absolute position of the eyes with respect to the target.

Some methodological details from different authors who tested the oculomotor behaviour of dyslexic and control subjects during sequential tracking of light stimuli are given in the following:

• Pavlidis (1981): LEDs; 4° apart (3 trials per subject); subjects: 10–16 y, 12 dyslexics with IQ above average but no further definition, 12 age-matched controls.

• Olson *et al.* (1983): a black character (space) against a white background, 5° apart (3 trials per subject), 8–13,7 y age-matched, 34 dyslexics not separated for discrepancy between verbal and performance IQ, 36 controls (reading on the average or above).

• Stanley *et al.* (1983): LEDs; 1° apart (10 trials); subjects: teenagers (12,6 y), 15 dyslexics with a low verbal IQ, 15 controls (reading above average).

• Brown *et al.* (1983): oscilloscope spot, 3.5° apart (5 trials); subjects: children (11 y), 34 dyslexics probably not separated for visuo-spatial or verbal problems, 33 controls (reading not lower than 1 y below grade level); he defined predictive eye movement as occurring 120 ms prior to or following the stimulus position change (some of them could have been ES).

• Black *et al.* (1984): single jumps of 15° (left or right), age range 6,0 to 16,9 (not matched but linear correlation analysis as a function of age for different parameers), 28 dyslexics with lower verbal IQ, 31 not age-matched controls (but linear correlation analysis as a function of age for different parameters) (reading above average).

- Fields *et al.* (1993): LEDs; 4.5° apart (probably 4 trials in total), intervals of 1 s or 330 ms; subjects: children (7–9 y), 12 dyslexics with a good verbal IQ, 12 controls (reading at average or above), 12 control low achievers (defined on the basis of a low verbal IQ).

Studies on reaction times to single light targets also yielded contradictory results. Some authors found the mean SRTs to be slower for dyslexic than for control subjects (Dossetor and Papaioannou 1975). Pirozzolo (1979) claimed that slower SRTs are characteristic for a subgroup of dyslexics with visuo-spatial problems. Adler-Grinberg and Stark (1978) and Black *et al.* (1984), on the other hand, found no differences in the saccadic latencies and velocities of dyslexic subjects compared with control subjects but they found saccadic intrusion in the smooth pursuit of dyslexics, as confirmed by a recent study (Eden *et al.* 1994). Unusual SRT distributions were observed in the gap and overlap tasks of dyslexic subjects compared with control children (Fischer and Weber 1990). The dyslexics were divided in four subgroups characterised by different types of latency distribution profiles. Group I had more ES than the controls in both tasks; group II exhibited *only* ES in both tasks; group III had slightly longer latencies to the right in the overlap task; group IV showed an increased number of ES in the gap task but slower latencies in the overlap trials.

The discrepant findings left the issue of abnormal saccadic eye movements in dyslexics unresolved. Methodological differences in the stimuli presentation and in the choice of the subjects' sample are critical for the interpretation of the results and may explain, at least in part, the contradiction. For instance, the definition of what 'dyslexic' means and how to reliably differentiate dyslexics from back-ward readers and from control subjects with a relatively bad reading performance can influence the outcome of oculomotor experiments. The official definiton of dyslexia is 'a disorder manifest by difficulty in learning to read despite conven-tional instruction, adequate intelligence and socio-cultural opportunity' (Critchley 1970). Some recent work, however, suggests that subjects form a normal distri-bution regarding their reading abilities including normally reading subjects and dyslexic subjects at the extreme end of the continuum (Shaywitz *et al.* 1992). This implies that a control child could have an average reading performance but intelligence well above average, so that the discrepancy between his/her achieve-ment in reading and the expected level on the basis of his/her IQ is significantly increased. If the saccadic performance correlates with reading ability in the same way as Stein has demonstrated for the control of vergence movements and binoc-ular fixation (Stein and Fowler 1993), this relatively 'bad' achiever would also show an unusual oculomotor behaviour. Given that a control group contains many of these cases, it would be more difficult to find significant differences between the eye movement performance of dyslexic and control children.

Finally, a source of inconsistency in the data is due to the finding of a considerable individual variability in eye movement performance (Fields *et al.*

1993; Olson *et al.* 1991; Brown *et al.* 1983). Yet, a higher correlation between a given eye movement pattern and a specific group of dyslexics can still be observed against a background of individual variable eye movement patterns (Fischer and Weber 1990; Biscaldi, Fischer and Aiple 1994).

Single case studies can be sometimes more helpful than studies with large samples of subjects in deciding whether the unusual eye movement patterns of a dyslexic person are merely a peripheral component of his/her reading difficulties or a meaningful peculiarity of his/her oculomotor system. Zangwill and Blakemore (1972) examined a single case of a young adult man with developmental dyslexia, intelligence above average and signs of mixed laterality. He had a strong tendency to make groups of regressive saccades during reading. This phenomenon could not be due to mere linguistic problems, since he could recognise and read single words correctly after tachistoscopic presentation. Ciuffreda *et al.* (1976) examined four subjects with reading problems. The findings suggest the complexity of the relation between reading quality and patterns of eye movements. One subject had complaints (such as blurring of text) during sustained reading but normal eye movements. For two subjects, classified as slow readers, fixations were either too long or too many. Regressions were present in one case but not in the other. Another subject, with a clear diagnosis of dyslexia, showed instability of fixation and an unusually high number of fixations during reading. The pattern of reading eye movements was contaminated with frequent reversed staircases. Interestingly, the number of regressions was different for the two eyes in monocular reading. Also Pirozzolo and Rayner (1978) described a case of Gerstmann syndrome with reversed staircase patterns in eye movements during reading that disappeared when the subject was reading text upside down. In one dyslexic subject it was demonstrated that his reading problems were caused by a selective attentional deficit (Rayner *et al.* 1989). Although the eye movements of this subject to meaningless targets seemed to be normal, this study clearly indicates that attentional mechanisms may also play an important role in dyslexia.

Psychometric subgroups

A problem concerning the subjects' sample is the definition of dyslexic subtypes insofar as the dyslexics of a given group show other cognitive impairments and/or make diverse types of reading and spelling errors. The most accepted classification of dyslexics in subgroups considers a larger group with mainly language and phonological problems and a less numerous group with visuo-spatial or visuo-perceptual impairments (Boder 1973; Mattis, French and Rapin 1975; Pirozzolo and Rayner 1981). A third small group with mixed language and visual problems was also identified by most authors.

In a review of different methods of grouping children with learning problems, the cluster analysis was proposed as a relatively unbiased methodological approach (Satz and Morris 1981). Using the neuropsychological variables of a large sample of school children, Satz and Morris found a subgroup of reading disabled children (about 14 per cent) with no neuropsychological impairment in any of the tests applied. According to their work, our subtyping approach for children (9–11 y) was also based on the presence or absence of cognitive impairments in addition to the reading and spelling disabilities (Biscaldi *et al.* 1994). The psychometric test battery consisted of the assessement of general non-verbal intelligence (Raven's progressive matrices); short-term memory span for verbally presented sequences of digits and non-words; auditive discrimination ability for non-words; and the measurement of concentration in an attentional-loading task. For the assessement of the reading and spelling abilities, standardised tests largely used in schools and in research laboratories in Germany were employed (see Biscaldi *et al.* 1994).

A child was classified as dyslexic if his/her reading and spelling scores were 1.5 standard deviations below his/her performance in the Raven test and, at the same time, below the average of their peers of the same school grade. Dyslexics with normal intelligence but with additional problems of the short-term memory span, in auditive discrimination ability and in concentrating (group D1; 9 subjects) were differentiated from dyslexics who yielded at least average results in the other psychometrical tests (group D2; 8 subjects). D1 children might form a heterogeneous group with respect to their different types of additional impairments, but the relatively small number of subjects (9) did not allow for further discrimination within the group. The D2 dyslexics, on the other hand, were similar to the 'unexpected' group of dyslexics identified by means of cluster analysis by Satz and Morris but their proportion was relatively high in our sample, perhaps because of the relatively small number of psychometric tests employed for the assessment of various cognitive abilities, or because of a bias in the choice of the subjects.

In another study, a group of teenagers (age 12–16 y) were tested (Biscaldi and Fischer 1994). In subjects of this age reading and spelling skills are supposed to be mostly or totally achieved. Although all dyslexic teenagers still showed a spelling level well below average, some of them had partly compensated for reading and evidently for other cognitive problems as well. Out of 16 dyslexics, only 5 were classified as D1 (very poor reading performance, performance below average in the Mottier and in the short-term memory test for sequences) and 11 were classified as D2 (reading performance below that of the control group but better than in group D1, performance at least on average in the other tests) (Biscaldi and Fischer 1994).

Finally, in a study which considered dyslexic and normally reading adult subjects (age 21–52 y) a group with a severe reading/spelling impairment (group B; 4 subjects) was identified (Fischer, Biscaldi and Otto 1993b). The other dyslexics had milder deficits (group A; 8 subjects), but their reading and spelling were still well below the performance of the control group. Some studies also indicate that dyslexic adults can show selective impairments in neuropsychological tests (Felton, Naylor and Wood 1990; Kinsbourne *et al.* 1991) but less work has been done to follow the general cognitive development of older dyslexics.

Reaction time and accuracy of saccades

As reviewed in the first part of the chapter, there are several neural subsystems serving the processes of fixation, selective attention and decision that control the preparation of saccades. These processes are recognisable in discrete peaks forming the SRT distribution. Therefore, besides other aspects of saccades, the SRTs have been studied most extensively. A basic question concerned the relative amount of express, fast regular and slow regular saccades in the SRT distributions of dyslexic compared with control subjects.

Single target tasks

The saccadic performance was measured in the overlap and in the gap task. In the latter, a temporal gap (200 ms) was introduced between the disappearance of the fixation point and the onset of the target. The target was displayed randomly at 4° to the left or right of the fixation point and 150 trials were collected for each subject in each single target task. Mean values of SRT and of other eye movement variables such as the standard deviation of the SRT, amplitude of the first saccade, number of corrective saccades and correction time were calculated for each subject and the groups were statistically compared using the *t*-test and the ANOVA (further methodological details can be found in Fischer *et al.* 1993b; Biscaldi *et al.* 1994; Biscaldi and Fischer 1994).

Figure 4.2 (parts (a) and (b)) gives a qualitative overview of the SRT data of the control subjects at different ages (each group contains 12 subjects). The saccadic populations are more or less recognisable in all three age groups (they are partly fused because the distribution results from pooled data of all subjects). The children show a clear separation between fast and slow regular saccades. However, in these young subjects each single peak is slightly shifted to slower values and the SRT distributions are more scattered in comparison with those of the teenagers and adults. Children make more anticipatory saccades (SRT< 90 ms, see also Fischer *et al.* 1993c) and their slow regular saccades end in a long tail with very slow latencies above 250 ms. Latencies below 140 ms are almost absent in the adult group. In the gap task (Figure 4.2(b)), children produce less anticipatory saccades and the number of saccades with very slow latencies is reduced. A peak of ES tends to dominate their distributions, whereas ES are less represented in the teenagers' and strongly reduced in the adults' distributions. There is a clear development of the SRT distributions from children to adults with the frequency of the different types of saccades varying with the age of the subjects.

Independently from the observations on the development of the SRTs, dyslexics showed in general significant deviations in most eye movement variables. Figure 4.3(a) displays the SRT data from the overlap paradigm for the D1 dyslexic children and teenagers and for the dyslexic adults of group A (see also Biscaldi *et al.* 1994; Fischer *et al.* 1993b). In general, these subjects tend to have slower mean SRTs and larger standard deviations than their age-matched control groups. The latency distributions are more scattered and have almost completely lost the characteristic bi- or trimodal structure visible in Figure 4.2. The number of anticipatory saccades is increased especially in the dyslexic children and teenagers. The D2 dyslexics of both age groups (Figure 4.3 (b)) have shorter SRTs and make clearly more ES in the overlap task than the corresponding control subjects. The dyslexic adults of group B show similar results to those observed in the younger dyslexic groups but their shorter mean latencies are accounted for by an increased number of anticipatory saccades rather than of ES. In Figure 4.3 there is no evidence for age-dependent changes in the SRT distributions as observed in the control subjects (Figure 4.2). The SRTs of the D1/A dyslexics reveal a maturational lag (scattered distributions, increased number of anticipatory saccades); the SRTs of the D2/B dyslexics show specific eye movement abnormalities such as an unusual increase of ES. The changes in the saccadic performance of dyslexic subjects seem to overcome the age-dependent development.

The data from the gap task do not reveal any significant difference between the dyslexics of groups D1 and A of the adults and the control group. In some cases, the SRTs were slightly prolonged and the standard deviations increased (data not shown). Figure 4.4 reveals that the proportion of ES is significantly increased for both target directions in the D2 dyslexics and, for saccades to the left, also in the dyslexic adults of type B. As a result, the mean SRTs are on the average 20 ms shorter than in the corresponding control groups. The comparison of Figure 4.2 (b) and Figure 4.4 shows in addition that the partial suppression of ES at greater age does not occur as effectively in dyslexics as in normally reading subjects.

Since the analysis of the SRTs was carried out separately for left and right directed saccades, we looked also at directional target effects in the SRT distributions. Among the control groups, only the children had significantly shorter SRTs for the right target in the overlap paradigm (see Figure 4.2(a)). A similar tendency was observed for the adults but it was not significant. Teenagers showed symmetric SRTs in the overlap task. In the gap task, all three groups exhibited symmetric SRT distributions (Figure 4.2(b)). So, control subjects have in general symmetric SRT distributions or a bias toward shorter SRTs to the right depending on age and type of paradigm but, as a group, they never display shorter SRTs to the left. The latter was observed in some cases among dyslexic subjects (group D1 of children, group B of adults). In all other cases the SRT distributions of dyslexics were symmetric (Figures 4.3 and 4.4).

Other eye movement abnormalities were found in the dyslexic subjects. Poor accuracy in reaching the target was observed in D1 as well as D2 dyslexics. For the group D1 the final saccadic amplitude scattered more than for the control subjects, and group D2 exhibited an increased number of undershoots. We looked also at the stability of fixation 200 ms before target onset (defined as mean eye velocity during this time) and we observed that dyslexics, especially those of group D1, had a significantly higher fixation instability than control subjects. Age-dependent differences were found for the number of overshoots in dyslexic subjects: dyslexic children made exclusively hypometric first saccades whereas the first saccades of the dyslexic teenagers could be also hypermetric (the number

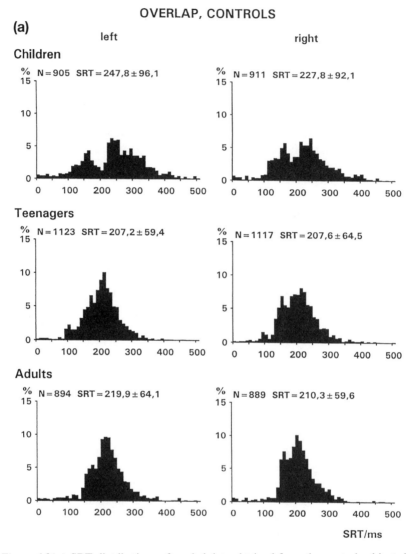

Figure 4.2(a) SRT distributions of pooled data obtained from the control subjects in the overlap paradigm.

Notes

The data of the 3 different age groups tested are plotted, separated for left and right directed saccades. The proportion of saccades in each 10 ms section is given in percent. Each subject in a distribution has contributed to form the peaks of fast regular and slow regular saccades. Children exhibit more scattered distribution than the older subjects.

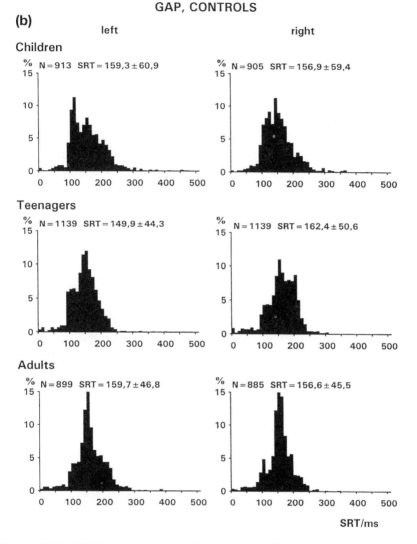

Figure 4.2(b) SRT distributions obtained in the gap paradigm.

Note

A first peak of express saccades (ES) is present in all three age groups but is considerably reduced in the groups of teenagers and adults.

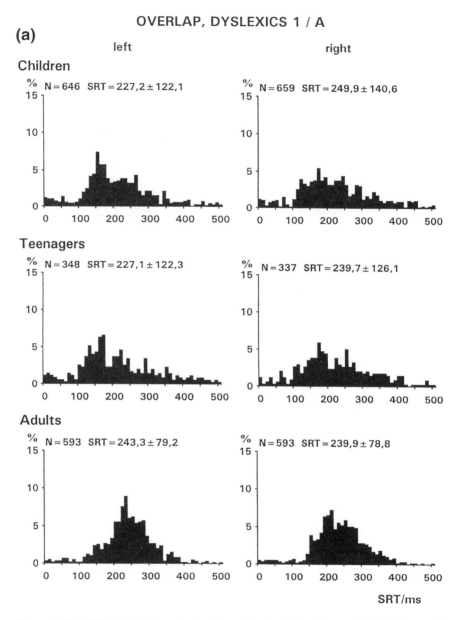

Figure 4.3(a) SRT distributions obtained from the dyslexics of groups D1 (children and teenagers) and A (adults) in the overlap paradigm.

Notes

The distributions are much more scattered than in the control subjects. The mean SRT is prolonged.

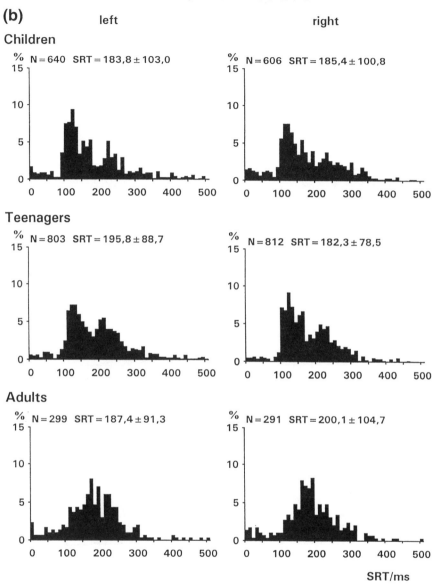

OVERLAP, DYSLEXICS 2 / B

Figure 4.3(b) SRT distributions of the dyslexics of groups D2 (children and teenagers) and B (adults).

Notes

The distributions exhibit a first clear peak of ES which is almost absent in the corresponding data of the control subjects. In the adults of group B, ES are reduced as compared with the younger groups.

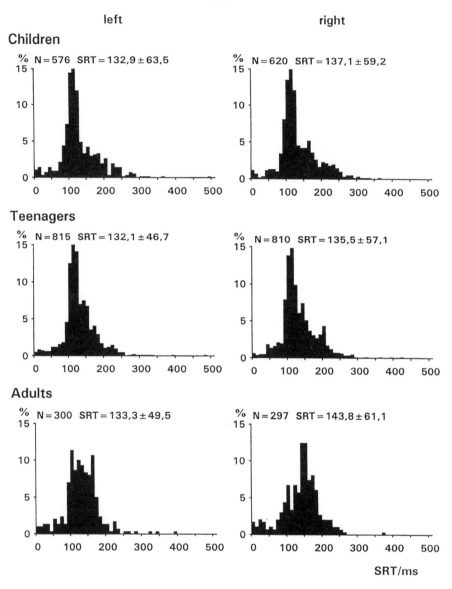

Figure 4.4 Data from the gap paradigm in dyslexics of groups D2 and B.

Notes

ES dominate the distributions. Notice the large peaks of ES in the children's and teenagers' data as compared with the control group (Figure 4.3 (b)). Adult dyslexics of group B also exhibit more ES than the control adults.

of overshoots was normal for teenage D2 dyslexics and significantly decreased for D2 children in comparison with control subjects).

A discriminant analysis with the overlap data determined which eye movement variables in this task allowed for a classification of the subjects in groups corresponding to those groups resulting from the psychometric tests. The discriminant analysis was run separately on the eye movement data of the children and of the teenagers and categorised almost all subjects correctly in their psychometric group of origin. In both cases the standard deviations of the SRT, the SRT, and the number of undershoots were selected by the analysis as best variables for the classification (Biscaldi and Fischer 1994).

Sequential tasks

Three sequential tracking tasks similar to those described by Pavlidis completed the experimental design. Thirty-five trials were available from each sequential tracking task. We analysed the number and amplitude of rightward and leftward (regressive) saccades and the mean fixation time between saccades made to five targets sequentially presented 4° apart.

All D2 dyslexics (independent of age) made more saccades than the control subjects. Hence, the mean fixation duration was shorter and the saccades had smaller amplitudes (Biscaldi *et al.* 1994; Biscaldi and Fischer 1994). The same behaviour was observed in group B of the adults (Fischer *et al.* 1993b). Regressions, on the other hand, were significantly increased only in the dyslexic teenagers of group D2. A selective increase of regressions in the dyslexic teenagers may be associated with the finding that they made a normal number of overshoots in the single target tasks whereas overshoots were completely absent in dyslexic children.

Only the dyslexic children of group D1 showed a tendency to make larger saccades than the control subjects. In addition, they sometimes overlooked targets so that the mean total time necessary to complete a trial was reduced. The frequency histograms of the occurrence of saccades in temporal relation to the targets displayed similarities with the SRT distributions obtained in the single target tasks: D1 subjects showed scattered and flat histograms in response to each target and D2 dyslexics exhibited narrow peaks situated 100–130 ms after the onset of each target.

Express saccade-makers

A significant increase in ES was found in two different subgroups of dyslexic children (Fischer and Weber 1990; Biscaldi *et al.* 1994), in a subgroup of dyslexic teenagers (Biscaldi and Fischer 1994) and of dyslexic adults (Fischer *et al.* 1993b). Interestingly, a large number of ES were also observed in the overlap paradigm where ES are usually less than 15 per cent. Almost 50 per cent of the dyslexics tested, especially of group D2, had more than 15 per cent ES in the overlap task.

When looking at the individual data from the overlap task, we identified subjects who produced more than 30 per cent ES. We called them ES-makers (Biscaldi *et al.* 1995; Biscaldi, Fischer and Stuhr 1996). Among a population of 166 subjects of different ages all tested with the overlap paradigm, ES-makers were estimated to be about 23 per cent of the dyslexic population and about 6 per cent of the population with normal reading and spelling performance. All the dyslexic ES-makers belonged to subgroup D2 or B of the adults (Biscaldi and Fischer 1994).

To test the fixation control on the saccade system of these uncommon subjects, a group of 6 dyslexic and 4 normally reading ES-makers was compared with 10 age-matched control subjects (less than 15 per cent ES in the overlap paradigm) in antisaccade and in memory-guided saccade tasks (Biscaldi *et al.* 1996). In the antisaccade tasks, the stimuli presentation was the same as in the gap and in the overlap standard tasks but the subject had to make a saccade to the side opposite to the target. In the memory-guided task, a target was briefly flashed to the left or right after 750 ms fixation but the subject was instructed to maintain fixation until fixation point offset. Only after its disappearance was a saccade required to the remembered target position.

Control subjects performed the memory-guided task and the antisaccade overlap task with an error rate lower than 20 per cent. Most of the ES-makers had considerable difficulties in suppressing visually-evoked saccades in both tasks. The dyslexic subjects, in particular, made more than 50 per cent cue-elicited saccades in the memory-guided task and more than 30 per cent prosaccades in the antisaccade overlap task. In the antisaccade gap task, the number of prosaccades reached 30 per cent in some control subjects and values between 43 per cent and 95 per cent in all ES-makers. An example of SRT distributions obtained in the different tasks from a dyslexic ES-maker (male, age 13 y) is given by Figure 4.5.

Since most ES-makers are male, it cannot be excluded that their unusual saccadic performance has a hereditary component. So far, we have found two fraternal pairs (brother and sister in one case and two brothers in the other case) who share this unusual oculomotor behaviour and reading/spelling problems. The father of the two brothers, also dyslexic, showed unimodal peaks centred at 140 ms (also to be considered as fast reactions in the overlap paradigm).

Despite the fact that the ES-makers could be easily separated from the control subjects by the number of erroneous prosaccades made in the antisaccade gap task, the hypothesis has to be tested whether they really form a separate group or rather whether the number of ES in the population follows a normal distribution with the ES-makers at the lower end of the continuum.

Discussion

The fixation system of the ES-makers

The behaviour of the ES-makers in the memory-guided task resembled very closely that of monkeys whose fixation neurons in the rostral dorsal part of the

Dyslexic express saccade-maker's reaction times

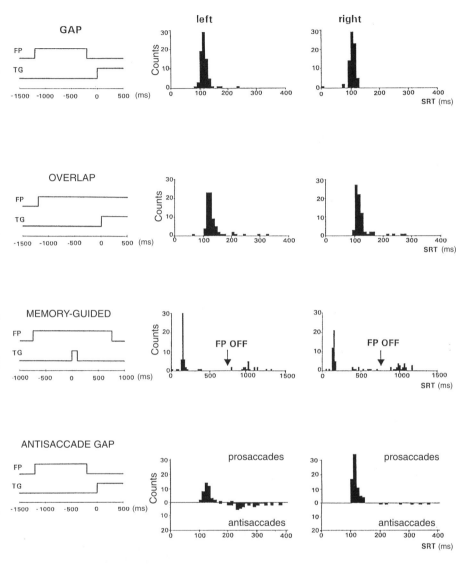

Figure 4.5 SRT distributions obtained in different tasks from a dyslexic ES-maker.

Notes

The temporal arrangement of the stimuli is shown at the left of the respective distributions. FP: fixation point, TG: target. From top to bottom: In the gap and overlap standard tasks the subject produced almost exclusively ES to both target directions. In the memory-guided task many saccades were erroneously executed before fixation-point offset (indicated by the arrow); these saccades had very fast latencies in the express range. In the antisaccade gap task, saccades were only sporadically directed to the hemifield opposite to the stimulus according to the instructions. The erroneous prosaccades were mostly ES.

superior colliculus were blocked by injection of muscimol (Munoz and Wurtz 1993). These collicular cells seem to belong to a diffuse fixation system involving cortical and subcortical structures. Fixation cells are found in area 7 of the parietal cortex (Sakata, Shibutani and Kawano 1980), in the prefrontal cortex (Bon and Lucchetti 1992), in the frontal eye field (Segraves and Goldberg 1987), and in the basal ganglia (Hikosaka and Wurtz 1983b). Some of these areas project to the superior colliculus. Thus, an abnormal function of the fixation system could be the basis for understanding the unusual behaviour of the ES-makers and the linkage between ES and dyslexia: dyslexic subjects may be impaired at a cortical level, whereas in normal reading ES-makers the fixation cells at the collicular level may show an abnormal functioning (Biscaldi *et al.* 1996). Some of the cortical structures mentioned above (the parietal cortex for instance, but also the basal ganglia) are known to be involved in the control of visual attention and indeed there must be a close interaction between the fixation system and the neural substrate of visual attention.

Visual attention has been proposed to be a main mechanism of the eye movement control during reading (Morrison 1984; Henderson and Ferreira 1990; Rayner 1995), although other models of oculomotor control have been suggested (O'Regan and Lévy-Schoen 1987; Weber and Fischer 1994). An abnormal functioning of the fixation system and probably of its modulation by attention (Munoz and Wurtz 1993) could at the same time be responsible for the generation of many ES in non-cognitive tasks (through abnormal disengagement and engagement mechanisms) and for difficulties in reading. In any case, it cannot be straightforwardly concluded that the oculomotor abnormalities are the cause of dyslexia.

Eye movement data from patients vs dyslexic subjects

Difficulties in performing an antisaccade task have been found in patients with unilateral lesions of the frontal cortex (Guitton, Buchtel and Douglas 1985) and in schizophrenic subjects (Abel, Levin and Holzman 1992). Patients with lesions involving the frontal eye fields were dramatically impaired in the antisaccade task and could not even correct their prosaccades once they had made an ES to the cue. They reacted toward the 'anti-side' only after a target was presented there. The saccades to the target had once again latency in the range of ES (Guitton *et al.* 1985). Another study showed that patients with frontal eye field lesions make almost only ES in the gap task, but not in the overlap task (Braun *et al.* 1992).

Schizophrenic subjects show an increase of ES in the gap task and, at the same time, saccadic intrusion in the smooth pursuit (Sereno and Holzman 1993). Currie *et al.* (1993) claimed that schizophrenic patients need longer gap durations to produce a normal number of ES but they did not distinguish between different types of eye movement behaviour in schizophrenia. Matsue *et al.* (1994) found that only schizophrenics with impaired smooth pursuit have an abnormal number of ES in the gap and also in the overlap task. Moreover, this group of schizophrenics also has difficulties in avoiding looking reflexively (with ES) at the stimulus in an antisaccade task. They suggested that the oculomotor behaviour of schizophrenics could be explained by dysfunction of the prefrontal cortex.

The SRTs of the D1 dyslexics, on the other hand, show some analogies with those obtained in patients with lesions of the dorsolateral parietal cortex (Braun *et al.* 1992). The flat form of the SRT distributions and the unusually high number of saccades with SRT > 400ms in these subjects give the impression that the saccade is not immediately triggered by the onset of the target. Since the posterior parietal lobe is involved in directing attention, the saccadic pattern of parietal patients has been interpreted as a consequence of a deficit in disengaging attention (Braun *et al.* 1992; Posner *et al.* 1984).

A deficit of selective visual attention in dyslexia?

There is other evidence that dysfunctions in selective attention are present in some reading disabled subjects (Rayner *et al.* 1989; Price and Humphreys 1993). It has been shown that dyslexics have difficulties in using cue informations (Brannan and Williams 1987) and that they have a large attentional focus and poor lateral masking (Geiger and Lettvin 1987). Yet, Geiger and Lettvin interpreted their results as an erroneous learned strategy (Geiger and Lettvin 1989). The parietal cortex, especially of the right hemisphere, has been assumed to underlie the poor vergence and binocular control observed in many dyslexics (Stein 1989). The hypothesis of a dysfunction of the parietal cortex has also been made in relation to the finding of a magnocellular defect in dyslexics (Lovegrove 1993; Livingstone *et al.* 1991), since the magnocellular pathway projects up to area MT which in turn is connected with the inferior parietal cortex (see Breitmeyer 1989). Concomitant phonological problems were also found in these subjects (Slaghuis, Lovegrove and Davidson 1993) and were explained in relationship to the transient channels dysfunction (Breitmeyer 1989). Finally, the prefrontal cortex may also play a role in reading disabilities (Kelly, Best and Kirk 1989): this cannot be excluded at least in dyslexics who show attentional deficits.

Saccade inaccuracy

It has been claimed that the poor vergence control in dyslexics leads to inaccuracy in the spatial localisation of small objects (Riddell, Fowler and Stein 1990). Eden *et al.* (1994) found instability of the left eye at the end of a saccade when dyslexics looked back and forth between two fixation targets, spaced at 10° of visual angle. These subjects had unstable central fixation as well. They explained that instability of the left eye is due to the difficulties dyslexics have in developing a strong reference eye and that it can lead to unstable fixation with more corrective movements. Problems in vergence movements could be a possible explanation for the saccadic inaccuracy of the dyslexic subject of our study (note that we analysed the data from the left eye). An alternative explanation is that the fixation system does not work in coordination with the saccadic system (i.e. disengagement from the fixation point does not occur at a consistent time after target onset). If fixation stability is impaired, small saccades bringing the fovea away from the fixation point are produced before target onset in many trials so that the target cannot be consistently reached.

Conclusions

Given that dyslexics as a group show abnormal eye movement patterns in non-cognitive tasks, the problem remains whether this is true for every dyslexic subject. In a recent study it has been claimed that 'it remains a controversy if dyslexia consists of distinct subtypes or rather there are variations in a continuum of cognitive and physiological abilities' (Shaywitz *et al.* 1992) (see also Eden *et al.* 1994). Perhaps there is a correlation between reading abilities and different patterns of oculomotor behaviour, but very large samples of subjects are needed to test for this hypothesis.

In conclusion, both the optomotor control and cognitive processes are needed in reading and they must be perfectly coordinated in time and space. If the control of the optomotor cycle does not work as effectively in dyslexics as it does in normally reading subjects this could also hinder the proper cognitive processes necessary for word recognition. The present data, however, do not necessarily imply that oculomotor abnormalities are the direct cause of dyslexia but rather that both the oculomotor abnormalities and the reading difficulties in specific groups of dyslexics may be the sign of inconsistent operation within central control mechanisms such as the fixation and the attention system.

Note

This work was supported by the DFG, SFB 325, TP C5 and TP C7.

References

Abel, L.A., Levin, S. and Holzman, P.S. (1992) 'Abnormalities of smooth pursuit and saccadic control in schizophrenia and affective disorders', *Vision Research*, 32, 1009–1014

Adler-Grinberg D. and Stark, L. (1978) 'Eye movements, scanpaths, and dyslexia', *American Journal of Optometry and Physiological Optics*, 55, 557–570

Biscaldi, M. and Fischer, B. (1994) 'Saccadic eye movements of dyslexics in non-cognitive tasks', in J. Ygge and G. Lennerstrand (eds), *Eye Movements in Reading* (pp. 245–259). Oxford: Pergamon Press.

Biscaldi, M., Fischer, B. and Aiple, F. (1994) 'Saccadic eye movements of dyslexic and normal reading children', *Perception*, 23, 45–64

Biscaldi, M., Fischer, B. and Stuhr, V. (1996) 'Human express saccade makers are impaired at suppressing visually-evoked saccades', *Journal of Neurophysiology*, 76, 199–214.

Biscaldi, M., Weber, H., Fischer, B. and Stuhr, V. (1995) 'Mechanism of fixation in man: evidence from saccadic reaction times', in J.M. Findlay, R. Walker and R.W. Kentridge (eds), *Studies in Visual Information Processing, Volume 6: Eye Movement Research Mechanisms, Processes and Applications* (pp. 145–155). Amsterdam: Elsevier-North-Holland.

Black, J.L., Collins, D.W., De Roach, J.N. and Zubrick, S. (1984) 'A detailed study of sequential saccadic eye movements for normal-and poor-reading children', *Perception and Motor Skills*, 59, 423–434.

Boch, R. and Fischer, B. (1986) 'Further observations on the occurrence of express-saccades in the monkey', *Experimental Brain Research*, 63, 487–494.

Boder, E. (1973) 'Developmental dyslexia: A diagnostic approach based on three atypical reading-spelling patterns', *Developmental Medicine and Child Neurology*, 15, 663–687.

Bon, L. and Lucchetti, C. (1992) 'The dorsomedial frontal cortex of the macaca monkey: fixation and saccade-related activity', *Experimental Brain Research*, 89, 571–580.

Brannan, J.R. and Williams, M.C. (1987) 'Allocation of visual attention in good and poor readers', *Perception and Psychophysics*, 41, 23–28.

Braun, D., Weber, H., Mergner, T. and Schulte-Mönting, J. (1992) 'Saccadic reaction times in patients with frontal and parietal lesions', *Brain*, 115, 1359–1386.

Breitmeyer, B.G. (1989) 'A visually based deficit in specific reading disability', *Irish Journal of Psychology*, 10, 534–541.

Brown, B., Haegerstrom-Portnoy, G., Adams, A.J., Yingling, C.D., Galin, D., Herron, J. and Marcus, M. (1983) 'Predictive eye movements do not discriminate between dyslexic and control children', *Neuropsychologia*, 21, 121–128.

Cavegn, D. (1994) 'Orienting, visual search and eye movements', *Perception Supplement*, 23, 12.

Chelazzi, L., Biscaldi, M., Corbetta, M., Peru, A., Tassinari, G. and Berlucchi, G. (1995) 'Oculomotor activity and visual spatial attention', *Behavioral Brain Research*, 71, 81–88.

Ciuffreda, K.J., Bahill, T.A., Kenyon, R.V. and Stark, L. (1976) 'Eye movements during reading: case reports', *American Journal of Optometry and Physiological Optics*, 53, 389–395.

Critchley, M. (1970) *The Dyslexic Child*. London: Heinemann

Currie, J., Joyce, S., Maruff, P., Ramsden, B., McArthgur-Jackson, C. and Malone, V. (1993) 'Selective impairment of express saccade generation in patients with schizophrenia', *Experimental Brain Research*, 97, 343–348.

Deubel, H. and Schneider, W. (1995) 'Saccade target selection and object recognition: evidence for a common attentional mechanism', *Vision Research*, in print.

Dossetor, D.R. and Papaioannou, J. (1975) 'Dyslexia and eye movements', *Language and Speech*, 18, 312–317.

Eden, G.F., Stein, J.F., Wood, H.M. and Wood, F.B. (1994) 'Differences in eye movements and reading problems in dyslexic and normal children', *Vision Research*, 34, 1345–1358.

Felton, R.H., Naylor, C.E. and Wood, F.B. (1990) 'Neuropsychological profile of adult dyslexics', *Brain and Language*, 39, 485–497.

Fields, H., Newman, S. and Wright, S.F. (1993) 'Saccadic eye movements in dyslexics, low achievers, and competent readers', in S.F. Wright and R. Groner (eds), *Studies in Visual Information Processing, Volume 3: Facets of Dyslexia and Its Remediation* (pp. 235–243). London: Elsevier Science Publishers.

Fischer, B. (1987) 'The preparation of visually guided saccades', *Reviews in Physiology, Biochemistry and Pharmacology*, 106, 1–35.

Fischer, B. and Boch, R. (1983) 'Saccadic eye movements after extremely short reaction times in the monkey', *Brain Research*, 260, 21–26.

Fischer, B. and Boch, R. (1985) 'Peripheral attention versus central fixation: modulation of the visual activity of prelunate cortical cells of the rhesus monkey', *Brain Research*, 345, 111–123.

Fischer, B. and Boch, R. (1991) 'Cerebral cortex', in R. Carpenter (ed.), *Vision and Visual Dysfunction, Volume 8: Eye Movements* (pp. 277–296). London: Macmillan Press.

Fischer, B., Boch, R. and Ramsperger, E. (1984) 'Express-saccades of the monkey: effect of daily training on probability of occurrence and reaction time', *Experimental Brain Research*, 55, 232–242.

Fischer, B. and Ramsperger, E. (1984) 'Human express saccades: extremely short reaction times of goal directed eye movements', *Experimental Brain Research*, 57, 191–195.

Fischer, B. and Ramsperger, E. (1986) 'Human express saccades: effects of randomization and daily practice', *Experimental Brain Research*, 64, 569–578.

Fischer, B. and Weber, H. (1990) 'Saccadic reaction times of dyslexic and age-matched normal subjects', *Perception*, 19, 805–818

Fischer, B. and Weber, H. (1992) 'Characteristics of "anti" saccades in man', *Experimental Brain Research*, 89, 415–424.

Fischer, B. and Weber, H. (1993) 'Express saccades and visual attention', *Behavioural Brain Research*, 16, 553–567.

Fischer, B., Weber, H. and Biscaldi, M. (1993a) 'The time of secondary saccades to primary targets', *Experimental Brain Research*, 97, 356–360

Fischer, B., Biscaldi, M. and Otto, P. (1993b) 'Saccadic eye movements of dyslexic adult subjects', *Neuropsychologia*, 31, 887–906.

Fischer, B., Weber, H., Biscaldi, M., Aiple, F., Otto, P. and Stuhr, V. (1993c) 'Separate populations of visually guided saccades in humans: reaction times and amplitudes', *Experimental Brain Research*, 92, 528–541.

Fischer, B., Gezeck, S. and Huber, W. (1995) 'The three-loop-model: A neural network for the generation of saccadic reaction times', *Biological Cybernetics*, 72, 185–196.

Geiger, G. and Lettvin, J.Y. (1987) 'Peripheral vision in persons with dyslexia', *New England Journal of Medicine*, 316, 1238–1243.

Geiger, G. and Lettvin, J.Y. (1989) 'Dyslexia and reading as examples of alternative visual strategies', in C. von Euler, I. Lundberg and G. Lennerstrand (eds), *Brain and Reading* (pp. 331–343). London: Macmillan.

Goldberg, M.E., Bushnell, M.C. and Bruce, C.J. (1986) 'The effect of attentive fixation on eye movements evoked by electrical stimulation of the frontal eye fields', *Experimental Brain Research*, 61, 579–584.

Guitton, D., Buchtel, H.A. and Douglas, R.M. (1985) 'Frontal lobe lesions in man cause difficulties in suppressing reflexive glances and in generating goal-directed saccades', *Experimental Brain Research*, 58, 455–472.

Henderson, J.M. and Ferreira, F. (1990) 'Effects of foveal processing difficulty on the perceptual span in reading: implications for attention and eye movement control', *Journal of Experimental Psychology: Learning, Memory and Cognition*, 16, 417–429.

Hikosaka, O. and Wurtz, R.H. (1983a) 'Effects on eye movements of a GABA agonist and antagonist injected into monkey superior colliculus', *Brain Research*, 272, 368–372.

Hikosaka, O. and Wurtz, R.H. (1983b) 'Visual and oculomotor functions of monkey substantia nigra pars reticulata. II. Visual responses related to fixation of gaze', *Journal of Neurophysiology*, 49, 1254–1267.

Hyönä, J. and Olson, R.K. (1995) 'Eye fixation patterns among dyslexic and normal readers: effect of word length and word frequency', *Journal of Experimental Psychology: Learning, Memory and Cognition*, 21, 1430–1440.

Jerabek, J. and Krejcova, H. (1991) 'Oculomotor and vestibular findings in developmental dyslexia', *Acta Otolaryngol* (Stockholm) Supplement, 513–514

Jüttner, M. and Wolf, W. (1994) 'Stimulus sequence effects on human express saccades described by a Markov model', *Biological Cybernetics*, 70, 247–253.

Kelly, M.S., Best, C.T. and Kirk, U. (1989) 'Cognitive processing deficits in reading disabilities: a prefrontal cortical hypothesis', *Brain and Cognition*, 11, 275–293.

Kinsbourne, M., Rufo, D.T., Gamzu, E., Palmer, R.L. and Berliner, A.K. (1991) 'Neuropsychological deficits in adults with dyslexia', *Developmental Medicine and Child Neurology*, 33, 763–775.

Klein, R.M. and Pontefract, A. (1994) 'Does occulomotor readiness mediate cognitive control of visual attention? Revisted', in C. Umilta and M. Moscovitch (eds), *Attention and Performance XV* (pp. 332–350). New York: Erlbaum.

Kowler, E., Anderson, E., Dosher, B. and Blaser, E. (1995) 'The role of attention in the programming of saccades', *Vision Research*, 35, 1897–1916.

Livingstone, M.S., Rosen, G.D., Drislane, F.W. and Galaburda, A.M. (1991) 'Physiological and anatomical evidence for a magnocellular defect in developmental dyslexia', *Proceedings of the National Academy of Science*, 88, 7943–7947.

Lovegrove, W. (1993) 'Do dyslexics have a visual defect?', in S.F. Wright and R. Groner (eds), *Studies in Visual Information Processing, Volume 3: Facets of Dyslexia and Its Remediation* (pp. 33–49). Amsterdam: Elsevier-North-Holland.

Mackeben, M. and Nakayama, K. (1993) 'Express attentional shifts', *Vision Research*, 33, 85–90.

Martos, F.J. and Vila, J. (1990) 'Differences in eye movement control among dyslexic, retarded and normal readers in the Spanish population', *Reading and Writing*, 2, 175–188.

Matsue, Y., Osakabe, K., Saito, H., Goto, Y., Ueno, T., Matsuoka, H., Chiba, H., Fuse, Y. and Sato, M. (1994) 'Smooth pursuit eye movements and express saccades in schizophrenic patients', *Schizophrenia Research*, 12, 121–130.

Mattis, S., French, J.H. and Rapin, I. (1975) 'Dyslexia in children and adults: Three independent neuropsychological syndromes', *Developmental Medicine and Child Neurology*, 17, 150–163.

Mayfrank, L., Mobashery, M., Kimmig, H. and Fischer, B. (1986) 'The role of fixation and visual attention in the occurrence of express saccades in man', *European Archives of Psychiatry and Neurological Sciences*, 235, 269–275.

Morrison, R.E., (1984) 'Manipulation of stimulus onset delay in reading: evidence for parallel programming of saccades', *Journal of Experimental Psychology: Human Perception and Performance*, 10, 667–682.

Munoz, D.P. and Wurtz, R.H. (1992) 'Role of the rostral superior colliculus in active visual fixation and execution of express saccades', *Journal of Neurophysiology*, 67, 1000–1002.

Munoz, D.P. and Wurtz, R.H. (1993) 'Fixation cells in monkey superior colliculus. II. Reversible activation and deactivation', *Journal of Neurophysiology*, 70, 576–589.

Nakayama, K. and Mackeben, M. (1989) 'Sustained and transient components of focal visual attention', *Vision Research*, 29, 1631–1647.

Nothdurft, H.C. and Parlitz, D. (1993) 'Absence of express saccades to texture or motion defined targets', *Vision Research*, 33, 1367–1383.

O'Regan, J.K. and Lévy-Schoen, A. (1987) 'Eye movement strategy and tactics in word recognition and reading', in M. Coltheart (ed.), *Attention and Performance XII: The Psychology of Reading* (pp. 363–383). Hillsdale, NJ: Erlbaum.

Olson, R.K., Conners, F.C. and Rack, J.P. (1991) 'Eye movements in dyslexic and normal readers', in J.F. Stein (ed.), *Vision and Visual Dysfunction, Volume 13: Vision and Vision Dyslexia* (pp. 243–250). London: Macmillan.

Olson, R.K., Kliegl, R. and Davidson, B.J. (1983) 'Dyslexic and normal readers' eye movements', *Journal of Experimental Psychology: Human Perception and Perform-ance*, 9, 816–825.

Pavlidis, G.T. (1981) 'Do eye movements hold the key to dyslexia?', *Neuropsychologia*, 19, 57–64.

Pirozzolo, F.J. (1979) *The Neuropsychology of Developmental Reading Disorders*. New York: Praeger Publishers.

Pirozzolo, F.J. and Rayner, K. (1978) 'Disorders of oculomotor scanning and graphic orientation in developmental Gerstmann syndrome', *Brain and Language*, 5, 119–126.

Pirozzolo, F.J. and Rayner, K. (1981) 'Language and brain: neuropsychological aspects of developmental reading disability', *School Psychology Review*, 10, 350–355.

Pirozzolo, F.J. and Rayner, K. (1988) 'Dyslexia: the role of eye movements in developmental reading disabilities', in C.W. Johnston and F.J. Pirozzolo (eds), *Neuro-psychology of Eye Movements* (pp. 65–80). Hillsdale, NJ: Lawrence Erlbaum Associates.

Posner, M.I. (1980) 'Orienting of attention', *Quarterly Journal of Experimental Psychology*, 32, 3–25.

Posner, M.I., Walker, J.A., Friedrich, F.J. and Rafal, R.D. (1984) 'Effects of parietal injury on covert orienting of attention', *Journal of Neuroscience*, 4, 1863–1874.

Price, C.J. and Humphreys, G.W. (1993) 'Attentional dyslexia: The effects of co-occuring deficits', *Cognitive Neuropsychology*, 10, 569–592.

Rayner, K. (1985) 'Do faulty eye movements cause dyslexia?', *Developmental Neuropsychology*, 1, 3–15.

Rayner, K. (1995) 'Eye movements and cognitive processes in reading, visual search, and scene perception', in J.M. Findlay, R. Walker and R.W. Kentridge (eds), *Eye Movement Research Mechanism, Processes and Applications* (Vol 6) (pp. 3–22). North Holland: Studies in Visual Information Processing.

Rayner, K., Murphy, L.A., Henderson, J.L. and Pollatsek, A. (1989) 'Selective attentional dyslexia', *Cognitive Neuropsychology*, 6, 357–378.

Reuter-Lorenz, P., Hughes, H.C. and Fendrich, R. (1991) 'The reduction of saccadic latency by prior offset of the fixation point: An analysis of the gap effect', *Perception and Psychophysics*, 49, 167–175.

Riddell, P.M., Fowler, M.S. and Stein, J.F. (1990) 'Spatial discrimination in children with poor vergence control', *Perception and Motor Skills*, 70, 707–718.

Robinson, D.L., Goldberg, M.E. and Stanton, G.B. (1978) 'Parietal association cortex in the primate: Sensory mechanisms and behavioral modulations', *Journal of Neuro-physiology*, 41, 910–932.

Rubino, C.A. and Minden, H.A. (1973) 'An analysis of eye movements in children with a reading disability', *Cortex*, 9, 217–220.

Sakata, H., Shibutani, H., and Kawano, K. (1980) 'Spatial properties of visual fixation neurons in posterior parietal association cortex of the monkey', *Journal of Neurophysiology*, 43, 1654–1672.

Saslow, M.G. (1967) 'Latency for saccadic eye movement', *Journal of the Optical Society of America*, 57, 1030–1033.

Satz, P. and Morris, R. (1981) 'Learning disability subtypes: a review', in F.J. Pirozzolo and M.C. Wittrock (eds), *Neuropsychological and Cognitive Processes in Reading* (pp. 109–141). New York: Academic Press.

Schiller, P.H., Sandell, J.H. and Maunsell, J.H. (1987) 'The effect of frontal eye field and superior colliculus lesions on saccadic latencies in the rhesus monkey', *Journal of Neurophysiology*, 57, 1033–1049.

Schiller, P.H., True, S.D. and Conway, J.L. (1979) 'Effects of frontal eye field and superior colliculus ablations on eye movements', *Science*, 206, 590–592.

Segraves, M.A. and Goldberg, M.E. (1987) 'Functional properties of corticotectal neurons in the monkey's frontal eye field', *Journal of Neurophysiology*, 58, 1387–1419.

Sereno, A.B. and Holzmann, P.S. (1993) 'Express saccades and smooth pursuit eye movement function in schizophrenic, affective disorder, and normal subjects', *Journal of Cognitive Neuroscience*, 5, 303–316.

Shaywitz, S.E., Escobar, M.D., Shaywitz, B.A., Fletcher, J.M. and Makuch, R. (1992) 'Evidence that dyslexia may represent the lower tail of a normal distribution of reading ability', *New England Journal of Medicine*, 326, 145–150.

Shepherd, M., Findlay, J.M. and Hockey, R.J. (1986) 'The relationship between eye movements and spatial attention', *Quarterly Journal of Experimental Psychology*, 38A, 475–491.

Shibutani, H., Sakata, H. and Hyvarinen, J. (1984) 'Saccade and blinking evoked by microstimulation of the posterior parietal association cortex of the monkey', *Experimental Brain Research*, 55, 1–8.

Slaghuis, W.L., Lovegrove, W.J. and Davidson, J.A. (1993) 'Visual and language processing deficits are concurrent in dyslexia', *Cortex*, 29, 601–615.

Sommer, M. (1994) 'Express saccades elicited during visual scan in the monkey', *Vision Research*, 34, 2023–2038.

Stanley, G., Smith, G.A. and Howell, E.A. (1983) 'Eye-movements and sequential tracking in dyslexic and control children', *British Journal of Psychology*, 74, 181–187.

Stark, L.W., Giveen, S.C. and Terdiman, J.F. (1991) 'Specific dyslexia and eye movements', in J. Stein (ed.), *Vision and Visual Dysfunction, Volume 13: Vision and Visual Dyslexia* (pp. 203–232). London: Macmillan.

Stein, J. (1989) 'Visuospatial perception and reading problems', *Irish Journal of Psychology*, 10, 521–533.

Stein J.F. and Fowler, M.S. (1993) 'Unstable binocular control in dyslexic children', *Journal of Research in Reading*, 16, 30–45.

Tam, W and Stelmach, L. (1993) 'Viewing behavior: Ocular and attentional disengagement', *Perception and Psychophysics*, 54, 211–222.

Weber, H. (1995) 'Presaccadic processes in the generation of pro and anti saccades in human subjects – a reaction time study', *Perception*, 24, 1265–1280.

Weber, H., Aiple, F., Fischer, B. and Latanov, A. (1992) 'Dead zone for express saccades', *Experimental Brain Research*, 89, 214–222.

Weber, H. and Fischer, B. (1994) 'Differential effects of non-target stimuli on the occurrence of express saccades in man', *Vision Research*, 34, 1883–1891.

Weber, H. and Fischer, B. (1995) 'Gap duration and location of attention focus modulate the occurrence of left/right asymmetries in the saccadic reaction times of human subjects', *Vision Research*, 19, 426.

Wenban-Smith, M.G. and Findlay, J.M. (1991) 'Express saccades: is there a separate population in humans?', *Experimental Brain Research*, 87, 218–222.

Zangwill, O.L. and Blakemore, C. (1972) 'Dyslexia: Reversal of eye movements during reading', *Neuropsychologia*, 10, 371–373.

5 Motor aspects of dyslexia

John Everatt, Sue McNamara, John A. Groeger and Mark F. Bradshaw

Introduction

It has been recognised for over a century that illiteracy is not invariably the consequence of lack of education or low intelligence. Some children with normal intelligence and adequate opportunity to learn have great difficulty in learning to read and spell. The term developmental dyslexia (the shorter form dyslexia will be used in this chapter) is used widely in contemporary accounts of this difficulty.

Dyslexia (translated roughly as a 'difficulty with words') is generally seen as a childhood difficulty with the acquisition of reading, spelling and writing skills (Miles 1993; Thomson 1990), although such literacy problems often extend into adulthood (see Bruck 1993; Miles 1993). Such disabilities may lead to profound problems/failure in academia, the consequences of which can, in certain cases, develop into emotional problems (see Edwards 1994; Miles and Varma 1995) or antisocial or criminal behaviour (e.g., Alm and Anderson 1995; Osmond 1993).

The clinical focus in both assessment and treatment of dyslexia has been on language skills, so many practitioners have come to view dyslexia primarily as a language deficit and, in particular, as a problem with phonological processing/awareness. Phonological awareness can be defined as the recognition of the speech sounds that comprise words. Such awareness is usually thought of in terms of an individual's ability to break down words into basic sounds (segmentation), combine sounds to form familiar or new words/sounds (sound blending), form or recognise rhymes or manipulate sounds to form new sounds or novel words. These skills require a precise understanding and manipulation of sound forms and are dependent upon the individual being able to accurately process phonological information. Additionally, phonological awareness may be a vital component in an individual's recognition of the connection between letters and sounds and therefore the process of decoding written text. The technique of 'sounding-out' a novel string of letters is an obvious area where phonological awareness would be useful. Poor phonological awareness or lower levels of phonological skill may lead to lower levels of reading ability. The phonological deficit hypothesis was proposed by the Haskin's Laboratory in the 1970s (see Liberman 1973), and refined by many researchers over the following years (see, for example, Snowling 1995; Stanovich 1988a). The main evidence provided for this theoretical viewpoint concerns differences between dyslexics and non-dyslexics on tasks requiring phonological processing (segmenting, blending, rhyming, etc.), the ability of poor phonological task performance to predict later reading problems, and the efficacy of instruction in phonemic skills to remediate or prevent serious reading problems (e.g. Bradley and Bryant 1983; Lundberg and Hoien 1989).

However, research has revealed deficits in tasks which have no linguistic/ phonological component. Such research has presented the possibility that dyslexia is associated with visual abnormalities (e.g. Lovegrove, Martin and Slaghuis 1986; Stein 1993), motor coordination problems (e.g. Nicolson & Fawcett, 1990; Wolff, Michel and Ovrut 1990), and problems with complex skill learning/ organisation (e.g. in driving: Groeger and Maguire, in press; organising/planning work and time-keeping: McLoughlin, Fitzgibbon and Young 1994; structuring pieces of written work: Miles and Gilroy 1996; Riddick 1996; Singleton 1996). Most of these non-linguistic deficits cannot easily be explained in terms of language processing problems (unless it is assumed that they are artifactual, see Stanovich 1988b). Other factors may underpin these deficits, or perhaps broader underlying learning difficulties give rise to both linguistic and non-linguistic aspects of dyslexia.

One of the common features of the non-linguistic consequences of dyslexia is that they involve either the coordination of visual and motor components of behaviour (hand–eye or eye movement coordination) or the combination of sequences of movements/processes and/or their precise control/planning. Such data have been used as the basic rationale for interventions involving the practice of basic movement behaviours (some entirely unrelated to literacy) to counteract some of the reading/writing difficulties experienced by dyslexics. The purpose of the present chapter is to review the evidence for these non-linguistic aspects of dyslexia and ascribe possible reasons for their existence. The chapter will include a basic introduction to motor deficits which have been associated with dyslexia and an overview of the development, architecture and processes involved in motor skills.

The incidence of motor deficits

While dyslexic children and adults do not appear to have overt neurological problems, they are often classified by neurologists and practitioners as clumsy. In terms of motor performance, dyslexics have been shown to have difficulty with static and dynamic balance, ball skills, manual dexterity, gross and fine motor control and the production of simultaneous movements. Additionally, there is evidence for a deficit in the motor skills required in speed of tapping, heel–toe placement, rapid successive finger opposition, and accuracy in copying. Dyslexic children, Denckla (1985) suggested, are characterised by a 'non-specific develop-mental awkwardness', so that even those children with dyslexia who show reasonable athletic or dance ability are poorly coordinated. This awkwardness may be outgrown by puberty, leading Denckla to argue for a maturational lag in the motor analyser that programmes timed sequential movements.

The percentage of dyslexic individuals presenting motor disabilities varies across studies and measures, but suggests a much higher incidence than that present within the general population. The study by Sudgen and Wann (1987), for example, suggests that around 30 per cent of children with learning difficulties have coordination difficulties compared with 5 per cent of academically able children. Brying and Michelsson (1984) found that approximately 20 per cent of the learning disabled group surveyed presented evidence of motor problems, whereas Klasen (1972) estimated that approximately 50 per cent of dyslexics sampled presented visual-motor deficits. Similarly, the motor problems experienced by the dyslexic individual may be long-term (e.g. Jaklewicz 1980) and inheritable (Regehr and Kaplan 1988).

Several lines of evidence for motor deficits among dyslexics exist. In terms of gross motor deficits, Haslum (1989) found that two motor skills (dyslexics were unable to throw a ball up, clap, and catch it again, and were less able to walk backwards in a straight line for six steps) were among the six variables that showed significant differences between dyslexic and non-dyslexic 10-year-olds. Nicolson and Fawcett (1996) in their Dyslexic Early Screening Test (DEST), argue that postural instability can distinguish the 4-year-old pre-reading dyslexic child from the non-dyslexic. Clearly, such views have important implications for identifying the dyslexic individual prior to academic failure and for the underlying cause of the disability. Similarly, McGlown (1984) presents evidence for a relationship between poor kinaesthetic awareness, impaired motor inhibition and dyslexia. In terms of fine motor behaviours, Wolff, Cohen and Drake (1984) found differences between dyslexics and controls in the timing of motor sequences, leading Wolff *et al.* (1990) to suggest that a failure to develop physical movement sequences may be linked to difficulties in reading and writing: such timing problems may be common to both literacy skills and the execution of simple, rhythmic motor tasks. Finally, there is considerable evidence that children with dyslexia are impaired in articulatory skills (see, for example, Snowling 1981), and the relationship between dyslexia and articulation problems is often used as an indicator of dyslexia (e.g. Miles 1993: Bangor Dyslexia Test (BDT)). Such evidence is usually considered as a phonological-related deficit; however, it could equally derive from an underlying motor problem. In the light of these non-linguistic based findings, it is important to consider alternative explanations for the difficulties dyslexics face.

Motor skills, timing and automaticity

One alternative to the phonological deficit hypothesis that may explain both phonological deficits and movement disabilities is derived from the recent research into the automaticity of motor skills in children with dyslexia (e.g. Nicolson and Fawcett 1990). Automaticity has been hypothesised as the final stage in learning any skill where performance becomes expert and less demanding in terms of resources (Shiffrin and Schneider 1977). Nicolson and Fawcett (1990) presented evidence that children with dyslexia were able to balance normally under single-task conditions, but when they were asked to perform a second task concurrently (such as counting or pressing a button on hearing a tone), their performance deteriorated significantly, contrary to that of non-dyslexic children in the sample. This led to the proposal that children with dyslexia have problems in skill automatisation (both motor and cognitive), but that for most skills the dyslexic can learn to mask their difficulties by a process of conscious compensation, leading to near-normal performance via greater effort. Problems remain in skills requiring rapid performance, the fluent interplay of a range of sub-skills, or when demands exceed available resources.

The automatisation deficit hypothesis predicts that there will be deficits not only in articulation skills but also in simple motor skills with no linguistic component, whereas, although the phonological deficit viewpoint could account for articulatory problems, other motor skills problems should be relatively mild and/or transient. To assess these predictions, Nicolson and Fawcett (1995) compared three groups of dyslexic children/adolescents with three groups of normally achieving children/adolescents matched for chronological age and IQ. Consistent with the automatisation deficit hypothesis, dyslexics presented severe problems in simple motor tasks, such as bead threading, which persisted into adolescence. These motor deficits were comparable in severity with articulation rate deficits.

A recent elaboration on these views proposes that dyslexia is related to a minor cerebellar weakness. Nicolson, Fawcett and Dean (1995) found their dyslexic subjects to be weaker than controls on a time estimation task which is believed to be an index of cerebellar functioning, but not on a control task involving estimations of loudness. Research by Keele, Ivry and colleagues (e.g. see Lundy-Ekman *et al.* 1991) suggests that the cerebellum operates an internal timing system which can be used in various tasks and may be a vital component of skilled movement behaviours.

The cerebellum may also play a role in refining motor programmes and controlling various rapid automated movements (such as rapid tracking saccades). It is known in the case of brain-injured patients that provided damage does not extend to the cerebellum, many of those skills which have become automatised are still available. As such, cerebellum dysfunctions may explain differences between dyslexics and non-dyslexics in the motor tasks assessed by Nicolson and Fawcett (1990, 1995). A weakness in the cerebellum may also account for phonological deficits and literacy problems. If cerebellum dysfunctions lead to articulation problems, and articulation expertise assists the process of becoming phonemically aware, then deficits here may lead to deficits on tasks which require precise phonological coding, such as reading. Additionally, if skilled reading/ writing requires sub-skills (such as word decoding) to become automatic, then the literacy abilities of the dyslexic will be further hindered.

Although further evidence and theoretical elaboration is required to establish the automaticity/cerebellum hypothesis as a viable alternative to the phonological deficit viewpoint, it does provide a link between literacy and motor deficits and provides a framework within which to consider reading/writing problems from the perspective of attentional resource-based processes. If such a link exists between literacy problems and motor deficits, detailed analysis of the processes which comprise skilled motor behaviours may be informative as to the basis of these deficits and provide some means to develop and assess the efficacy of procedures to remediate these deficits.

Sequencing skills

Movements can be thought of as comprising the three components of timing, force and sequencing, which may be dissociable (Lundy-Ekman *et al.*, 1991). Deficits in one area (e.g. timing) may not be associated with deficits in a second (force or sequencing). The data presented in the previous sections suggest that dyslexics show deficits in tasks requiring precise timing or time estimation. However, problems with learning and reproducing sequential information have also been related to dyslexia. For example, a number of dyslexia assessments include measures of memory or digit span; see Miles (1993) or Nicolson and Fawcett (1996), and the ACID profile (which includes deficits in digit span) of the WISC is a widely referenced characteristic of dyslexia (see Vargo, Grosser and Spafford 1995). An assessment of memory span requires the dyslexic to repeat a series of items (usually digits) presented to them in random and increasingly larger strings, the subject's task being to repeat each string in the correct sequence. Similarly, a recent study by Plaza and Guitton (1997) reported the single case of an 11-year-old dyslexic boy who showed a discrepancy between sequential and simultaneous skills. This subject found it difficult to imitate hand movements and to repeat digits and words in sequential order. These authors also report that they have observed such sequential failure in the cognitive profiles of several other dyslexic children. However, assessments of dyslexics' ability to learn and produce sequential information suggest that such deficiencies may not be an underlying characteristic of all dyslexics.

In this study, 20 dyslexic and 23 non-dyslexic adult subjects performed a variation of the Nissen and Bullemer (1987) serial reaction time task. Subjects were presented with four blocks of 120 trials. Each trial consisted of an asterisk appearing at any one of four locations on a computer screen, the subject being asked to press one of four buttons associated with the position of the asterisk; the left-most location was associated with the left-most button, the central-left location was associated with the central-left button, etc. The first three blocks comprised ten repetitions of a 12-trial sequence, recognition of which would mean that the subject would be able to predict the position of the next item. However, subjects were not informed of the existence of this sequence and the start and finish of each sequence was unmarked, giving the impression of a continuous series of 120 trials. Also, the sequence was devised such that more than two responses needed to be linked to allow prediction; for example, which location followed location 1 was determined by the location preceding location 1. The final, fourth block comprised a random series of 120 trials making predictions regarding the position of any subsequent trial impossible. Under these conditions,

Table 5.1 Mean scores, with standard deviations in brackets, of dyslexic and non-dyslexic subjects for both errors and times across the three sequenced trial blocks (blocks 1 to 3) and the random trial block (block 4)

	Dyslexics		Non-dyslexics	
	Times	Errors	Times	Errors
Block 1	464.00	4.90	376.60	7.48
	(318.26)	(4.13)	(173.63)	(18.52)
Block 2	359.16	4.15	335.13	3.43
	(138.76)	(2.83)	(118.77)	(3.60)
Block 3	340.83	4.90	340.57	3.70
	(109.21)	(3.08)	(103.98)	(4.00)
Block 4	404.25	10.75	415.51	6.22
	(104.21)	(7.44)	(98.51)	(4.68)

subjects showed consistent improvement in performance throughout those blocks which comprised the repeating sequence; the sequence aided performance. When the random trials were introduced, however, performance deteriorated to levels comparable to the start of the procedure. These performance characteristics suggest that the subjects learned the sequence (whether or not they were able to verbalise the sequence) and used this knowledge when responding. This task provided a means to assess the ability of dyslexic individuals to learn and use a series of simple sequenced responses to a visual stimulus.

Comparisons of the dyslexic and non-dyslexic subjects indicated improvements in performance across the sequential trials and decrements in performance when these were replaced by random trials (see Table 5.1). In terms of response times, there were significant differences between blocks 1 and 2 (dyslexic, $F_{(1,19)} = 5.48$, $p = .03$; non-dyslexics, $F_{(1,22)} = 4.40$, $p = .05$), though less evidence for improvements between blocks 2 and 3 (dyslexics, $F_{(1,19)} = 3.24$, $p = .09$; non-dyslexics, $F_{(1,22)} < 1$). Errors indicated no evidence for differences between blocks 1 and 2 nor blocks 2 and 3 for either group (dyslexics, blocks 1 and 2: $F_{(1,19)} = 1.34$, $p = .26$; dyslexics, blocks 2 and 3: $F_{(1,19)} = 1.24$, $p = .28$; non-dyslexics, blocks 1 and 2: $F_{(1,22)} = 1.10$, $p = .31$; non-dyslexics, blocks 2 and 3: $F_{(1,22)} < 1$). However, performance deteriorated between blocks 3 and 4, differences being significant for both dyslexics (time: $F_{(1,19)} = 34$, $p < .001$; errors: $F_{(1,19)} = 18$, $p < .001$) and non-dyslexics (time: $F_{(1,22)} = 49$, $p < .001$; errors: $F_{(1,22)} = 13$, $p < .002$). Under the present non-linguistic conditions (the stimulus could be defined simply by its spatial location), these dyslexic adults seemed as able as their non-dyslexic peers to learn and produce a sequence of response.

Similarly, in clinical settings, it is not the case that dyslexic children perform worse than their non-dyslexic peers when required to reproduce information presented sequentially. For example, in a task which required children to indicate, in order, a series of locations on a computer screen using movements and presses of the mouse (the task was based upon that used in the CoPS programme; see Singleton and Thomas 1994), dyslexic 8- to 11-year-olds were as quick and as accurate as similar aged non-dyslexics. Given that sequencing tasks can be identified where dyslexics' performance can be equivalent to non-dyslexics, differences between dyslexics and non-dyslexics in sequencing tasks such as digit span could be due to procedural factors. To assess this possibility, a separate group of dyslexics and non-dyslexics were given three digit span tasks. Each task comprised a series of digits which the child had to reproduce in the correct order. The number of digits within each series was increased to the point where the child failed twice to repeat the digits in correct order. Tasks varied dependent upon the mode of response required. In the first task, the subject had to write down the digits. In the second, a verbal response was required. In the final task, the subject was asked to point to tiles on which were written the digits 1 to 9. Span size also varied across these three conditions. Analyses indicated an interaction between task (written, oral versus pointing) and group (dyslexic versus non-dyslexic): $F_{(2,102)} = 3.45, p < .04$. Although the span of the dyslexics was lower in the verbal (dyslexics mean = 5.00, SD = 0.95; non-dyslexics mean = 5.53, SD = 0.92; $t_{(51)} = 2.85, p < .01$) and written (dyslexics mean = 4.76, SD = 1.04; non-dyslexics mean = 5.47, SD = 0.76; $t_{(51)} = 2.04, p < .05$) conditions, this had increased to comparable levels in the pointing condition (dyslexics mean = 5.57, SD = 0.99; non-dyslexics mean = 5.66, SD = 0.87; $t_{(51)} = 0.33, p = .74$). Again, these data suggest that the ability to sequence information is not deficient within these dyslexics under all performance characteristics.

The development of movement skills

A second way of investigating possible links between motor difficulties and developmental dyslexia, and one which is more in keeping with the views of Denckla (1985) for a maturational lag and the procedures of movement remediation practices, is to consider the normal development of motor skills and explore how they might be related to the difficulties experienced by the dyslexic.

Throughout their development, children undergo surprisingly rapid changes in their movement skills. The often jerky, inefficient movements of the infant change to the more efficient, smooth attempts of older children. These observable differences between infancy and childhood are due both to maturation and learning, resulting in more efficient motor control and response organisation in older children.

Motor development can be thought of as a process that begins before birth and continues throughout adult life. Early movement sequences are considered to be biologically determined due to their dependence on physiological and neurological maturation. Skilled movements, in contrast, are dependent on the combination of maturation, practice and learning. On the basis of the broad similarity in the progression of movement behaviour and the way in which children achieve new motor skills, it has been argued that all children progress through a relatively similar developmental sequence, although the rate of progression may vary. Individual differences apparent in children's development and behaviour may be explained by the interaction of internal and external factors (Fischer and Farrar 1988).

Internal factors that contribute to differences in the rate of motor development in children are differences in growth and biological maturation, cognitive capacity, personality and motivation. For example, improvements in cognitive capacity with maturation may allow children to direct their attention to relevant sources of movement information which will facilitate the learning of more complex skills. External factors which affect motor development include the amount of stimulation received by the child. Placing visually attractive objects within the reach of the infant results in the appearance of visually guided reaching movements earlier than in babies who were not provided with stimulating visual environments.

Observable developmental changes in movement behaviour can be ordered into a hierarchy, progressing from relatively simple movements to complex skills. The developmental sequence starts with reflexive responses which the infant cannot control and progresses to highly skilled movements which are dependent on motor learning and control factors. Reflex actions such as the early grasp reflexes that are present in newborn infants elicit predetermined finger movements that will be incorporated into many more advanced skills – including the ability to grasp, manipulate and release objects which provide the child with the necessary movement patterns to learn fine motor skills such as handwriting. Similarly, the postural reflexes are necessary for normal motor development, with many being used and modified to assist in the maintenance of postural stability throughout life. Such automated units of movement have been argued to form the basic building blocks of many complex and skilled movements. It is possible that any arrest in motor development at any of these stages may be linked with the arrest of the complex skills necessary for the acquisition of reading and writing (see, for example, the discussion in relation to dyslexia and learning disabilities in Hepper 1994 and McGlown 1984).

Neurobehavioural perspectives

Together with touch, the vestibular system is one of the sensory systems that develops earliest. This system responds to movement of the head and provides us with information about body position and motion in relation to ourselves and to the external environment. Such information is essential for the majority of motor skills since they depend upon the maintenance of postural stability. The sensory organs responsible for vestibular information are located within the labyrinth of the inner ear. Information from the vestibular system is important in the maintenance of balance, but also plays a role in eye, head and neck movements and the maintenance of muscle tone: reflexive motor commands issued by the vestibular nucleus are distributed to the motor nuclei of cranial nerves involved with eye, head and neck movements, while descending instructions along the vestibulospinal tracts of the spinal cord adjust peripheral muscle tone to complement the reflexive movements of the head and neck.

The kinaesthetic system is important because it provides information about bodily movement without reference to the external receptors of vision and audition. Such information is essential for the maintenance of an appropriate posture, for the control of muscle tone and the coding of movement information which may assist the learning of skilled movements. Children who have been diagnosed as dyslexic often have a low body awareness in comparison to their non-dyslexic peers. If they have low muscle tone, they usually appear to be 'floppy' or weak, or they may compensate for low tone and poor body awareness by tensing their muscles and hyperextending their joints to provide them with increased kinaesthetic information.

Developmental changes in children's movement behaviour, especially with regard to knowledge about their bodies, are partly dependent upon the ability to integrate and interpret sensory information based upon past experiences. As children become more competent in visual and kinaesthetic perceptual processes, they are able to make increasingly more accurate judgements about the speed and direction of moving objects and to perform more complex movements. Improvements in processing sensory information may underlie age-related changes in motor development. In this way, infants are able to develop more mature motor patterns and movement behaviours (see Lazlo and Bairstow 1985). The integration of kinaesthetic and visual information is also essential to the maintenance of postural stability which has itself been linked to dyslexia (Nicolson and Fawcett 1996). Deficits in sensory processes (for example, within the visual system, see Eden *et al.* 1996; Livingstone *et al.* 1991) may be linked to developmental delays or deficits in motor behaviours. In a replication of the findings for differences between dyslexics and non-dyslexics in motion perception (see Everatt, Bradshaw and Hibbard, in press), screening procedures employed to ensure appropriate classification of subjects into dyslexic and non-dyslexic groups included assessments of a history of motor co-ordination problems. Interestingly, those who indicated a history of motor problems performed worse on the measures of motion perception. Although these data are little better than anecdotal, they suggest a possible link between the underlying visual deficits associated with dyslexia and motor problems. More formal assessments of these possible links are being undertaken at present.

Motor learning theory

Sensory information appears to be vital to our ability to learn and control movements, providing one of the components necessary for the central representation of movement in motor memory/motor schemas. When people learn any new skill, their primary concern is with acquiring the movement necessary for its performance. Practice leads to a refinement of the actions, the phasing (timing between different components in the movement), the amount of force, and the spatial accuracy of the movement. In these early stages of acquiring motor skills, attention is focused on a small aspect of the task. This usually means that in newly-learnt skills there is a tendency to simplify the movement by reducing the number of different components it comprises. Well-learnt skills, conversely, may be performed with low attentional demands because some or all aspects of the task can be performed automatically or via the implementation of some stored motor programme. Deficits in attention and/or the process of making a behaviour free from attentional resource limitations (see Everatt *et al.* Chapter 1 of this volume) may therefore be related to poor acquisition of motor skills.

Generalised motor programmes are assumed to contain prestructured commands for many movements that may be varied by applying specific parameters, such as the overall duration, force, muscle selection and spatial location, to effect the desired movement. In handwriting, for example, the shape of the letter may be invariant, but if the overall force is increased, then the size of the letter will be larger. Motor schema theory, on the other hand, may provide an explanation of how movements are learned, and how memory processes may play an integral role in the connection between motor deficits and learning disabilities. For example, Schmidt (1988) suggests that when a movement generated by a generalised motor programme is performed, all aspects of that movement are temporarily stored in memory. Problems dyslexics experience with movement behaviours may be linked to their oft-cited problems with short-term memory (e.g. Rugel 1974). Deficits in memory may have important implications for the speed with which an individual processes movement-related information and for the number of components of a task which can be combined into a smooth sequence. However, not all dyslexics experience difficulties with processing sequential information (see previous section on this topic) or memory span (e.g. Torgeson and Houck 1980), and as with attentional processes, studies comparing the motion co-ordination abilities of those dyslexics with and without deficits in memory span are required to assess this potential link between dyslexia and movement disorders.

One of the consequences of improved information processing ability in older children (such as more efficient encoding, rehearsal and organisation of motor functions) is that they become better at learning and controlling ongoing movement sequences and are able to perform and learn more complex sequences of skilled movements.

Motor control and inhibitory processes

An understanding of motor coordination probably requires a knowledge of the ways in which joint combinations are selected from the large repertoire of possible combinations. The individual achieves control over the many possible muscle actions of the body by grouping them into an organised system of constraints (see Newell and Barclay 1982). This control can be conceptualised as comprising three stages. In the first phase, children utilise sensory feedback to learn about their environment and to acquire basic control of movements. The second phase can be thought of as involving integrative processing resulting in greater knowledge of the body and a heightened ability to control it while interacting in the environment. An increased ability to process information from internal and external sources and in planning motor responses characterise this phase. The final phase involves learning and advanced control of movements, particularly of the spatial-temporal aspects of complex movements.

The nervous system has two kinds of neurons, excitory and inhibitory. The inhibitory system serves many purposes in behaviour: curbing impulsiveness, attending to one task over a period of time, interrupting overlearned responses, decreasing distractibility, overriding automatic responses such as reflexes, and maintaining an appropriate level of arousal. In one way or another, some or all of these abilities appear to be deficient in learning-disabled children implying a common inhibitory control deficiency and/or a functional deficiency in the ability to allocate appropriate attention to task-relevant information.

In clinical settings, dyslexic children are often described as presenting difficulties with tasks requiring changes in motor tempo. Observations of dyslexic children attempting to draw a line slowly or walk slowly suggest that they have difficulties overriding highly learned responses. The dyslexic child tends to perform tasks in a very stereotypical manner and experiences problems when variations in routine behaviours are introduced. Similarly, overactive primitive postural reflexes (Tonic Neck Reflex, Tonic Labyrinthine Reflex) are often associated with learning disabled children (McGlown 1984; Goddard 1996), and may be another manifestation of a general lack of inhibitory control. Postural reflexes represent relatively inflexible neural organisations which are normally inhibited and succeeded by more mature, voluntary purposive movements. The notion of a general inhibitory control deficit in learning disabled children might account for many of the observable movement behaviour problems that typify this population. However, as with many other areas, research investigating the relationship between inhibitory mechanisms and motor skills deficits is insufficient formally to judge the views of McGlown (1984) and others.

Intervention studies

Despite considerable evidence linking movement disorders and dyslexia, there is little to suggest that improvements in motor behaviours per se will lead to improved academic skills. Reviews from Critchley and Critchley (1978), to Kavale and Mattson (1983), to Myers and Hammill (1990) all conclude that attempting to remediate the poor academic abilities of dyslexics by the implementation of some programme to improve motor behaviour will not meet with success. Nevertheless, a number of courses exist which use techniques to improve basic movement behaviours as a quintessential feature of their programme (e.g., Bertrand 1997; Goddard 1996). A reason given for the continued use of motor training programmes is that they improve the academic skills of a proportion of children, and even those who do not show such improvements may gain benefits in terms of self-esteem and motivation (Cratty 1996). The former reason may be supported by data which suggest there are sub-groups of learning disabled children with motor disabilities. For example, Lubs et al. (1991) divided the learning disabled children they assessed into several sub-groups based upon the presence or absence of motor problems. Within the sub-groups which showed motor problems, one presented motor planning problems along with academic abilities, and a second suggested problems related to dyspraxia. These two groups were similar in that they both experienced problems in executing complex serial skills, although the latter seemed able to acquire these skills over a long period of time. One possible direction for future research into the efficacy of movement-based remediation techniques is the a priori differentiation of the learning disabled children into such sub-groups.

Overview: movement disorders and dyslexia

In summary, a body of research can be presented to suggest links between dyslexia and movement or coordination difficulties. Dyslexics may show a range of problems from difficulties in basic gross physical tasks, such as tying shoe laces, to deficits in fine motor and articulatory skills. It has been suggested that a failure to develop physical movement sequences may be linked to sequencing difficulties in reading and writing, although the findings reported within this chapter suggest that some process other than those related to the learning and use of sequential information may be the underlying cause of these problems; timing components may be a more likely candidate.

Alternative candidates which might lead to associations between dyslexia and motor deficits were proposed in the chapter. These concentrated on visual and attentional processes, the theme of this book, and suggest the possibility that movement deficits might be a consequence of some underlying dysfunction as much as literacy skills. However, the scarcity of empirical studies in this area means that formal assessment of these possibilities is inappropriate at this point in time.

Neurobehavioural studies could also point to a link between movement difficulties and dyslexia. For example, differences in the ability to process rapidly changing or moving stimuli have been used as evidence for abnormalities found in the magnocellular visual system of reading-disabled individuals. These same deficits could lead to poor movement performance given the link between sensory processes and the acquisition of complex movements. There is also evidence for links between dyslexia and poor kinaesthetic awareness, postural instability and impaired motor inhibition. The arrest of motor development in any of these respects might lead to poor acquisition of the complex skills required in reading and writing. However, again, research assessing these possibilities is necessary. If such developmental problems exist, remediation therapies which tackle these movement deficits might help to reduce the difficulties dyslexics experience in reading and writing. To date, studies of such therapies have presented negative results and it may be that more refined programmes are required, based on some analysis of the individual movement problems experienced by the dyslexic.

References

Alm, J. and Andersson, J. (1995) 'Reading and writing difficulties at prisons in the county of Uppsala', report of the Dyslexia Project of the National Labour Market Board of Sweden.

Bertrand, L. (1997) 'Support for dyslexic children in Luxembourg', in R. Salter and I. Smythe (eds), *The International Book of Dyslexia*. London: EDA & WDNF.

Bradley, L. and Bryant, P.E. (1983) 'Categorising sounds and learning to read: A causal connection', *Nature*, 301, 419–421.

Bruck, M. (1993) 'Word recognition and component phonological processing skills of adults with childhood diagnosis of dyslexia', *Developmental Review*, 13, 258–268.

Brying, G. and Michelsson, K. (1984) 'Neurological and neuropsychological deficiencies in dyslexic children with and without attentional disorders', *Developmental Medicine and Child Neurology*, 26, 765–773.

Cratty, B.J. (1996) 'Coordination problems among learning disabled children: Meanings and implications', in B.J. Cratty and R.L. Goldman (eds), *Learning Disabilities: Contemporary Viewpoints*. Amsterdam: Harwood Publishers.

Critchley, M. and Critchley, E.A. (1978) *Dyslexia Defined*. London: Heinemann Medical Books.

Denckla, M.B. (1985) 'Motor coordination in dyslexic children: Theoretical and clinical implications', in F.H. Duffy and N. Geschwind (eds), *Dyslexia: A Neuroscientific Approach to Clinical Evaluation*. Boston: Little, Brown.

Eden, G.F., VanMeter, J.W., Rumsey, J.M., Maisog, J.M., Woods, R.P. and Zeffiro, T.A. (1996) 'Abnormal processing of visual motion in dyslexia revealed by functional brain imaging', *Nature*, 382, 66–69.

Edwards, J. (1994) *The Scars of Dyslexia: Eight Case Studies in Emotional Reaction*. London: Cassell.

Everatt, J., Bradshaw, M.B. and Hibbard, P.B. (in press) 'Visual processing and dyslexia', *Perception*.

Fischer, K.W. and Farrar, M.J. (1988) 'Generalisation about generalisations: How a theory of skill development explains both generality and specificy', in A. Demetriou (ed.), *The Neo-Piagetian Theories of Cognitive Development*. North Holland: Elsevier.

Goddard, S. (1996) *A Teacher's Window into the Child's Mind*. Eugene, OR: Fern Ridge Press.

Groeger, J.A. and Maguire, R.L. (in press) 'Dyslexia and driving: Controlled processing of control skills?', in G.B. Grayson (ed.), *Behavioural Research in Road Safety VI*. London: Transport Research Laboratory.

Haslum, M.N. (1989) 'Predictors of dyslexia', *Irish Journal of Psychology*, 10, 622–630.

Hepper, P.G. (1994) *Noise Fetus*. Hove: LEA.

Jaklewicz, H. (1980) 'Follow-up studies on dyslexia and dysorthographia', *Psychiatria Polska*, 14, 613–619.

Kavale, K. and Mattson, P. (1983) 'One jumped off the balance beam: Meta-analysis of perceptual-motor training', *Journal of Learning Disabilities*, 16, 166–173.

Klasen, E. (1972) *The Syndrome of Specific Dyslexia*. Maryland: University Park Press.

Lazlo, J.L. and Bairstow, P.J. (1985) *Perceptual-motor Behaviour: Developmental Assessment and Therapy*. London: Holt, Rinehart & Winston.

Liberman, I.Y. (1973) 'Segmentation of the spoken word and reading acquisition', *Bulletin of the Orton Society*, 23, 65–77.

Livingstone, M.S., Rosen, G.D., Drislane, F.W. and Galaburda, A.M. (1991)

'Physiological and anatomical evidence for a magnocellular deficit in developmental dyslexia', *Proceedings of the National Academy of Sciences, USA*, 88, 7941–7947.

Lovegrove, W.J., Martin, F. and Slaghuis, W. (1986) 'A theoretical and experimental case for a visual deficit in specific reading disability', *Cognitive Neuropsychology*, 3, 225–267.

Lubs, H.A., Duara, R., Levin, R., Lubs, M.L., Rabin, M., Kushch, A. and Gross-Glenn, K. (1991) 'Dyslexia sub-types: Genetics, behavior and brain imaging', in D.D. Duane and D.B. Gray (eds), *The Reading Brain: The Biological Basis of Dyslexia*. Maryland: New York Press.

Lundberg, I. and Hoien, T. (1989) 'Phonemic deficits: A core symptom of developmental dyslexia?', *Irish Journal of Psychology*, 10, 579–592.

Lundy-Ekman, L., Ivry, R., Keele, S. and Woollacott, M. (1991) 'Timing and force control deficits in clumsy children', *Journal of Cognitive Neuroscience*, 3, 367–376.

McGlown, D. (1984) *Developmental Reflexive Rehabilitation*. London: Taylor & Francis.

McLoughlin, D., Fitzgibbon, G. and Young, V. (1994). *Adult Dyslexia: Assessment, Counselling and Training*. London: Whurr.

Miles, T.R. (1993) *Dyslexia: The Pattern of Difficulties*, second edition. London: Whurr.

Miles, T.R. and Gilroy, D.E. (1996) *Dyslexia at College*. London: Routledge.

Miles, T.R. and Varma, V. (eds) (1995) *Dyslexia and Stress*. London: Whurr.

Myers, P.I. and Hammill, D.D. (1990) *Learning Disabilities: Basic Concepts, Assessment Practices and Instructional Strategies*. Texas: Pro-Ed.

Newell, K.M. and Barclay, C.R. (1982) 'Developing knowledge about action', in J.A.S. Kelso and J.E. Clark (eds), *The Development of Motor Control and Coordination*. Chichester: Wiley.

Nicolson, R.J. and Fawcett, A.J. (1990) 'Automaticity: A framework for dyslexia research?', *Cognition*, 35, 159–182.

Nicolson, R.J. and Fawcett, A.J. (1995) 'Dyslexia is more than a phonological disability', *Dyslexia: An International Journal of Research and Practice*, 1, 19–36.

Nicolson, R.J. and Fawcett, A.J. (1996) *DEST Manual*. London: The Psychological Corporation.

Nicolson, R.J., Fawcett, A.J. and Dean, P. (1995) 'Time estimation deficits in developmental dyslexia: Evidence for a cerebellar involvement', *Proceedings of the Royal Society*, 259, 43–47.

Nissen, N.J. and Bullemer, P. (1987) 'Attentional requirements of learning: Evidence from performance measures', *Cognitive Psychology*, 19, 1–32.

Osmond, J. (1993) *The Reality of Dyslexia*. London: Cassell.

Plaza, M. and Guitton, C. (1997) 'Working memory limitations, phonological deficit, sequential disorder and syntactic impairment in a child with severe developmental dyslexia', *Dyslexia: An International Journal of Research and Practice*, 3, 93–108.

Regehr, S.M. and Kaplan, B.J. (1988) 'Reading disability with motor problems may be an inherited sub-type', *Pediatrics*, 82, 204–210.

Riddick, B. (1996) *Living with Dyslexia*. London: Routledge.

Rugel, R.P. (1974) 'WISC subtest scores of disabled readers', *Journal of Learning Disabilities*, 7, 57–64.

Schmidt, R.A. (1988) *Motor Control and Learning*, second edition. Champaign, IL: Human Kinetics Publishers.

Shiffrin, R.R. and Schneider, W. (1977) 'Controlled and automatic human information processing: II. Perceptual learning, automatic attending, and general theory', *Psychological Review*, 84, 127–190.

Singleton, C. and Thomas, K. (1994) 'Computerised screening for dyslexia', in C. Singleton (ed.), *Computers and Dyslexia*. Hull: University of Hull.

Singleton, C.H. (1996) 'Dyslexia in higher education: issues for policy and practice', in C Stephens (ed.), *Dyslexia Students in Higher Education: Practical Responses to Student and Institutional Needs*: Huddersfield: University of Huddersfield.

Snowling, M.J. (1981) 'Phonemic deficits in development dyslexia', *Psychological Research*, 43, 219–234.

Snowling, M.J. (1995) 'Phonological processing and developmental dyslexia', *Journal of Research in Reading*, 18, 132–138.

Stanovich, K.E. (1988a) 'Explaining the differences between the dyslexic and the garden-variety poor reader: The phonological-core variable-difference model', *Journal of Learning Disabilities*, 21, 590–604.

Stanovich, K.E. (1988b) 'The right and wrong places to look for the cognitive locus of reading disability', *Annals of Dyslexia*, 154–177.

Stein, J. (1993) 'Visuospatial perception in disabled readers', in D.M. Willows, R.S. Kruk and E. Corcos (eds), *Visual Processes in Reading and Reading Disabilities*. Hillsdale, NJ: Erlbaum.

Sudgen, D. and Wann, C. (1987) 'The assessment of motor impairment in children with moderate learning disabilities', *British Journal of Educational Psychology*, 57, 225–236.

Thomson, M.E. (1990) *Developmental Dyslexia*. London: Whurr

Torgeson, J.K. and Houck, D.G. (1980) 'Processing deficiencies of learning-disabled children who perform poorly on the digit span test', *Journal of Educational Psychology*, 72, 141–160.

Vargo, F.E., Grosser, G.S. and Spafford, C.S. (1995) 'Digit span and other WISC-R scores in the diagnosis of dyslexia in children', *Perceptual and Motor Skills*, 80, 1219–1229

Wolff, P.H., Cohen, C. and Drake, C. (1984) 'Impaired motor timing control in specific reading retardation', *Neuropsychologia*, 22, 587–600.

Wolff, P.H., Michel, G.F. and Ovrut, M. (1990) 'Rate and timing precision of motor coordination in developmental dyslexia', *Developmental Psychology*, 26, 349–359.

6 Anatomy, circuitry and plasticity of word reading

Michael I. Posner, Yalchin G. Abdullaev,
Bruce D. McCandliss, and Sara C. Sereno

Introduction

The last several years have seen remarkable changes in our understanding of how high level human skills are organised in the brain. Much of this new information has depended upon neuroimaging methods to reveal areas of the brain active in various cognitive tasks, particularly in visual word recognition. Converging evidence from techniques such as positron emission tomography (PET), functional magnetic resonance imaging (fMRI), and the recording of brain event related potentials (ERPs) strongly suggests that specific brain areas are closely linked to distinct aspects of word recognition. In this chapter, we do not dwell on the methodological issues surrounding these techniques, although we do recognise the limitations that accompany each of them. Our focus, instead, is to gather together what we currently know about brain areas and word reading – how neural systems are organised, how they change during learning and acquisition, and how abnormalities in their circuitry may help us in understanding reading difficulties.

Most of the neuroimaging data that we cite involves the processing of individual visual words. Our goal, however, is to understand the very complex yet seemingly effortless task of reading text. The study of eye fixations during normal reading provides a natural connection between reading individual words and reading continuous text. The eye movement record provides information about the duration, location and order of eye fixations. Eye movements can be recorded under normal reading conditions or in situations in which portions of the text are altered in some way (e.g. restricting the text that is available on a given fixation). With these techniques, it is possible to infer the type and amount of processing that occurs on a word during a single eye fixation. We argue that the duration of eye fixations during normal reading provides evidence about the time taken for individual words to access their internal lexical and semantic representations. By combining evidence of functional anatomy with studies of the time course of activation we are able to relate the process of lexical access to the fixation pattern of reading text. We further discuss how experience with words influences these internal representations and speculate on problems that arise in acquiring the skill of reading.

We begin our analysis in the next section with information from eye movement studies of reading. This work was summarised by Rayner and Pollatsek (1989) and a chapter in the current volume is devoted to this topic (see Pollatsek *et al.*, Chapter 8). Our treatment focuses on those aspects related to lexical processing within the confines of a single fixation. In the third section we review anatomical evidence, mainly from PET studies, that suggests possible brain areas associated with component processes of word recognition. These processes include analysis of visual features, orthography, phonology, and semantics. This area, too, has been subject to recent reviews (Démonet, Wise and Frackowiak 1993; Posner and Carr 1992; Posner and Raichle 1994). We also introduce, where possible, converging data from neuronal depth recordings in patients. In the fourth section we turn to the organisation of these areas in real time. Studies using scalp recording of brain ERPs yield estimates of the time of activation of component processes and insights into the circuitry of visual word processing. In the fifth section we review efforts to study changes in the anatomy and circuitry of word reading that accompany learning. Finally, we briefly consider the significance of these results with skilled readers for understanding various forms of dyslexia.

Eye fixations and reading

During normal, skilled reading, the eyes typically remain fixed on a given word for about a quarter of a second. This places temporal constraints on word recognition and can thus assist in interpreting research using a real-time measure of brain activity such as recording ERPs during single word presentations.

In the typical eye movement paradigm, eye movements are monitored as subjects read text. The duration of eye fixations as well as the overall pattern of fixations are used to determine the underlying processes of word recognition, sentence processing and text comprehension. The eye movement technique offers certain advantages over other techniques in investigating on-line language processing. First, reading is a natural task and eye movements are a normal part of reading. Subjects do not have to make decisions about the words they read or name them aloud as they do in other experimental procedures. Yet, it is well-documented that the processing of a word in text is, in fact, reflected in its fixation time (see Rayner and Sereno 1994, for a review).

Readers typically fixate for about 200–250 ms, saccade forward about 6–8 character spaces, and make regressions (look back in the text) about 10–15 per cent of the time. While there is considerable variability within each of these measures, the variability is closely related to the characteristics of the text (easy vs difficult) and the reader (beginning vs skilled). For example, if a text is difficult, fixations are longer, saccades are shorter, and there are more regressions. The eye movement technique is remarkably sensitive to processing difficulties. Effects are reflected not only in the total number of fixations or the overall reading rate, but typically appear within the confines of a single fixation on a word. For example, the eye movement measure is able to capture the on-line difficulties associated with (1) within-word structural information (Lima 1987; Inhoff 1989),

(2) word-level variables such as word frequency (Rayner and Duffy 1986; Sereno 1992), regularity (Sereno and Posner 1995), and lexical ambiguity (Duffy, Morris and Rayner 1988; Rayner and Frazier 1989; Sereno, Pacht and Rayner 1992), and (3) extra-word variables such as contextual predictability (Carroll and Slowiaczek 1986; Zola 1984), temporary syntactic ambiguities (Frazier and Rayner 1982; Rayner, Carlson and Frazier 1983) and discourse integration (O'Brien *et al.* 1988).

Given that the fixation time on a word in reading reflects its processing difficulty and the fact that an eye movement is necessarily programmed at some point before the end of the fixation, a more precise estimate of the time-course of word recognition can be made by determining *what* causes the eyes to move and *when* this occurs. With respect to the 'what' question, two different classes of models have emerged over the past 20 years to account for eye movement control in reading (for a review see Rayner, Sereno and Raney 1995). Cognitive control models maintain that generating an eye movement is strongly linked to the lexical processing of the currently fixated word (e.g. Morrison 1984; Pollatsek and Rayner 1990; Sereno 1992). Oculomotor models, on the other hand, claim that lower level factors such as fixation location mainly govern the decision to move the eyes (e.g. Kowler and Anton 1987; McConkie *et al.* 1988; McConkie *et al.* 1989; O'Regan and Levy-Schoen 1987). We believe the weight of evidence, alluded to above, favours a cognitive control model. With respect to the 'when' question, the time elapsed between a decision to move the eyes and an actual eye movement – the oculomotor latency – has been estimated to be about 150 ms (Rayner *et al.* 1983).[1]

Perhaps the best way to demonstrate how eye movements temporally constrain lexical processing is to dissect the time course of a single fixation on a word in reading. Figure 6.1 depicts a time-line of a 275 ms fixation. While fixations in reading are often shorter than this, we have chosen this duration to reflect the somewhat artificial situation in which a reader obtains foveal but no prior parafoveal view of a word.[2] Certain constraints placed on the 'front-end' and 'back-end' of the fixation serve to narrow the window during which lexical processing occurs (see Figure 6.1). At the front-end, when a stimulus is visually presented, it takes roughly 60 ms for that information to travel from the retina to higher cortical areas. At this point, lexical processing can begin. At the back-end, oculomotor latency, the time needed to program and execute an eye movement, limits the interval during which a sufficient degree of lexical processing must be achieved. That is, since eye fixations reflect lexical processing, such processing must be largely completed in order to 'trigger' the next eye movement. Oculomotor latency is estimated to be around 150 ms in duration. Finally, once a signal is given to move the eyes, about 20 ms elapses before the eye muscles are activated and the saccade begins.

Figure 6.1 also summarises the timing of activations within hypothesised functionally distinct anatomical areas that is discussed in the following sections. There are assumptions and uncertainties in the anatomy and circuitry that we review. However, we suggest a first approximation to coordinate the programming

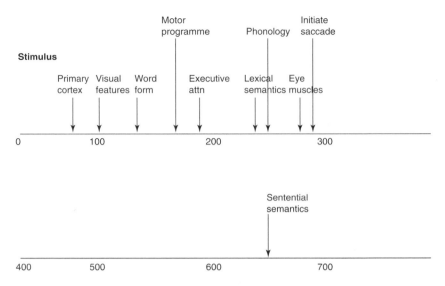

Figure 6.1 Time line for processing during word reading.

Notes

Fixation starts at time 0 and saccade to new word at 275 ms. Constructed from data on fixation times in normal reading, PET and ERP studies of word reading.

of eye movement in reading with concurrent activity in the brain. In the argument that follows, we propose that saccade programming is linked to the status of perceptual word processing in left occipital cortex that engages an 'executive' attentional system. Meanwhile, higher-level semantic information accruing at more anterior sites exerts an influence, which may sometimes affect the eye movement programme already in progress. This analysis provides a reasonable time course by which semantic activity may influence the fixation time of the eye.

Functional anatomy of word reading

It is now possible to determine in some detail the brain areas that can be activated during fixation of a single word. The basic strategy is to consider the cognitive operations that constitute reading the word. Usually visual, phonological, semantic and attentional operations are thought to be crucial (LaBerge and Samuels 1974; Posner 1978). Our goal is to describe the brain areas active during each operation. By comparing differences in cerebral blood flow when a given operation is required with a condition when that operation is not required, one can seek to determine the brain areas involved (see Posner and Raichle 1994 for extensive illustrations of this logic). The methods adopted so far for imaging blood flow changes during reading have been positron emission tomography (PET) and functional magnetic resonance imaging (fMRI) (see Toga and Mazziotta 1995 for a discussion of these methods). There are problems that accompany these techniques. The temporal resolution of methods that rest on blood flow do not allow temporal information in the range required by Figure 6.1. Other difficult issues about the use of these methods, that have been discussed in the literature, are the choice of an appropriate task control condition and the validity of the subtractive method (see, for example, Démonet *et al*. 1993; Sergent *et al*. 1992). While caution about these issues is appropriate we also believe that the considerable amount of convergence between methods that we describe below suggests important progress is being made.

Visual word form

The first cortical processing of a visual word must òccur in primary visual cortex. However, comparisons of blood flow activity – when subjects are instructed to look at words versus only at a fixation point – have shown that most of the blood flow differences occur in the left and right hemisphere extrastriate visual areas (see Posner and Raichle 1994 for a review). Figure 6.2 summarises these activations in left and right occipital lobe from a number of blood flow studies and depth electrical recordings studies.

The right hemisphere activation appears to be common to orthographically legal or illegal letter strings and false fonts and is, therefore, not unique to words or letters. The left extrastriate activations are more specific. In one study, areas of the ventral occipital-temporal junction were activated by words and orthographically regular nonwords, but not by consonant strings (Petersen *et al*. 1990). The specificity of this activation suggests that this region is sensitive to the visual organisation of letters permitted within alphabetic languages and, hence, it has been called the 'visual word form' area. Presumably, this organisation is developed as a child learns to read. In the fifth section we will examine the development of this area in childhood and the degree of plasticity it shows with new learning (see pp. 154-155).

There has also been some dispute about the location of the visual word form area (Howard *et al*. 1992; Menard *et al*. 1996). In a PET study, reading words aloud was compared with saying a single word, 'crime', when a false font was presented. This comparison was thought to provide a better experimental condition than passive viewing of words because subjects were required to respond to each event. In order to take care of the motor activity in reading, the control condition also needed to include vocalisation, hence the use of saying a word to a false font. This condition produced activation of a left lateral temporal area, but little or no evidence of the visual word form area discussed above. A study comparing passive presentation of visual words with fixation control conditions also found activation in the lateral temporal lobe near the angular gyrus but little activity in the medial occipital lobe.

Depth recorded ERP studies have shown areas of the medial inferior occipital and temporal lobe (near the word form area described above, see black triangles in Figure 6.2) active during the processing of visual letters and words but not other familiar stimuli like faces (Nobre, Allison and McCarthy 1994).

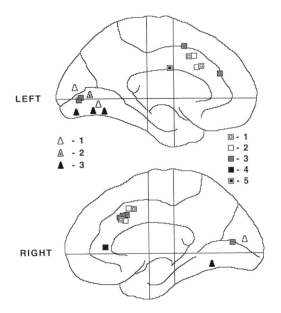

Figure 6.2 Views of medial left (upper) and right (lower) cortices with the review of cortical areas related to visual word form (triangles) and attention (squares).

Notes

Visual word form related areas (triangles):

1 – visual words vs fixation point, PET (Petersen *et al.* 1989);
2 – visual words vs fixation point (Petersen *et al.* 1989), visual words and pseudowords vs consonant strings and false fonts, PET (Petersen *et al.* 1990);
3 – visual words and pseudowords vs faces, depth-ERP (Nobre *et al.* 1994).

Attention-related areas (squares):

1 – use generation vs reading aloud single nouns, semantic categorisation with low probability vs high probability of target words, visual (Petersen *et al.* 1988, 1989; Posner *et al.* 1988); same as in Figure 6.3–1;
2 – use generation vs repeating aloud single nouns, auditory (Petersen *et al.* 1988, 1989; Posner *et al.* 1988); same as in Figure 6.3–2;
3 – incongruent vs congruent in Stroop task, PET (Pardo *et al.* 1990);
4 – Stroop task vs naming the colours of crosses, PET (Bench *et al.* 1993);
5 – Stroop task vs naming the colours of bars, PET (George *et al.* 1994).

These findings support the medial occipito-temporal visual word form described above. Taken together these findings suggest a network of left lateralised areas, where the most posterior medial activations might be involved in processing letters while the more medial activations process orthographically regular words and nonword strings. We now believe that the left lateralised activation (Howard *et al.* 1992; Menard *et al.* 1996) near the angular gyrus study involves a more general posterior response to familiar words when they are actively processed as language, but is not the earliest stage involved in the synthesis of letters into a visual word form.

Phonological processing

In cognitive psychology a distinction has been made between at least two types of phonological coding in reading. One type, input or acoustic phonology, is related to recoding the visual word into a form similar to its auditory input. Another type is more closely related to production and is termed output or articulatory phonology. Studies of cerebral blood flow have provided evidence of both forms of coding. When subjects were asked to determine if a pair of visual words rhymed (Petersen *et al.* 1989) an area of the left superior temporal lobe located anterior to the angular gyrus was found to be active (Figure 6.3). A very close area was active when auditory words were presented. It seems reasonable to assume that this area is related to recoding a visual word into its phonology (input phonology). This area was not found to be active during reading words aloud or during semantic tasks. These findings supported the view that phonological encoding of visual words is an optional part of word reading and that an

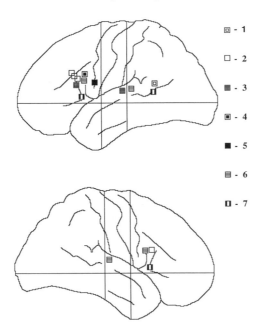

Figure 6.3 Review of different studies demonstrating cortical areas related to phonological encoding.

Notes

1 – rhyming visual words, PET (Petersen *et al.* 1988; Posner *et al.* 1988);
2 – phonologically similar vs different pseudowords in visual lexical decision, neuronal activity (Bechtereva *et al.* 1991);
3 – auditory phoneme monitoring, PET (Démonet *et al.* 1992);
4 – phonetic categorisation of visual letters, PET (Sergent *et al.* 1992);
5 – rhyming auditory syllables, PET (Zatorre *et al.* 1992);
6 – rhyming visual letters, PET (Paulesu *et al.* 1993);
7 – rhyming visual pseudowords, fMRI (Shaywitz *et al.* 1995).

alternative, direct visual-to-semantic route is used in recognising familiar words (Coltheart 1978).

In recent years, this view has been questioned and a more central role for phonological processing has been advocated (Lukatela and Turvey 1994a, 1994b; Lesch and Pollatsek 1993, 1995; Perfetti, Bell and Delaney 1988; Van Orden, Pennington and Stone 1990).

It has also been found that more anterior areas are activated in the phonological task, particularly when pseudoword input is used (Bechtereva, Abdullaev and Medvedev 1991; Démonet *et al.* 1992; Paulesu, Frith and Frackowiak 1993; Petersen and Fiez 1993; Sergent *et al.* 1992; Shaywitz *et al.* 1995; Zatorre *et al.* 1992). This region is close to Broca's area and is likely to involve processes that are closer to the output phonology of the letter string. In one of these studies (Shaywitz *et al.* 1995) activation of posterior temporo-parietal areas was found in addition to the anterior activation (Figure 6.3).

As far as we are aware, no study has provided strong evidence showing the exact functions of the anterior and posterior phonological areas nor the degree of automaticity of their activation. As we shall see, the rather late time course of the frontal activity in phonological tasks (Bechtereva *et al.* 1991), suggests that this area is related to output phonology. It seems safe to conclude that these studies have been generally supportive of cognitive views of separable areas involved in acoustic (input phonology) and articulatory (output phonology) encoding of visually presented words.

Semantic analysis

Frontal areas

When subjects are asked to provide the use for a visually presented noun versus just naming the noun, there is additional activation in four areas: (1) left anterior inferior prefrontal cortex, (2) anterior cingulate (3) left temporo-parietal cortex (Wernicke's area) and (4) right lateral cerebellum (see Figure 6.4). Two of these are left lateralised and appear to be intimately related to language. The first is a left inferior frontal activation that is anterior and overlaps Broca's area (left frontal regions in Figure 6.4). This area has been implicated in nearly every auditory or visual study requiring an analysis of word meaning. For example, when subjects were asked to determine if each of a set of words was an animal name compared to a passive word viewing condition, this area was active although no explicit output was required (Posner *et al.* 1988). Thus, activation here does not appear to be uniquely associated with verb generation, although its location within the frontal lobe and activation of homologous areas in the right hemisphere during other forms of generation have led some to conclude that it is related to the act of generation (e.g. Démonet *et al.* 1993).

In the first PET studies using semantic analysis tasks for words, the only left activation was prefrontal (Petersen *et al.* 1988). When the task was replicated using fMRI, both left and right prefrontal activations were found in some subjects,

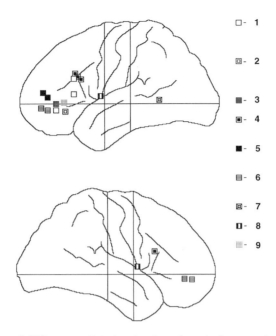

Figure 6.4 Review of different studies showing lateral cortical areas related to semantic tasks.

Notes

1– use generation vs reading aloud visual nouns, semantic categorisation of visual words, PET (Petersen *et al.* 1988, 1989; Posner *et al.* 1988);

2 – use generation vs repeating aloud auditory nouns, PET (Petersen *et al.* 1988, 1989; Posner *et al.* 1988);

3 – visual words vs pseudowords in passive presentation, PET (Petersen *et al.* 1990);

4 – visual words vs pseudowords in lexical decision task, neuronal activity (Bechtereva *et al.* 1991);

5 – semantic classification of visual words; lexical decision of visual words and phrases, neuronal activity (Abdullaev and Bechtereva, 1993);

6 – verb generation vs reading aloud visual nouns, fMRI (McCarthy *et al.* 1993);

7 – use generation vs reading aloud visual nouns, PET (Raichle 1994; Raichle *et al.* 1994);

8 – use generation vs reading aloud visual nouns, PET, activity in insula shown here as its projection to the surface; it is higher during reading aloud than during use generation (Raichle 1994; Raichle *et al.* 1994);

9 – semantic classification of visual words, PET (Kapur *et al.* 1994).

while in other subjects only unilateral left prefrontal activations were found (McCarthy *et al.* 1993).

Depth electrodes were also used to study neuronal activity of the left prefrontal cortex (areas 46 and 10) in a patient during semantic tasks (Abdullaev and Bechtereva 1993). During a lexical decision task between words and pseudo-words, cells in this prefrontal cortical area showed significant differences related to word meaning. The same cells demonstrated stronger responses related to semantic processing in the task of discriminating visual concrete and abstract words (Figure 6.4). These semantic differences appeared at about 200 ms and remained present to 700 ms. Neuronal activity of this left prefrontal area was also studied during an object naming task and in two mental arithmetic tasks. In these tasks no significant task-related responses were found, demonstrating functional selectivity of at least these cells in semantic processing of words. The neuronal responses of cells in the left prefrontal cortical region during tasks involving the semantics of words, but not in picture naming or mental arithmetic, show the selective involvement of these cells in the circuitry performing semantic encoding and support the previous PET findings. This functional selectivity of the left anterior inferior frontal cortex for semantic processing has been also shown by fMRI (Demb *et al.* 1995).

Review of cortical areas activated in semantic tasks shown in Figure 6.4 demonstrates good convergence of data from different methods such as PET, fMRI and neuronal activity. Comparison of this review map with the map of phonological operations shown in Figure 6.3 allows separation of two function-ally distinct areas within this left frontal region. One is within the anterior inferior prefrontal cortex where no phonology-related activity was found, and another within a slightly more superior posterior part closer to Broca's area where both semantic and phonological operations have been localised in many recent studies (Figures 6.3 and 6.4).

Wernicke's area

Wernicke's area is in the left dominant temporo-parietal cortex and has been related to language in nineteenth-century clinical-anatomical comparisons based on lesion analyses. It may include one or more of Brodmann's areas 22, 37, 39 and/or 40 (Kertesz, Harlock and Coates 1979; Selnes *et al.* 1985), damage may cause so-called fluent, or Wernicke's aphasia with impairment in uttering or comprehending meaningful sentences.[3]

Cognitive studies have provided some constraints about the nature of such lesions for the processing of individual words. Milberg and associates in several studies (see, for example, Milberg *et al.* 1995) found that semantic priming of individual words does occur in patients diagnosed as Wernicke's aphasics even though they have semantic paraphasias in speech. Dronkers (personal com-munication), however, reported that the most severe chronic Wernicke's aphasics showed semantic priming in object but not in word tasks. At least under some conditions, patients exhibiting Wernicke's aphasia do process the meaning of words rather automatically, but do not carry out the strategic processing normally present in these tasks (Milberg *et al.* 1995).

Although the initial studies using PET during the generate uses task did not show activation in Wernicke's area, subsequent studies have shown such activa-tion. The most likely problem with the initial study was that words were presented once per second. When this rate was slowed to one word every 1.5 seconds (Raichle *et al.* 1994), or when more than one use had to be generated, clear activation of Wernicke's area was found (see Figure 6.4). Some of these findings appear to be similar to the cognitive studies in which lesions of Wernicke's area are associated with more complex semantic processing than the automatic access to single word meanings. The significance of this is discussed further under 'circuitry' when we consider the temporal relationship between the lateral frontal and posterior activations.

Attention

Another area found active during the use generation task was the anterior cingulate on the frontal midline (see Figure 6.2). Midline frontal activation has been found in many tasks involving active attention and/or responses by the subject. When the task involves an immediate motor output, as in reading words aloud or responding rapidly to input, activation tends to be more superior in the supplementary motor areas. However, even quite passive tasks (e.g. listening to words or determining if words are animal names) in which no motor response is required or when motor activity is subtracted out (as in use generation minus reading aloud subtraction) activation in the anterior cingulate is produced. Nor does this activation depend upon the task having a linguistic structure, since activation of the cingulate occurs when subjects are making complex visual classification (Corbetta *et al.* 1990).

For these reasons anterior cingulate activation has often been thought to be related to a higher form of attention. Indeed it was to test this idea that Pardo *et al.* (1990) studied the Stroop effect since it is regarded as a kind of 'gold standard' of attention tasks given the conflict between the word name and ink colour. They found strong activation in the cingulate, and subsequent studies of the Stroop effect have had similar results (Bench *et al.* 1993; George *et al.* 1994). Cingulate activation was also found in a wide variety of nonlinguistic tasks that could be summarised as requiring controlled processes of asking subjects to take note of a particular event (see Posner and Rothbart 1992). As in other attention networks (Posner and Petersen 1990) there is likely to be a network of areas involved that appear to include elements of the basal ganglia and lateral and orbital frontal areas. It seems likely that lateral frontal areas play the role of representing particular kinds of information; for example word associations, in the case of the left lateral frontal area active in the generate task.

Circuitry

We have discussed the many brain areas implicated in various word tasks revealed mainly through functional imaging. These include areas involving visual, phonological, semantic and attentional aspects of word processing. We now ask when and in what order these areas become active during the processing of visual words. This amounts to development of a circuitry of visual word processing.

To study this issue, we have used high density scalp recording of brain electrical activity with normal subjects (Tucker *et al.* 1994). Figure 6.5 (lower right) shows a two-dimensional representation of the scalp surface with a rough indication of placement of the 64 electrodes. ERPs are stimulus-locked averages

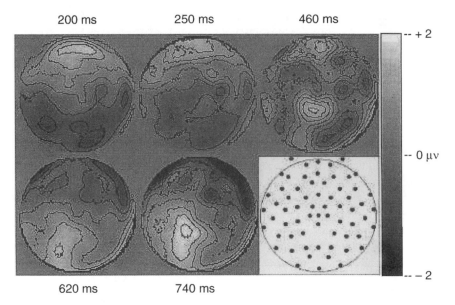

Figure 6.5 Electrical potential fields at varying points following a visual word.

Notes

The potentials indicate the difference between the generate and repeat conditions. Bright areas indicate areas of large positive differences and dark areas indicate negative differences. Location of 64-channel array is in the lower right. For each circular map the upper portion is frontal lobes and lower portion occipital lobes, the left hemisphere is to the left and right hemisphere to the right. The time slices displayed in Figure 6.5 are chosen to illustrate activation of the cingulate (upper left); cingulate and left frontal activation (upper middle); reduced overall activation with start of Wernicke's area (upper right); clear activation of Wernicke's area (lower left); and continued activation of Wernicke's area (lower middle)

of the electroencephalogram (EEG) across many presentations of stimuli and have a long history in cognitive studies (see Rugg and Coles 1995 for a recent thorough review). They provide a continuous record, obtained simultaneously at many different scalp locations, of electrical changes related to ongoing cognitive processing. ERPs are sensitive to exogenous and endogenous properties of stimuli. Because ERPs are recorded through the scalp and skull, and because the surface of the brain is convoluted, accurate localisation of surface potentials to underlying neural sources – what has been termed the 'inverse solution' – is rather difficult. One approach to obtain both precise temporal and neuroanatomical information is to link together results from comparable ERP and PET studies.[4]

We focus on ERP work that has been performed in our laboratory at the University of Oregon. In all but one of these studies, EEG was collected via a 64-channel electrode net (a 32-channel system was used in Compton *et al.* 1991). In addition, original mastoid referenced data were transformed into averaged referenced data prior to analysis (Tucker *et al.* 1994).[5]

Early visual areas

As discussed in the last section, PET studies showed that all types of letter strings activated right prestriate and parietal areas, whereas only word-like stimuli activated homologous left hemisphere areas. In an early ERP (32-channel) study in our lab, Compton *et al.* (1991) presented words and consonant strings under four task conditions: (1) passive viewing; (2) thickened letter segment detection; (3) case mismatch detection; and (4) lexical decision. They observed that the P100 (first positive wave of the ERP with a peak latency of about 100 ms) was larger over right hemisphere scalp sites than left ones for all types of strings. This amplitude difference occurred in all tasks and started at about 50 ms. Compton *et al.* suggested that the surface potential asymmetry reflected an analysis of high level visual features common to the perception of any visual input.

Compton *et al.* also observed a difference between words and consonant strings in the N1 or first negative wave (consonant strings were more negative), beginning at about 125 ms post-stimulus and somewhat lateralised in left hemisphere scalp sites. They proposed that the N1 differences over posterior temporal sites were related to visual word form activation, the asymmetry suggestive of a posterior midline source. In a study designed to test changes in ERPs over several weeks (McCandliss, Posner and Givón 1997) found a difference between words and consonant strings similar in form to Compton's but starting at about 170 ms and stable over the weeks of testing. Additional support for a left posterior locus for word processing was reported by Dehaene (1996), in which spelled digits activated primarily left posterior areas while arabic digits activated bilateral areas. The time course was similar to that reported by Compton *et al.* In an intracranial ERP study, Nobre and McCarthy (1994) found that the posterior fusiform gyri produced large negativities around 200 ms in response to all types of letter strings but not to other visual objects or patterns. In addition it appears that attention can influence this visual area. In a visual spatial attention task (attend left or attend right), Heinze *et al.* (1994) found activation of the ipsilateral posterior fusiform gyrus using PET and, in an analogous ERP study, a corresponding modulation of the P1 over posterior sites starting at 80 ms.

There is some evidence that lexical influence may come even earlier than in the above studies. Sereno, Rayner and Posner (1998) found that words differed from both pseudowords and consonant strings (which did not differ from each other) in the P100 as early as 100 ms following input (nonwords were more positive). These lexicality differences appeared bilaterally in posterior parietal scalp sites. The word targets themselves varied as a function of word frequency and regularity (spelling–sound correspondence). Sereno *et al* found that high and low frequency words differed from each other in the N1, as early as 132 ms, bilaterally in occipital and anterior parietal scalp sites. They also analysed eye movement data from a reading study in which the same target words (high and low frequency regular and exception words) appeared in sentences, and argued that the combined ERP and eye movement results indicate a very early time course of lexical processing.

These data argue the case that important lexical distinctions having to do with word-like stimuli occur within 100–150 ms after input rather than that posterior regions may be more left lateralised for words than for appropriate control stimuli. These activations are fast enough to precede the initiation of eye movements.

Later non-visual activations

To investigate the time course of phonological processing, McCandliss, Pollatsek and Posner (1993) compared ERPs to visual words under conditions which either emphasised phonological coding or emphasised passive viewing. In each trial, two visual words were presented sequentially, and ERPs were collected to the first word. In the phonological encoding task, subjects had to decide whether the first and second words rhymed. In the passive task, subjects ignored the first word and made a decision about the number of letters in the second word. Comparing ERPs recorded under these two task conditions revealed differences in superior central scalp sites starting around 250 ms after input. This activation pattern at the scalp reflects a parallel to the posterior phonological activation found in PET studies of visual words in which the task conditions of rhyme judgement and passive viewing were compared. The ERP results suggest that subjects are able to bias the degree of phonological processing applied to a visual word within the first 250 ms of processing. Given the above discussion of the time dynamics of eye fixations, this effect appears to be occurring too late to potentially affect fixation durations. It is possible that the increased phonological processing required by the rhyme judgement task influences post-access processing of phonological information rather than the early phonological processes which influence eye movements during reading.

To investigate the temporal dynamics of the PET activations associated with higher level semantics, Snyder *et al.* (1995) presented visual words and subjects either named them or generated a use. ERPs in these two conditions were subtracted from each other. There was an increase in frontal positivity starting around 180 ms. Snyder *et al.* used this scalp difference to localise potential neural generators by means of Brain Electrical Source Analysis (BESA) algorithms (Scherg and Berg 1993). They found that these data were best fit by a single generator on the frontal midline, a location that matched the anterior cingulate activation found in PET. By 220 ms, BESA required an additional generator to account for the scalp difference. This source was in the left frontal cortex, matching the left frontal regions activated in PET. Around 600 to 700 ms, ERP differences were found over left temporo-parietal regions and BESA computed a generator matching the PET activation in Wernicke's area. Finally, around 800 ms, ERP differences over anterior temporal regions (right greater than left) were attributed to insular activation in PET

Halgren *et al.* (1994), in an intracranial ERP study with neurosurgical patients, found some evidence supporting the time course outlined above. In their study the anterior cingulate elicited a positive wave around 190 to 200 ms, and they found activity in the left inferior frontal gyrus area 46 at about 280 ms was evoked by words but not by faces.

Modulation

We have attempted to summarise the likely time course of activation of the functional anatomy in visual word reading (see Figure 6.1). Visual feature analysis occurs from about 50 to 100 ms after input and the perceptual word form is synthesised from letters by about 150 ms. By 180 ms, frontal attentional areas become active and by 220 ms, frontal semantic areas are activated. Regions associated with output phonology and Wernicke's area are active only later. Overall, these findings suggest that frontal areas involved in the generation of word uses as well as visual areas related to the visual word form are active early enough to trigger eye movement programming. Since in the routine reading of familiar visual words PET studies suggest that frontal areas are generally not strongly activated, it seems most likely that eye movements are triggered initially by activation of a network of posterior visual word form areas, but could be modified by frontal areas.

The early activation of the anterior cingulate suggests that much of the later processing can be modulated by attention. Indeed, we have examined some aspects of this form of control. The attention system could be used to activate any of these anatomical areas and thus reorder the priority of the cognitive operations involved. For example, when subjects were asked whether a word was natural and had a thick letter, activation over frontal semantic areas was amplified early in processing while the posterior feature areas were amplified later; when subjects were asked whether the word had a thick letter and was natural, there was early posterior and later frontal amplification (Posner and Raichle 1994). These findings suggest that the location of mental operations remain relatively fixed but the order can be changed by attentional networks.

Plasticity

There are many forms of plasticity in brain mechanisms underlying reading. These are outlined in Figure 6.6. We have already referred to the moment-to-moment changes that occur when people attend to or give priority to different

PLASTICITY

Time	Cause	Example	Mechanism
Millisecond shifts	Attention	Conjunctions	Amplification
Seconds to minutes	Practice	Generate task	Pathway
Days to weeks	Item learning	Lexical items	Connections
Weeks to months	Rule learning	Orthography	Structures
Months to years	Development	Attention system	Control structures

Figure 6.6 Forms of brain plasticity exhibited at different time scales.

mental operations. However, learning that takes place over longer periods of time must involve modifications of neural structures and circuitry. We examine three examples of learning visual words: first, the effects of practice in the generate task; second, the acquisition of an artificial language by undergraduate students; and third, a cross-sectional developmental look at the acquisition of literacy in children. The consequences of learning are assessed by changes in the patterns of ERPs.

Practice effects

When subjects are asked to generate uses for the same list of nouns on repeated occasions, they show great improvements in the speed of output as though the task has become automated (Raichle *et al.* 1994). In PET, when generate is compared to repeat (naming the noun), in addition to increased activation in anterior cingulate, left frontal, Wernicke's and right cerebellar regions, there is also decreased activation in the insula. The insula, which lies hidden behind the anterior end of the temporal lobe, is activated in word naming, but this activity is suppressed during novel word generation. As the same list is practised, the activations unique to generation disappear and the insular activation increases, resembling word naming. Thus, automating the computation not only leads to faster RTs and reduced interference but also to an apparent (temporary) change in the brain circuits that underlie the task. Abdullaev and Posner (1997) performed the same study using high density scalp-recorded ERPs and found a marked reduction of activation in cingulate and frontal as well as Wernicke's regions with practice. There was some tendency for activation to be reduced more in frontal scalp regions than in Wernicke's area. Subjects were also asked to generate novel responses to the list of nouns they already practised. In this condition, a positivity was found at about the same time as in Wernicke's area, but in a right homologous scalp area to the Wernicke activation. Cognitive studies have suggested that remote association might involve right hemisphere activation (Nakagawa 1991). We do not yet know the boundary conditions under which briefly generating weak associations will produce the additional circuitry found in the Abdullaev and Posner study. However, the data do suggest very specific changes in circuitry depending upon the momentary strength of association.

Second language acquisition

In a recent ERP study, McCandliss, Posner and Givón (1997) investigated the changes that took place as learning transformed novel words of a new language into well-recognised items. The Keki artificial language study (Yang and Givón 1993) created an artificial language of 68 words. This language was taught to undergraduates via visual and auditory displays in a laboratory setting for 2 hours per day, 5 days per week, over a period of 5 weeks. Subjects were tested in three separate sessions that included reaction time measures (Yang and Givón 1993) and scalp electrical recordings (McCandliss *et al.* 1997) administered after 0, 20, and 50 hours of training.

The reaction time task (Yang and Givón 1993) involved same–different matching of two successive visual strings (presented in opposite case letters). Stimuli were familiar English words, Keki words, or Keki control strings designed to look like Keki words. There was a consistent advantage in reaction times for English words over Keki control strings at all three testing intervals (the word superiority effect). Yang and Givón found that a similar benefit developed for Keki words during the course of the 5 weeks of learning. In the first session, before any training, reaction times for Keki words and Keki control strings did not differ. After 20 hours of training, reaction times for Keki words were significantly faster than for Keki control strings, and after 50 hours of training, reaction times to Keki words were equivalent to those for English words. This result supports the notion that after 5 weeks of training, Keki words were being processed similarly to English words in some respects.

In the ERP experiment (McCandliss *et al.* 1997), consonant strings were added to the stimulus set to examine posterior brain responses linked to visual word form processing. Randomly mixed blocks of stimuli were presented during each testing session under three different task instructions: (1) passive viewing; (2) thickened letter feature detection; and (3) semantic judgement (i.e. 'Is stimulus something tangible?'). McCandliss *et al.* first examined ERPs to English words and consonant strings. In all three testing sessions, responses to consonant strings were more negative than to English words over left and right posterior electrode sites between 170 and 230 ms. Although the latency of this effect is slightly later than the original word/consonant effect reported by Compton *et al.* (1991), the direction of the effect and the scalp distribution pattern are similar and suggest brain sources associated with visual word form processing.

To test for plasticity in the processing of Keki words, ERP responses to Keki words and Keki control strings collected after 0, 20, and 50 hours of training were compared to the baseline conditions of the English words and consonant strings. Results of this analysis revealed that Keki and Keki control did not differ significantly from each other in any session. As a group, these stimuli fell between the values obtained for the English and consonant strings, and were significantly different from each of these two baselines.

The pattern of results for a window from 170–230 ms suggests that ERP differences between stimulus types might be related to findings of medial extra-striate activation in PET studies by word-like versus consonant strings. They also show that this posterior visual word form area is not sensitive to the amount of learning in this experiment. Over the course of training there was a dramatic shift in the familiarity of the Keki strings over their controls, as demonstrated by the reaction time data. However, the 50 hours of training had no measurable impact on the visual word form response. On the other hand, it appears that orthographic regularity had a large impact on this measure. The orthography that was used to form the Keki words and the Keki control words resembled English in many respects, but had some unique qualities as well.

The impact of the 50 hours of training was also examined in a later window from 280 to 360 ms. In this later time period, responses to Keki and Keki control strings fell between the values obtained for consonant strings and English words. The positive response to Keki in this time window changed dramatically compared with the other types of stimuli. In the first session responses to Keki words and Keki control strings did not differ, but both were more positive than to English words. Over the course of training, a difference emerged between the Keki and Keki control, such that response to Keki strings came to resemble the response to English words, while response to Keki controls and consonant strings remained more positive than to English words. After 50 hours of training, the positive response to Keki words was equivalent to that for English words, and was significantly different from both Keki control and consonant strings. The difference which emerged between Keki words and Keki control strings was broadly distributed over posterior and frontal sites (left greater than right).

The 280–360 ms window results demonstrate that a 5-week training manipulation had systematic effects upon the ERPs to novel words. This ERP difference between Keki and Keki controls reflects a type of item-specific learning. McCandliss *et al.* (1997) suggest that because the magnitude of this learning effect was greatest under task demands that required semantic judgements, semantic processes might play a substantial role in the changes observed in ERPs to the Keki strings.

In summary, the Keki project examined changes in reaction time and brain electrical responses resulting from a controlled set of learning experiences. After 5 weeks of training, reaction time performance on Keki words resembled that for English words and was reliably faster than for Keki control strings. After 170 ms, stimulus differences appeared which were consistent with posterior word form activation, but these differences seemed unaffected by the learning manipulation and the task manipulation. After about 280 ms, the effects of learning were found over frontal and posterior sites, and this learning effect appeared strongest when subjects attended to the meanings of the words.

These findings illustrate differences in the way brain circuitry involved in processing visual words is modified. We believe that the approach used in this study will allow examination of many questions of how different forms of learning are represented in the changes in brain circuitry.

Initial literacy

A series of studies has sought to follow the development of initial word skills in 4, 7, and 10-year-old children using high density electrodes to trace changes in circuitry (McCandliss 1997). For all children, words and consonant strings were presented in both a passive viewing and a thickened letter segment detection task. The 4-year-old children could not read, but the 7 and 10-year-old children could read many words. For these older children, we separated ERPs to words they read well from words which were not in their vocabularies. After an initial testing session, these older children were taught the meanings of some of the unfamiliar words, and given several sessions of practice reading them. ERPs were collected both before and after these practice sessions.

Although there were many interesting results from these studies, we mention only the most critical. The 4-year-olds showed no evidence of a special response to words, however, we did find that their posterior areas behaved in a way similar to adults. For example, when the active task (thickened letter segment detection) was compared with passive viewing, the P2 showed increased positivity around 250 ms, a pattern very similar to that obtained with adults.

The 7-year-olds showed strong ERPs over the entire head to all letter strings. There was also some evidence that the degree of frontal activation depended on whether the words were familiar or unfamiliar. However, when consonant strings and words were compared, there was no evidence of the early visual word form scalp signature found in adults. Although the children clearly could read many words, it may well have been that they had not yet developed the very specific structures that allow for rapid and automatic integration of the familiar visual letters into visual chunks or units.

Only with the 10-year-olds was there evidence of the adult scalp signature of word form activation. ERPs to consonant strings significantly differed from those to words over posterior temporal sites. These effects were more distinct after learning. Some cognitive literature suggests the word superiority effect develops between second and fifth grade level (see Carr and Posner 1995 for a review). Perhaps these cognitive findings are a reflection of the development of a visual word form system.

In summary, there seems to be evidence for all the levels of reorganisation proposed in Figure 6.6. Attention can reactivate and temporarily reorder anatomically distinct computations; automation can influence the specific circuitry used in word processing; and learning can guide pathway organisation over brief periods or over many years of experience. The combination of non-invasive high-density electrical recording and identification of areas of activation through PET and fMRI provides a set of tools to examine brain mechanisms underlying all these forms of learning and development.

Dyslexia

The group of disorders associated with processing written language is called dyslexia or in its most radical form alexia. The diagnosis of dyslexia occurs when visual deficits, memory disturbances, poor education, general mental retardation, low IQ, or other reasons have been excluded. When dyslexia is related to a recent brain lesion (e.g. stroke, tumor, trauma, etc.) it is called acquired dyslexia. When dyslexia has no acute neurological history and becomes evident from early childhood in the first years of education it is called developmental dyslexia.

Substantial advances have been made in the study of acquired dyslexia and a number of separate disorders have been dissociated; some specific to reading, others not (Shallice 1988). For example, damage to left posterior brain regions can produce letter-by-letter reading. This disorder seems specific to the word form system and, in its purest form, may have relatively little impact on activities other than reading. A person with this disorder may develop strategies to re-code individual letters into their sounds in order to recognise words. On the other hand, neglect dyslexia, in which spatially-defined parts of the input are not 'perceived', greatly hinders reading but is not at all specific to reading. The use of neuro-imaging techniques should aid in understanding the various compensatory methods that can help to restore some of the lost skills.

Developmental dyslexia is more complex because failure to learn to read may involve cultural or instructional factors, perhaps in combination with more subtle deficits in underlying anatomy. It is more prevalent in males and left-handers and may have a genetic component. One theme of this chapter is that learning to read, itself, influences the organisation within and between brain areas. Thus, the interaction of educational and neurological factors in literacy is basic to understanding the difficulties that may arise in its acquisition. Developmental dyslexics show a variety of disorders which do not appear to share a unitary, underlying cause. For example, while erratic eye movements in reading may be symptomatic of some dyslexics, it cannot be said that poor eye movement control causes dyslexia. On the other hand, problems such as perceiving auditory sequences or recognising the onsets of phonemes (Tallal, Stark and Mellits 1985) may reflect more general language deficits.

We expect that theoretically motivated studies of dyslexia will reveal the difficulties that can occur and inform teachers more completely of methods to overcome them. We anticipate that studies of the anatomy and circuitry of normal fluent word recognition such as those we have reviewed can assist in under-standing the multiple disorders that might impair the acquisition and performance of reading.

Summary

In this chapter we have sought to summarise the contributions of neuroimaging in understanding the high-level skill of reading. We recognise that many of these findings require assumptions, some of which are disputed. None the less, we believe our time-line of the internal computations that occur during an eye fixa-tion on a single word is an important contribution, even if some details are proven wrong in future studies. We find that activation of word-specific visual codes and attention to those codes occurs early enough to influence the programming of an eye movement to a following word. Since attentional networks do not appear active during reading words aloud it seems that the visual word form is the most important input to eye movement programming. Activation of semantic areas of the frontal lobe may occur in time to modify eye movements, so that average fixation duration may reflect the influence of the meaning of the current lexical item. These results and the methods they are based upon move us forward toward a detailed understanding of the brain mechanisms involved in a complex, highly skilled activity such as reading.

Notes

This research was supported by grants from the James S. McDonnell Foundation, Pew Memorial Trusts and W.M. Keck Foundation to the Center for the Cognitive Neuroscience of Attention and by ONR Contract 0014-89-J3013 to the University of Oregon. This chapter represents a genuine collaboration of the four authors who contributed different areas of expertise to its development. The authors would like to thank many colleagues at the University of Oregon who assisted in aspects of this research effort.

1 Estimations of oculomotor latency have typically come from visual search experiments or from ones in which subjects must fixate specified locations in a given order. In reading, the reader controls the location of the next fixation, and it may very well be the case that oculomotor latency is reduced in this context. It is also possible that global reading strategies (e.g. fast vs slow reading of the same text) could affect oculomotor latency (O'Regan and Levy-Schoen 1987).

2 The cost associated with viewing words foveally in reading without benefit of parafoveal preview has been estimated to be about 35 ms for average length words (Blanchard, Pollatsek and Rayner 1989). This was determined by comparing fixation time on a word under a normal reading condition to a condition that prevents parafoveal preprocessing of that word (e.g. initially substituting a string of Xs for the word until it is directly fixated).

3 There is still much dispute about what constitutes Wernicke's aphasia, what brain areas when damaged or destroyed produce it, and the differences between acute and chronic forms (see Dronkers (1995) for a discussion of these issues).

4 One solution to this problem was proposed by Dale and Sereno (1993) in which they combined complementary electro- and magnetoencephalography (EEG and MEG) data with MRI structural information to achieve both high temporal and spatial resolution.

5 Mastoid referencing assumes that there is no activity that occurs at the mastoid site. If such activity exists, it will be reflected in varying degrees across the other electrodes. In average referencing, each electrode is referenced to the average voltage over the entire scalp surface. Theoretically, the average voltage is zero if the entire scalp is sampled.

References

Abdullaev, Y.G. and Bechtereva, N.P. (1993) 'Neuronal correlate of the higher-order semantic code in human prefrontal cortex in language tasks', *International Journal of Psychophysiology*, 14, 167–177.

Abdullaev, Y.G. and Posner, M.I. (1997) 'Time course of activating brain areas in generating verbal associations', *Psychological Science*, 8, 56–59.

Bechtereva, N.P., Abdullaev, Y.G. and Medvedev, S.V. (1991) 'Neuronal activity in frontal speech area 44 of the human cerebral cortex during word recognition', *Neuroscience Letters*, 124, 61–64.

Bench, C.J., Frith, C.D., Grasby, P.M., Friston, K.J., Paulesu, E., Frackowiak, R.S.J. and Dolan, R.J. (1993) 'Investigations of the functional anatomy of attention using the Stroop test', *Neuropsychologia*, 31, 907–922.

Blanchard, H.E., Pollatsek, A. and Rayner, K. (1989) 'The acquisition of parafoveal word information in reading', *Perception and Psychophysics*, 46, 85–94.

Carr, T. & Posner, M.I. (1995) 'The impact of learning to read on the functional anatomy of language processing', in B. De Gelder and J. Morais (eds), *Language and Literacy: Comparative Approaches* (pp. 267–294). Cambridge, MA: MIT Press.

Carroll, P. and Slowiaczek, M.L. (1986) 'Constraints on semantic priming in reading: A fixation time analysis', *Memory and Cognition*, 14, 509–522.

Coltheart, M. (1978) 'Lexical access in simple reading tasks', in G. Underwood (ed.), *Strategies of Information Processing* (pp. 151–216). London: Academic Press.

Compton, P.E., Grossenbacher, P., Posner, M.I. and Tucker, D.M. (1991) 'A cognitive-anatomical approach to attention in lexical access', *Journal of Cognitive Neuroscience*, 3, 304–312.

Corbetta, M., Miezin, F.M., Dobmeyer, S., Shulman, G.S. and Petersen, S.E. (1990) 'Attentional modulation of neural processing of shape, color, and velocity in humans', *Science*, 248, 1556–1559.

Dale, A.M. and Sereno, M. (1993) 'Improved localization of cortical activity by combining EEG and MEG with MRI cortical surface reconstruction: A linear approach', *Journal of Cognitive Neuroscience*, 5, 162–176.

Demb, J.B., Desmond, J.E., Wagner, A.D., Vaidya, C.T., Glover, G.H. and Gabrieli, J.D. (1995) 'Semantic encoding and retrieval in the left inferior prefrontal cortex: a functional MRI study of task difficulty and process specificity', *Journal of Neuroscience*, 15, 5870–5878.

Dehaene, S. (1996) 'The organization of brain activations in number comparison', *Journal of Cognitive Neuroscience*, 8, 47–68.

Démonet, J.-F., Chollet, F., Ramsay, S., Cardebat, D., Nespoulous, J.N., Wise, R., Rascol, A. and Frackowiak, R.S.J. (1992) 'The anatomy of phonological and semantic processing in normal subjects', *Brain*, 115, 1753–1768.

Démonet, J.-F., Wise, R. and Frackowiak, R.S.J. (1993) 'Language functions explored in normal subjects by positron emission tomography: A critical review', *Human Brain Mapping*, 1, 39–47.

Dronkers, N. (1995) 'A new brain region for coordinating speech articulation', *Nature*, 384, 159–161.

Duffy, S.A., Morris, R.K. and Rayner, K. (1988) 'Lexical ambiguity and fixation times in reading', *Journal of Memory and Language*, 27, 429–446.

Flowers, D.L., Wood, F.B. and Naylor, C.E. (1991) 'Regional cerebral blood flow correlates of language processes in reading disability', *Archives of Neurology*, 48, 637–643.

Frazier, L. and Rayner, K. (1982) 'Making and correcting errors during sentence comprehension: Eye movements in the analysis of structurally ambiguous sentences', *Cognitive Psychology*, 14, 178–210.

George, M.S., Ketter, T.A., Parekh, P.I., Rosinsky, N., Ring, H., Casey, B.J., Trimble, M.R., Horwitz, B., Herscovitch, P. and Post, R.M. (1994) 'Regional brain activity when selecting response despite interference: An $H_2{}^{15}O$ PET study of the Stroop and an emotional Stroop', *Human Brain Mapping*, 1, 194–209.

Halgren, E., Baudena, P., Heit, G., Clarke, M., Marinkovic, K. and Chauvel, P. (1994) 'Spatio-temporal stages in face and word processing: 2. Depth-recorded potentials in the human frontal and Rolandic cortices', *Journal of Physiology*, 88, 51–80.

Heinze, H.J., Mangun, G.R., Burchert, W., Hinrichs, H., Scholz, M., Münte, T.F., Gos, A., Scherg, M., Johannes, S., Hundeshagen, H., Gazzaniga, M.S. and Hillyard, S.A. (1994) 'Combined spatial and temporal imaging of brain activity during visual selective attention in humans', *Nature*, 372, 543–546.

Howard, D., Patterson, K., Wise, R., Brown, W.D., Friston, K., Weiller, C. and Frackowiak, R. (1992) 'The cortical localization of the lexicons', *Brain*, 115, 1769–1782.

Inhoff, A.W. (1989) 'Lexical access during eye fixations in reading: Are word access codes used to integrate lexical information across interword fixations?', *Journal of Memory and Language*, 28, 444–461.

Kapur, S., Rose, R., Liddle, P.F., Zipursky, R.B., Brown, G.M., Stuss, D., Houle, S. and Tulving, E. (1994) 'The role of the left prefrontal cortex in verbal processing: Semantic processing or willed action?', *NeuroReport*, 5, 2193–2196.

Kertesz, A., Harlock, W. and Coates, R. (1979) 'Computer tomographic localization, lesion size, and prognosis in aphasia and nonverbal impairment', *Brain and Language*, 8, 34–50.

Kowler, E. and Anton, S. (1987) 'Reading twisted text: Implications for the role of saccades', *Vision Research*, 27, 45–60.

LaBerge, D. and Samuels, S.J. (1974) 'Toward a theory of automatic information processing in reading', *Cognitive Psychology*, 6, 293–323.

Lesch, M.F. and Pollatsek, A. (1993) 'Automatic access of semantic information by phonological codes in visual word recognition', *Journal of Experimental Psychology: Learning, Memory and Cognition*, 19, 285–294.

Lesch, M.F. and Pollatsek, A. (1995) 'Evidence for the use of assembled phonology in accessing the meaning of printed words', manuscript submitted for publication.

Lima, S.D. (1987) 'Morphological analysis in reading', *Journal of Memory and Language*, 26, 84–99.

Lukatela, G. and Turvey, M.T. (1994a) 'Visual lexical access is initially phonological: 1. Evidence from associative priming by words, homophones, and pseudohomophones', *Journal of Experimental Psychology: General*, 123, 107–128.

Lukatela, G. and Turvey, M.T. (1994b) 'Visual lexical access is initially phonological: 2. Evidence from phonological priming by homophones and pseudohomophones', *Journal of Experimental Psychology: General*, 123, 331–353.

McCandliss, B.D. (1997) 'Experience based changes in cortical responses to written words', doctoral dissertation, University of Oregon.

McCandliss, B.D. Pollatsek, S. and Posner, M.I. (1993) 'Attention to phonological and semantic codes in processing visual words', poster presented at the West Coast Attention Meeting, Eugene, OR, May.

McCandliss, B.D., Posner, M.I. and Givón, T. (1997) 'Brain plasticity in learning visual words', *Cognitive Psychology*, 33, 88–110.

McCarthy, G., Blamire, A.M., Rothman, D.L., Gruetter, R. and Shulman, R.G. (1993) 'Echo-planar magnetic resonance imaging studies of frontal cortex activation during word generation in humans', *Proceedings of the National Academy of Sciences of the USA*, 90, 4952–4956.

McConkie, G.W., Kerr, P.W., Reddix, M.D. and Zola, D. (1988) 'Eye movement control during reading: I. The location of initial eye fixations on words', *Vision Research*, 28, 1107–1118.

McConkie, G.W., Kerr, P.W., Reddix, M.D., Zola, D. and Jacobs, A.M. (1989) 'Eye movement control during reading: II. Frequency of refixating a word', *Perception and Psychophysics*, 46, 245–253.

Menard, M.T., Kosslyn, S.M., Thompson, W.L., Alpert, N.M. and Rauch, S.L. (1996) 'Encoding words and pictures: A positron emission tomography study', *Neuropsychologia*, 34, 185–194.

Milberg, W., Blumstein, S., Katz, D., Gershberg, R. and Brown, T. (1995) 'Semantic facilitation in aphasia: effects of time and expectancy', *Journal of Cognitive Neuroscience*, 7, 33–50.

Morrison, R.E. (1984) 'Manipulation of stimulus onset delay in reading: Evidence for parallel programming of saccades', *Journal of Experimental Psychology: Human Perception and Performance*, 10, 667–682.

Murtha, S., Chertkow, H., Dixon, R., Beauregard, M. and Evans, A. (1995) 'Anticipatory phonetic activation in silent word reading: Evidence from backward masking', *Journal of Memory and Language*, 27, 59–70.

Nakagawa, A. (1991) 'Role of anterior and posterior attention networks in hemisphere asymmetries during lexical decisions', *Journal of Cognitive Neuroscience*, 3, 313–321.

Neville, H.J., Mills, D.L. and Lawson, D.S. (1992) 'Fractionating language: Different neural subsystems with different sensitive periods', *Cerebral Cortex*, 2, 244–258.

Nobre, A.C., Allison, T. and McCarthy, G. (1994) 'Word recognition in the human inferior temporal lobe', *Nature*, 372, 260–263.

Nobre, A.C. and McCarthy, G. (1994) 'Language-related ERPs: Scalp distributions and modulation by word type and semantic priming', *Journal of Cognitive Neuroscience*, 6, 233–255.

O'Brien, E.J., Shank, D.M., Myers, J.L. and Rayner, K. (1988) 'Elaborative inferences during reading: Do they occur on-line?', *Journal of Experimental Psychology: Learning, Memory, and Cognition*, 14, 410–420.

O'Regan, J.K. and Levy-Schoen, A. (1987) 'Eye-movement strategy and tactics in word recognition and reading', in M. Coltheart (ed.), *Attention and Performance XII: The Psychology of Reading* (pp. 363–383). London: Erlbaum.

Pardo, J.V., Pardo, P.J., Janer, K.W. and Raichle, M.E. (1990) 'The anterior cingulate cortex mediates processing selection in the Stroop attentional conflict paradigm', *Proceedings of the National Academy of Sciences of the USA*, 87, 256–259.

Paulesu, E., Frith, C.D. and Frackowiak, R.S.J. (1993) 'The neural correlates of the verbal component of working memory', *Nature*, 362, 342–345.

Perfetti, C.A., Bell, L.C. and Delaney, S. (1988) 'Automatic (prelexical) phonetic activation in silent word reading: Evidence from backward masking', *Journal of Memory and Language*, 27, 59–70.

Petersen, S.E. and Fiez, J. (1993) 'PET studies of language', in M.E. Raichle (organiser), *New Views of Cognition: 1993 Short Course 2 Syllabus* (pp. 22–31) Washington, DC: Society for Neuroscience.

Petersen, S.E., Fox, P.T., Posner, M.I., Mintun, M. and Raichle, M.E. (1988) 'Positron emission tomographic studies of cortical anatomy of single-word processing', *Nature*, 331, 585–589.

Petersen, S.E., Fox, P.T., Posner, M.I., Mintun, M. and Raichle, M.E. (1989) 'Positron emission tomographic studies of the processing of single words', *Journal of Cognitive Neuroscience*, 1, 153–170.

Petersen, S.E., Fox, P.T., Snyder, A.Z. and Raichle, M.E. (1990) 'Activation of extrastriate and frontal cortical areas by visual words and word-like stimuli', *Science*, 249, 1041–1044.

Pollatsek, A. and Rayner, K. (1990). 'Eye movements and lexical access in reading', in D. Balota, G.B. Flores d'Arcais and K. Rayner (eds), *Comprehension Processes in Reading* (pp. 143–163). Hillsdale, NJ: Erlbaum.

Posner, M.I. & Abdullaev, Y.G.(1996) 'What to image?: Anatomy, circuitry and plasticity of human brain function', in A.W. Toga and J.C. Mazziotta (eds), *Brain Mapping: The Methods* (pp. 407–421). London: Academic Press.

Posner, M.I. and Carr, T.H. (1992) 'Lexical access and the brain: Anatomical constraints on cognitive models of word recognition', *American Journal of Psychology*, 105, 1–26.

Posner, M.I., Petersen, S.E., Fox, P.T. and Raichle, M.E. (1988) 'Localization of cognitive operations in the human brain', *Science*, 240, 1627–1631.

Posner, M.I. and Petersen, S.E. (1990) 'The attention system of the human brain', *Annual Review of Neuroscience*, 13, 25–42.

Posner, M.I. and Raichle, M.E. (1994) *Images of Mind: Exploring the Brain's Activity*. New York: W.H. Freeman & Co. (Scientific American Library, NY).

Posner, M.I. and Rothbart, M.K. (1992) 'Attention and conscious experience', in A.D. Milner and M.D. Rugg (eds), *The Neuropsychology of Consciousness* (pp. 91–112). London: Academic Press.

Price, C.J., Wise, R.J.S., Watson, J.D.G., Patterson, K., Howard, D. and Frackowiak, R.S.J. (1994) 'Brain activity during reading: The effects of exposure duration and task', *Brain*, 117, 1255–1269.

Raichle, M.E. (1994) 'Images of the mind: Studies with modern imaging techniques', *Annual Review of Psychology*, 4, 333–356.

Raichle, M.E., Fiez, J.A., Videen, T.O., MacLeod, A.M.K., Pardo, J.V. and Petersen, S.E. (1994) 'Practice-related changes in human brain functional anatomy during non-motor learning', *Cerebral Cortex*, 4, 8–26.

Rayner, K., Carlson, M. and Frazier, L. (1983) 'The interaction of syntax and semantics during sentence processing: Eye movements in the analysis of semantically biased sentences', *Journal of Verbal Learning and Verbal Behavior*, 22, 358–374.

Rayner, K. and Duffy, S.A. (1986) 'Lexical complexity and fixation times in reading: Effects of word frequency, verb complexity, and lexical ambiguity', *Memory and Cognition*, 14, 191–201.

Rayner, K. & Frazier, L. (1989) 'Selection mechanisms in reading lexically ambiguous words', *Journal of Experimental Psychology: Learning, Memory, and Cognition*, 15, 779–790.

Rayner, K. and Pollatsek, A. (1989) *The Psychology of Reading*. Englewood Cliffs, NJ: Prentice-Hall.

Rayner, K. and Sereno, S.C. (1994) 'Eye movements in reading: Psycholinguistic studies', in M.A. Gernsbacher (ed.), *Handbook of Psycholinguistics* (pp. 57–81). New York: Academic Press.

Rayner, K., Sereno, S.C. and Raney, G.E. (1995) 'Eye movement control in reading: A comparison of two models', *Journal of Experimental Psychology: Human Perception and Performance*, in press.

Rayner, K., Slowiaczek, M.L., Clifton, C., Jr and Bertera, J.H. (1983) 'Latency of sequential eye movements: Implications for reading', *Journal of Experimental Psychology: Human Perception and Performance*, 9, 912–922.

Rugg, M.D. and Coles, M.G.H. (eds) (1995). *Electrophysiology of Mind*. Oxford: Oxford University Press.

Scherg, M. and Berg, P. (1993) *Brain Electrical Source Analysis. Version 2.0.* NeuroScan, Inc.

Selnes, O.A., Knopman, D.S., Niccum, N. and Rubens, A.B. (1985) 'The critical role of Wernicke's area in sentence repetition', *Archives of Neurology*, 17, 549–557.

Sereno, S.C. (1992) 'Early lexical processes when fixating a word in reading', in K. Rayner (ed.), *Eye Movements and Visual Cognition: Scene Perception and Reading* (pp. 304–316). New York: Springer-Verlag.

Sereno, S.C., Pacht, J.M. and Rayner, K. (1992) 'The effect of meaning frequency on processing lexically ambiguous words: Evidence from eye fixations', *Psychological Science*, 3, 296–300.

Sereno, S.C., Rayner, K. and Posner, M.J. (1998) 'Establishing a time-line of word recognition: Evidence from eye movements and event-related potentials', *Neuroreport*, 9, 2195–2200.

Sergent, J., Eric, Z., Levesque, M. and MacDonald, B. (1992) 'Positron emission tomography study of letter and object processing: Empirical findings and methodological considerations', *Cerebral Cortex*, 2, 68–80.

Shallice, T. (1988) *From Neuropsychology to Mental Structure*. New York: Cambridge University Press.

Shaywitz, B.A., Shaywitz, S.E., Pugh, K.R., Constable, R.T., Skudlarski, P., Fulbright, R.K., Bronen, R.A., Fletcher, J.M., Shankweller, D.P., Katz, L. and Gore, J.C. (1995) 'Sex differences in the functional organization of the brain for language', *Nature*, 373, 607–609.

Snyder, A.Z., Abdullaev, Y.G., Posner, M.I. and Raichle, M.E. (1995) 'Scalp electrical potentials reflect regional cerebral blood flow responses during processing of written words', *Proceedings of the National Academy of Sciences of the USA*, 92, 1689–1693.

Tallal, P., Stark, R.E. and Mellits, D. (1985) 'The relationship between auditory temporal analysis and receptive language development: evidence from studies of developmental language disorder', *Neuropsychologia*, 23, 537–544.

Thacher, R.W. (1992) 'Cyclic cortical reorganization during childhood', *Brain and Cognition*, 24, 51–73.

Toga, A.W. and Mazziotta, J.C. (1995) *Brain Mapping: The Methods*. New York: Academic Press.

Tucker, D.M. (1993) 'The geodesic sensor net', *Electroencephalography and Clinical Neurophysiology*, 87, 154–163.

Tucker, D.M., Liotti, M., Potts, G.F., Russell, G.S. and Posner, M.I. (1994) 'Spatio-temporal analysis of brain electrical fields', *Human Brain Mapping*, 1, 134–152.

Van Orden, G.G., Pennington, B.F. and Stone, G.O. (1990) 'Word identification in reading and the promise of subsymbolic psycholinguistics', *Psychological Review*, 97, 488–522.

Yang, L. and Givón, T. (1993) 'Tracking the acquisition of L2 Vocabulary: The Keki language experiment (Tech. Rep. No. 93–11)', University of Oregon, Institute of Cognitive and Decision Sciences.

Zatorre, R.J., Evans, A.C., Meyer, E. and Gjedde, A. (1992) 'Lateralization of phonetic and pitch discrimination in speech processing', *Science*, 256, 846–849.

Zola, D. (1984) 'Redundancy and word perception during reading', *Perception and Psychophysics*, 36, 277–284.

7 Filtering performance by good and poor readers

Raymond M. Klein and Barbara D'Entremont

Introduction

Over the years, reading difficulties experienced by otherwise normal individuals have been attributed to underlying deficits in a wide variety of cognitive components necessary for successful reading. At one time visual factors were thought to be paramount (Vellutino 1979) but, subsequently, the emphasis shifted to deficits in verbal processing (such as verbal short term memory (Jorm 1983), and phonological coding (Mann, Liberman and Shankweiler 1980; Olson 1985), so much so that the view that developmental dyslexia has at its root a deficit in phonological processing or awareness became a predominant orthodoxy. There have been challenges to the dyslexia-as-phonological-deficit orthodoxy, most notably Tallal's proposal of a temporal processing deficit (Tallal 1980; Tallal and Stark 1982; for a review see Farmer and Klein 1995) and Breitmeyer's (1980) proposal of, and Williams' and Lovegrove's empirical support for, a visual transient system deficit (Lovegrove, Martin and Slaghuis 1986; Williams and LeCluyse 1990). Several findings in the literature on visual information processing and reading disability (which we review in the next section), suggested to us that a revival of interest in the hypothesis that many poor readers may suffer from a selective attentional deficit would be a worthwhile strategy. Studies (Brannan and Williams 1987; Enns, Bryson and Roes 1995), which have begun to show differences in attentional processes between good and poor readers, encourage this strategy.

Can an attentional deficit resolve an old puzzle?

It has been claimed that poor readers are deficient in the encoding of location information (Mason 1980; Mason, Pilkington and Brandau 1981). Mason (1980), for example, looked at good and poor readers' ability to identify letters when their location was uncertain or indicated by a pre-cue. In one condition, she presented a stimulus consisting of three dollar signs and a letter that was preceded and followed by a masking stimulus. The subject's task was to identify the letter (which could occur in any of the four positions). Poor readers were worse than good readers on this task, which Mason describes as 'identification dependent on localisation'. In a second condition, a cue was provided in the pre-mask which indicated where the target would appear. Here, once the cue was processed, localisation was not required. When location information was provided by the cue, the difference between the two groups disappeared. Mason interpreted this as evidence for a deficit in locating the target.

In a contradictory study by Manis and Morrison (1982), subjects were required to decide whether a target had appeared previously in a five-letter array and when they correctly detected the presence of a target they reported its location. They found that poor readers were much worse than good readers at the yes/no detection task. However, when they had detected the target, poor readers were equivalent to good readers in localising it. The conclusion they drew from this study was that there was no deficit in encoding location.

The Mason (1980) and Manis and Morrison (1982) results can be reconciled by re-examining the evidence in terms of attentional differences between good and poor readers. The cue in Mason's study served to focus attention away from the distractors and on to the position where the target would appear. The poor readers had a lower performance in the absence of this cue. In Manis and Morrison (1982) there were no cues to aid the poor readers so they performed worse at attending to array items (cf. Brannan and Williams 1987) and thus at determining whether the target was present. However, once they had attended sufficiently to detect the target, they were equally efficient at localising it.

In an unpublished manuscript, Briand and Bryson hypothesised that the good readers in the Mason study may have been better able than the poor readers to use the static and dynamic segregation cues that were available in her displays to allocate attention to the region of the target letter. To test this idea they varied whether or not these cues were present. They replicated Mason's finding of worse performance by poor readers as long as there was change at each possible location between the pre/post masking display and the target array (no dynamic segregation cue). When the only change was at the target location, the poor readers did not show a deficit, presumably because the change served as a spatial cue for attention. Although this pattern is consistent with the proposal that poor readers have difficulty in *orienting* attention, we prefer, and in this chapter will test, an alternative explanation for their results based on difficulties in *filtering* distracting information.

Kahneman, Treisman and Burkell (1983) reported that the appearance of distractors, not their mere presence, interferes with the processing of a target. The appearance of new events requires new processing, and if more than one event occurs, there is competition for attention. Four events may be regarded as the appearance of three distractors along with the target. If poor readers have difficulty filtering distractors, they would be expected to be more affected by the presence of distractors than good readers. However, if there is only one event, there is no competition for attention and no reduction in performance should be observed.

Rationale

It is possible, therefore, that poor readers do not filter out distracting information as efficiently as good readers. In addition to their problems ignoring distractors in the above cited studies, a number of other studies provide results consistent with the idea that poor readers may have a filtering problem. For example, poor readers have been shown to have difficulty identifying embedded letters (Bouma and Legein 1977) and to be 'field dependent' on embedded figures tests, meaning that they have difficulty separating figure from ground (Witken *et al.* 1962). Similarly, reading disabled children had difficulty ignoring irrelevant red words inserted in the spaces between lines of text (Willows 1974). Finally, Geiger and Lettvin (1987) showed that adult dyslexic readers were more susceptible to the masking effects of peripheral information than were normal readers.[1] This result could be due to attention or to differences in the interaction between foveal and parafoveal information. In the experiment reported below all stimuli are presented at the same eccentricity. Hence, if a difference between good and poor readers is obtained it can be attributed unambiguously to attentional mechanisms.

The present study used a version of the Eriksen filtering task (Eriksen and Hoffman 1972; Miller 1991) to test the hypothesis that good and poor readers differ in their ability to ignore or filter distracting information. Several studies which have examined the component processes of poor readers have found that many rely more heavily on orthographic coding than phonological coding (Boder 1972; Mann *et al.* 1980; Olson, 1985; Olson *et al.* 1990). Therefore, phonological and orthographical coding were assessed to determine if these skills are correlated with the ability to control attention as measured in the filtering task.

In our implementation of the filtering task, subjects were required to identify one of two digits (the digits 1 or 2) by pressing a corresponding button. The target appeared at the top or bottom of an imaginary circle (12 o'clock or 6 o'clock position). Distractors which were either the same as (compatible) or different from (incompatible) the target appeared at one of three distances from the target, measured along the circumference of the circle. The degree of distractor processing was operationalised by subtracting the reaction time (RT) to identify the target with compatible distractors present (C_{RT}) from the RT to identify the target with incompatible distractors present (I_{RT}). This score ($I_{RT} - C_{RT}$) will be referred to as the flanker compatibility effect (FCE; see Miller 1991). Typically the FCE is large for near distractors (within 0.5 degrees) and it decreases with increasing distractor distance (D'Aloisio and Klein 1990). If good readers show the normal pattern while poor readers do not, it will indicate that poor readers do not filter normally.

Method

Subjects

The Nelson-Denny Reading Test (Form D) and the Cognitive Failures Questionnaire (CFQ, consisting of 25 questions about common events of

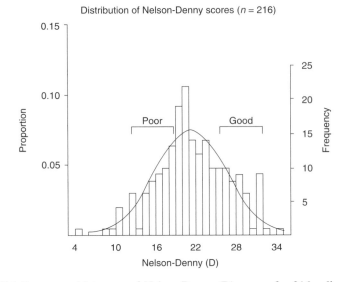

Figure 7.1 Frequency histogram of Nelson-Denny (D) scores for 216 college students, showing regions from which the good and poor readers used in the present study were drawn.

forgetfulness which people often experience, see Broadbent *et al.* 1982) were administered to 216 introductory psychology students. The CFQ was administered because of previous claims that absentminded individuals have difficulty focusing attention (Brennan 1988; Broadbent, Broadbent and Jones 1986). The distribution of Nelson-Denny scores for this sample is shown in Figure 7.1. Good and poor readers were recruited on the basis of their Nelson-Denny scores, as follows: 17 subjects (9 male, 8 female) scoring above the 80th percentile on norms provided with the test were selected to serve as good readers, and 15 subjects (7 male, 8 female) with scores in the 13th–33rd percentiles were selected to serve as poor readers. Subjects' verbal and performance IQ were estimated using the Vocabulary and Block Design subtests of the Wechsler Adult Intelligence Scale (WAIS) since these are the best predictors of verbal and performance IQ (Wechsler 1944). All subjects were native English speakers with normal or corrected to normal vision.

Apparatus and stimuli

Visual stimuli were presented on a computer (PDP-11/23)-driven Tektronix 604 oscilloscope with fast phosphor. Responses were made on a two-button response board with the index finger controlling the left button and the middle finger controlling the right button (or vice versa for left-handed subjects).

The target and distractor stimuli used in the filtering task consisted of the digits 1 or 2, each subtending 0.23 degrees of visual angle horizontally and 0.28 degrees vertically. The digits appeared on an imaginary circle with a radius of 1.1 degrees, as shown in Figure 7.2. Component reading skills (orthographic-to-phonological recoding and sight vocabulary) were measured using two lists of letter string pairs (Olson 1986).[2] In one list, which we will call the phonological task, the letter string pairs were both nonwords but one sounded like a word (e.g. kake, dake). Because neither letter string is visually familiar, the subject must determine each string's pronunciation in order to decide which one sounds like a real word. In the other list, which we will call the orthographical task, one letter string was a word and one was not, but they both had the same pronounciation (e.g. rain, rane). Because the strings do not differ in the pronunciation that would be assembled via orthographic-to-phonological coding, familiarity with the orthographic strings is necessary to solve this task. The letter strings ranged from 3 to 12 letters in length and any one pair did not necessarily have the same number of letters in each string.

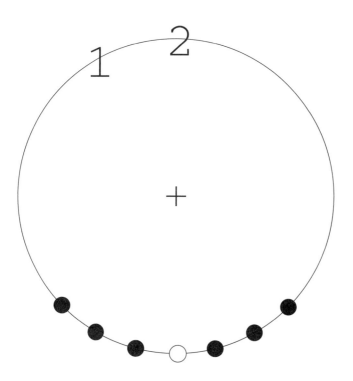

Figure 7.2 Layout of the display used in the filtering task.

Notes

All digit stimuli were displayed on a virtual circle (the circle in the display is for illustrative purposes and was not displayed to participants) with a diameter of 1.1 degrees. Targets appeared randomly at the top or bottom of the virtual circle and a single distractor was placed in one of the 3 nearby locations. A sample display (medium incompatible) is shown in the upper portion of the figure. On the lower part of the figure are shown the possible target (open circle) and distractor (closed circles) locations for 6 o'clock targets.

Procedure

The filtering task was administered first, followed by the component reading skills and the verbal performance IQ tests.

In the filtering task, the targets appeared at either the top or bottom of an imaginary circle (i.e. at 12 o'clock and 6 o'clock). Irrelevant distractor digits appeared at one of 3 distances (0.3, 0.6, and 0.9 degrees) from the target in either a clockwise or counterclockwise direction (see Figure 7.2). Subjects were instructed to respond to '1' targets by pressing the left button and '2' targets by pressing the right button. They were told to ignore the distractors. Each trial began with a fixation point at the centre of the screen for 1 second followed by the test display for 200 ms. After a brief inter-trial interval the fixation point reappeared, signalling the beginning of the next trial. The main variables were distractor type (compatible/incompatible) and distractor distance (near, medium and far). The order of the presentation of conditions was randomised. There was one practice block (48 trials) to familiarise the subject with the task (8 trials in each condition: compatible distractor – three distances, and compatible distractor – three distances), and one test block (144 trials: 24 trials in each condition).

In the component reading skills task, the letter strings appeared one above the other on the screen. In the phonological task, subjects were asked to press one of two vertically arranged response keys corresponding to the position (above/below fixation) on the screen which displayed a letter string that sounded like a word. In the orthographical task, they were asked to press the button corresponding to the position of the letter string which was a real word. Following the onset of fixation the test stimulus was displayed for 200 ms. There were 10 practice trials and 55 test trials for each task. The order in which the two tasks was presented was counterbalanced across subjects.

Results and discussion

IQ, CFQ and reading scores

The findings relating IQ, CFQ and reading scores are shown in Table 7.1. Both verbal and performance IQ as well as CFQ scores were subjected to 2×2 (reading ability × gender) ANOVAs. As might be predicted, poor readers had significantly lower verbal IQs than good readers. There were no differences for performance IQ or CFQ. Within-group correlations between these variables and the Nelson-Denny reading scores were calculated. For the poor readers, there was a significant negative correlation between reading score and the CFQ, $r = -0.702$, indicating that among the selected poor readers, self-reported absentmindedness (high CFQ scores) was associated with *poor* reading comprehension. There was no correlation between CFQ and reading ability in the good readers or in the two groups combined. Due to the possible importance of the CFQ/reading relation in the poor readers, it was decided to return to our original sample of 216 students to see if it would be replicated. There were 53 cases in the original sample whose Nelson-Denny scores fell in the range of the poor readers used in this experiment

Table 7.1 IQ and cognitive failures scores for good and poor readers and their correlations with reading scores

	Mean		
	Good	*Poor*	*F*
Verbal IQ	124.3	105.4	18.27[a]
Performance IQ	120.2	120.8	0.01
CFQ	39.6	36.5	0.59

	Correlations with ND	
	Good	*Poor*
CFQ	0.18	−0.702[a]
Verbal IQ	0.37	−0.028
Performance IQ	0.35	0.024

Note
[a] $p < .01$

(10 < ND < 19). For this larger sub-sample of poor readers, the correlation was −0.29 ($p = .036$), indicating that there may be a general trend among poor readers for the more absentminded to be worse at reading.

Filtering Task

The reaction time (RT) and accuracy data (see Table 7.2) from the filtering task were subjected to $2 \times 2 \times 3 \times 2$ (good/poor reader × gender × distance × distractor type) ANOVAs. In the analysis of reaction times, there were main effects of distance ($F_{(2, 56)} = 15.36$, $p < .01$) and distractor type ($F_{(1, 28)} = 30.49$, $p < .01$) and a significant interaction between these variables ($F_{(2, 56)} = 4.27$, $p < .05$).[3] In the analysis of accuracy there were no significant effects or interactions. Thus the typical FCE, as described in the introduction, was obtained: RT was slower

Table 7.2 Reaction times (and accuracy) for good and poor readers in the distractor task

	Near		Medium		Far	
	C	*I*	*C*	*I*	*C*	*I*
Good						
RT (ms)	666.0	738.3	645.8	671.6	652.9	665.2
% Correct	93.18	94.94	93.24	97.65	95.94	96.65
Poor						
RT (ms)	679.6	714.5	662.3	695.8	658.4	689.3
% Correct	92.67	93.13	92.93	94.27	93.47	94.53

Note
C = compatible; I = incompatible

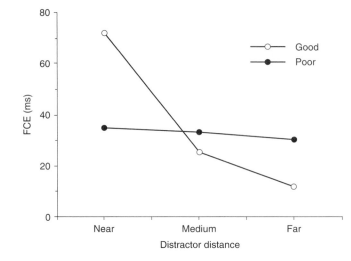

Figure 7.3 Flanker compatibility effect (FCE = incompatible minus compatible RT) for good and poor readers as a function of distractor distance.

with incompatible distractors than compatible distractors, with this effect (i.e. $I_{RT} - C_{RT}$) decreasing as distance increased.

This pattern, however, is qualified by a significant interaction between reading level, distance and distractor type ($F_{(2, 56)} = 3.36, p < .05$). Inspection of the data (see Figure 7.3) indicates that the poor readers did not show the typical decrease in interference across the distance that was shown by the good readers. Separate ANOVAs conducted on the data from the good and poor readers confirmed this pattern. There was a significant interaction between distance and distractor type for the good readers ($F_{(2, 32)} = 7.88, p < .01$) but not for poor readers ($F_{(2, 28)} < 1$).

To provide a single measure of the *pattern* of filtering performance as a function of distractor distance shown by individual subjects, the FCE at the medium and far distances was averaged and subtracted from the FCE at the near distance. To the extent that a subject shows the typical pattern, this measure, which we will call FCE′, will be positive, and for subjects who show little change in the FCE with distance FCE′ will be near zero. An ANOVA performed on FCE′ revealed a significant difference between the good (FCE′ = 53.2 ms) and poor (FCE′ = 2.8 ms) readers ($F_{(1,30)} = 6.67, p = .015$).

Component reading skills

Reaction time and accuracy from the phonological and orthographical component reading skills tasks (shown in Table 7.3) were analysed separately using 2×2 (reading level × gender) ANOVAs. For RT there were significant effects of reading level, with good readers significantly faster at both tasks (phonological $F_{(1, 28)} = 10.40, p < .01$; orthographical $F_{(1, 28)} = 6.69, p < .05$). In the analysis of accuracy, the poor readers were significantly less accurate than the good readers

Table 7.3 Reaction times, accuracies and efficiency scores for good and poor readers on component reading skills tasks

	Good			*Poor*		
	RT	*%C*	*Eff.*	*RT*	*%C*	*Eff.*
Phonological	1750	91.5	1924.8	2143	85.7	2534.1
Orthographical	977	97.1	1009.1	1106	95.2	1162.8

in the phonological task ($F_{(1, 28)} = 5.79$, $p < .025$). The apparent group difference in the orthographical task was only marginally significant ($F_{(1,28)} = 3.3$, $.05 < p < .1$). No other effects were significant. To generate a single, overall measure of performance efficiency for each task, we divided each subject's mean RT in each task by its corresponding accuracy (proportion correct) (see Townsend and Ashby 1983 for justification of this transformation). These scores were subjected to a mixed ANOVA which, in addition to the expected main effects of reading level and task, revealed a significant interaction between these variables ($F_{(1,28)} = 9.06$, $p < .01$), indicating that the performance disadvantage shown by the poor readers was greater on the phonological than on the orthographical task.

In light of the work by Castles and Coltheart (1993) we thought it would be interesting to look at the relative performance of our sample of poor readers on the two component reading skills tasks to see if sub-groups with presentations corresponding to phonological and surface dyslexia might be apparent. Performance of all subjects on these two tasks is represented in scatterplot form in

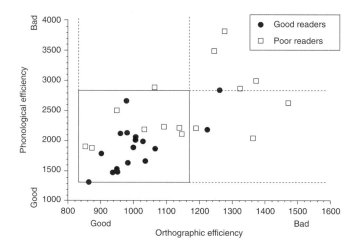

Figure 7.4 Scatterplot showing poor readers' scores on the orthographical and phonological skill tasks.

Note

The box displays the region where 90% of the normal data fall.

Figure 7.4. The mean and standard deviation of scores of the good readers were used to develop confidence intervals that should include 90 per cent of good readers. Note that many poor readers fall outside the normal range on both tasks and quite a few fall within the normal range on both tasks. Poor readers who are normal on the phonological skills task and below normal on the orthographic skills task might be classified as showing a surface dyslexic pattern: they appear to have normal skill in orthographic-to-phonological conversion and worse than normal skill in recognising visual words. Three of the poor readers fall into this category. Poor readers who are normal on the orthographical skills task and below normal on the phonological skills task might be classified as showing a phonological dyslexic pattern: they appear to have normal skill in recognising visual words and worse than normal skill performing orthographic-to-phonological conversion. One of the poor readers falls into this category. Filtering performance of these four individuals was examined to see if there were any interesting relations between reading skill asymmetry and visual attention; none was apparent.

Correlations

The relationship between performance on the component reading skills, reading ability and our measure of attentional focusing (FCE′) was examined for the entire sample and for the two reading levels separately (see Table 7.4). In all the analyses, performance on the two component reading skills tasks was positively correlated. Across both groups good performance on these tasks was strongly associated with high reading scores (note that good performance in the RT and efficiency measures is reflected in LOW scores). This relation is also present when the groups are analysed separately, however, due to reduced power or restricted range, none of the effects is significant in the separate analyses.

Conclusion

The good and poor readers in our study differ in their ability to control the region of attended information or to ignore information outside the focus of attention (Figure 7.2). Good readers showed the typical pattern with distractors nearest the target having a large influence on performance that drops off as the distractor distance increases. In contrast, for poor readers the effect of distractors remained constant regardless of their distance from the target. This pattern can be described in terms of differences in filtering, one mechanism hypothesised to underlie selective attention (Broadbent 1958; LaBerge and Brown 1989). Kahneman *et al.* (1983), for example, likened the filtering of distractors to the casting of a shadow over the distracting information. LaBerge and Brown's theory of attention (1989) provides a more elaborated framework within which the differences we have observed might be explained. In their model, information flow from a selected position increases relative to other locations but in addition to this target enhancement mechanism, there is a filtering mechanism which operates by

Table 7.4 Correlations among measures of orthographical coding, phonological coding, reading and the pattern of distractor interference

	Orthographical			Phonological			Reading
	RT	*%C*	*Eff.*	*RT*	*%C*	*Eff.*	
(a) All subjects combined							
FCE′	−0.12	0.01	−0.12	−0.13	0.18	−0.17	0.34[d]
Ortho RT				0.68[a]			−0.47[a]
Ortho %C					0.55[a]		0.37[c]
Ortho eff.						0.65[a]	−0.52[a]
Phono RT							−0.51[a]
Phono %C							0.44[b]
Phono eff.							−0.55[a]
(b) Good readers							
FCE′	−0.06	−0.17	−0.02	0.16	−0.20	0.21	−0.33
Ortho RT				0.64[a]			−0.05
Ortho %C					0.58[b]		0.42[d]
Ortho eff.						0.66[a]	−0.17
Phono RT							−0.06
Phono %C							0.38
Phono eff.							−0.16
(c) Poor readers							
FCE′.	0.18	−0.15	0.20	0.05	0.18	−0.06	−0.21
Ortho RT				0.60[a]			−0.35
Ortho %C					0.45[d]		0.25
Ortho eff.						0.49[d]	−0.40
Phono RT							−0.21
Phono %C							0.09
Phono eff.							−0.17

Notes
FCE′ = FCE at near location minus the average FCE at the medium and far locations
[a]$p < .01$; [b]$p < .025$; [c]$p < .05$; [d]$p < 1$

opening channels large enough to allow one piece, or chunk, of information to pass through at a time. The filter operates on a winner-take-all principle such that when the information flow from one location sufficiently exceeds that from the others, a corresponding channel opens to allow only the selected (target) information to pass through. In terms of this model, it could be the inhibitory mechanism that is different, and possibly deficient, for the poor readers, a difference that might result in an increase in the the minimum size of the opened channel.

Converging evidence for the existence of a deficit of this sort can be found in a case study of a severe dyslexic. This subject was required to read text with restricted windows of text (Rayner *et al.* 1989). These researchers found that the dyslexic subject actually read better than controls when the window size was restricted and everything outside the window was uniform (e.g. all Xs). When the distracting information in the periphery was eliminated, the dyslexic performed better than the normal readers, suggesting that when they were present he was unable to filter the words outside fixation.

Rayner *et al.*'s study, however, cannot be directly compared with ours because of the difference in the displays and the uniqueness of their subject. Nevertheless, their study does provide indirect evidence for a hypothesis which asserts that poor readers may experience less interference from distractors at near distances and more interference at far distances than good readers.

Our poor readers were worse at both phonological and orthographical coding, but the difference was greater on the phonological task, which was particularly evident in the efficiency measure, a result consistent with the findings of other researchers (Mann *et al.* 1980; Olson, 1985; Olson *et al.* 1989). We also found that phonological and orthographical coding were correlated highly with each other for good and poor readers, which is consistent with recent studies of dyslexic and non-dyslexic twins showing that both abilities are substantially heritable (Olson, Forsberg and Wise 1994). One likely reason for this high correlation is that reading experience is highly important for the development of both kinds of representation (phonological and orthographic), and hence factors that tend to influence the amount of reading experience would lead to a positive correlation in these two component skills. Thus when a child has a decoding deficit (which could be based on poor phonemic awareness, see e.g. Olson *et al.* 1994, or visual attention, see below), they may find reading difficult and hence read infrequently.

Our findings suggest that poor readers filter irrelevant material differently from good readers. They do not, however, provide a direct insight into the mechanism of this relationship nor do they imply that there is a causal connection from this attentional difference to the difference in reading ability. Causal connections of this sort are difficult to establish (see Farmer and Klein 1995; 485–487, for a discussion of various strategies), and some discussion of the plausibility of, not to mention directionality of, a causal link between a filtering deficit and reading skill is warranted before a costly and time consuming effort is initiated.

One way to link the idea of a filtering deficit to a reading deficit might be to assume that following a shift in fixation all newly foveated and neighbouring letters and words constitute new events. The filtering problem, then, would involve premature activation of neighbouring units whose processing must be suppressed until the selected, or attended, unit is fully analysed. In this context it is important to note that the size of the units that the reader must process, e.g. sub-syllabic, syllabic, word, phrase, will vary with the reader's level of skill. The poor readers we have tested exhibit a filtering mechanism that results in distractors receiving the same level of processing regardless of their distance from the target (within the range of 0.3 to 0.9 degrees). Thus, when reading, it might be difficult for poor readers to ignore letter clusters which are near the cluster they are currently analysing, or to ignore words which are near the attended word. In development, a difficulty focusing attention on letter clusters might interfere with the acquisition of the orthographic rules and their relation to phonology. As these problems are overcome, a difficulty focusing attention on the word one is analysing might interfere with the general task of reading. We believe that either or both of these interference effects might be on the pathway from an attentional deficit to a reading disability.

The alternative direction of causal connection, from poor reading to a filtering deficit, must also be considered. Individuals who are poor readers probably read much less often than individuals who are good readers. Perhaps reading experience is a particularly effective form of exercise for the filtering mechanism described above. The more practised individuals are at examining small, high contrast print with the relatively short exposures and subsequent masking that, due to rapid sequences of saccades, characterise skilled reading, the more efficiently their filtering mechanism may operate.[4] Perhaps the most convincing strategy for choosing between these two alternative directions (filtering deficit → reading deficit vs reading deficit → filtering deficit) would be to conduct a longitudinal study in which the filtering performance of prelinguistic children was determined, and their acquisition of reading skill subsequently tracked.

An alternative approach is to look for converging evidence. Gernsbacher (1993) reviews her work showing that less skilled readers are less efficient than skilled readers at suppressing a variety of forms of irrelevant information, such as: (a) the inappropriate meanings of ambiguous words; (b) the incorrect forms of homophones; (c) the typical but absent members of scenes; and (d) words superimposed on pictures. Because the less skilled readers did not seem to differ from skilled readers in the activation of contextually appropriate information (which in the LaBerge and Brown (1989) sense would correspond to their enhancement mechanism), Gernsbacher concluded that poor readers suffer from a general deficit in suppression mechanisms. Our finding of a difference between good and poor readers in a simple visual filtering paradigm converges nicely with Gernsbacher's findings. Moreover, because for some of Gernsbacher's tasks (e.g. suppressing pictures from scenes) it is difficult to see how experience at reading could lead to better suppression, we feel that a causal connection from filtering to reading provides a more plausible account. On the basis of our finding together with Gernsbacher's, we believe a strong case is made that some poor readers suffer from a deficit in the control of inhibitory mechanisms thought to be important in selective attention (Houghton and Tipper 1994; Klein and Taylor 1994), and that this deficit may play a causal role in their reading disability.

Notes

1 Geiger and Letvin (1987) also proposed that normal and dyslexic readers differ in the shape of the acuity gradient around fixation. Their suggestion that dyslexics have a shallower fall-off in acuity, with better performance than normals in the periphery, has not been replicated (Klein *et al.* 1990; Goolkasian and King 1990) and their evidence in support of this suggestion was probably compromised by their failure to encourage and ensure correct fixation (Klein *et al.* 1990).

2   The authors wish to acknowledge appreciation to R.K. Olson for providing these lists.
3   There was a significant interaction between gender and distractor type such that the females showed a larger FCE than the males ($F_{(1, 28)}$ = 4.53, $p < .05$). The overall interference score ($I_{RT} - C_{RT}$) for males was 21.2, for females it was 47.9. Because this pattern was uninfluenced by reading score, we will not discuss it further.
4   A third general possible relation is that there is no direct causal link in either direction. For example, the difficulty with reading and the difficulty with filtering might be independently caused by a third factor. We find this implausible, though perhaps the reader will attribute this to a lack of imagination.

References

Boder, E. (1972) 'Developmental dyslexia: Prevailing diagnostic concepts and a new diagnostic approach', *Progress in Learning Disabilities*, 293–320.

Bouma, H. and Legein, Ch.P. (1977) 'Foveal and parafoveal recognition of letters and words by dyslexics and by average readers', *Neuropsychologia*, 15, 69–80.

Breitmeyer, B.G. (1980) 'Unmasking visual masking: A look at the "why" behind the veil of "how"', *Psychological Review*, 87, 52–69.

Brannan, J.R. and Williams, M.C. (1987) 'Allocation of visual attention in good and poor readers', *Perception and Psychophysics*, 41, 23–28.

Brennan, M. (1988) 'Attentional variation as predicted by type A behaviour pattern and cognitive failure', unpublished master's thesis, Dalhousie University, Halifax, Nova Scotia.

Briand, K. and Bryson, S. 'Letter encoding under spatial uncertainty in skilled and unskilled readers', unpublished manuscript.

Broadbent, D. (1958) *Perception and Communication*. London: Pergamon Press.

Broadbent, D.E., Cooper, P.E., Fitzgerald, P. and Parkes, K.R. (1982) 'The cognitive failures questionnaire (CFQ) and its correlates', *British Journal of Clinical Psychology*, *21, 1–16*.

Broadbent, D.O., Broadbent, M. and Jones, J. L. (1986) 'Performance correlates of self-reported cognitive failure and of obsessionality', *British Journal of Clinical Psychology*, 25, 285–298.

Castles, A. and Coltheart, M. (1993) 'Varieties of developmental dyslexia', *Cognition*, 47, 149–180.

D'Aloisio, A. and Klein, R.M. (1990) 'Aging and the deployment of visual attention', in J. Enns (ed.) *The Development of Attention: Research and Theory*. Amsterdam: North-Holland.

Enns, J., Bryson, S. and Roes, C. (1995) 'Searching for letter identity and location by disabled readers', *Canadian Journal of Experimental Psychology*, 49, 357–367.

Eriksen, C.W. and Hoffman, J.E. (1972) 'Temporal and spatial characteristics of selective encoding from visual displays', *Perception and Psychophysics*, 12, 201–204.

Farmer, M.E. and Klein, R.M. (1995) 'The evidence for a temporal processing deficit linked to dyslexia: A review', *Psychonomic Bulletin and Review*, 2, 460–493.

Geiger, G. and Lettvin, J.Y. (1987) 'Peripheral vision in persons with dyslexia', *New England Journal of Medicine*, 316, 1238–1243.

Gernsbacher, M.A. (1993) 'Less skilled readers have less efficient suppression mechanisms', *Psychological Science*, 4, 294–298.

Goolkasian, P. and King, J. (1990) 'Letter identification and lateral masking in dyslexic and average readers', *American Journal of Psychology*, 103, 519–538.

Houghton, G. and Tipper, S.P. (1994) 'A model of inhibitory mechanisms in selective attention', in D. Dagenbach and T.H. Carr (eds), *Inhibitory Processes in Attention, Memory and Language*. San Diego, CA: Academic Press.

Jorm, A.F. (1983) 'Specific reading retardation and working memory: A review', *British Journal of Psychology*, 74, 311–342.

Kahneman, D., Treisman, A. and Burkell, J. (1983) 'The cost of visual filtering', *Journal of Experimental Psychology: Human Perception and Performance*, 9, 510–522.

Klein, R., Berry, G., Briand, K., D'Entremont, B. and Farmer, M. (1990) 'Letter identification declines with increasing retinal eccentricity at the same rate for normal and dyslexic readers', *Perception and Psychophysics*, 47, 601–606.

Klein, R.M. and Taylor, T.L. (1994) 'Categories of cognitive inhibition with reference to attention', in D. Dagenbach and T.H. Carr (eds), *Inhibitory Processes in Attention, Memory and Language*. San Diego, CA: Academic Press.

LaBerge, D. and Brown, V. (1989) 'Theory of attentional operations in shape identification', *Psychological Review*, 95, 101–124.

Lovegrove, W., Martin, F. and Slaghuis, W. (1986) 'A theoretical and experimental case for a visual deficit in specific reading disability', *Cognitive Neuropsychology*, 3, 225–267.

Manis, F.R. and Morrison, F.J. (1982) 'Processing of identity and position information in normal and disabled readers', *Journal of Experimental Child Psychology*, 33, 74–86.

Mann, V.A., Liberman, I.Y. and Shankweiler, D. (1980) 'Children's memory for sentences and word strings in relation to reading ability', *Memory and Cognition*, 8, 329–335.

Mason, M. (1980) 'Reading ability and the encoding of item and location information', *Journal of Experimental Psychology: Human Perception and Performance*, 6, 89–98.

Mason, M., Pilkington, C. and Brandau, R. (1981) 'From print to sound: Reading ability and order information', *Journal of Experimental Psychology: Human Perception and Performance*, 7, 580–591.

Miller, J. (1991) 'The flanker compatibility effect as a function of visual angle, attentional focus, visual transients, and perceptual load: A search for boundary conditions', *Perception and Psychophysics*, 49, 270–288.

Olson, R.K. (1985) 'Disabled reading processes and cognitive profiles', in U.B. Gray and J. Kavanagh (eds), *Biobehavioural Measures of Dyslexia* (pp. 215–242). Maryland: York Press.

Olson, R.K., Forsberg, H. and Wise, B. (1994) 'Genes, environment, and the development of orthographic skills', in V.W. Berginger (ed.), *The Varieties of Orthographic Knowledge I: Theoretical and Developmental Issues* (pp. 27–41). Dordrecht: Kluwer.

Olson, R.K., Wise, B., Conners, F., Rack, J. and Fulker, D. (1989) 'Specific deficits in component reading and language skills: Genetic and environmental influences', *Journal of Learning Disabilities*, 22, 339–348.

Olson, R.K., Wise, B., Conners, F. and Rack, J. (1990) 'Organization, heritability, and remediation of component word recognition and language skills in disabled readers', in T.H. Carr and B.A. Levy (eds), *Reading and its Development: Component Skills Approaches*. Academic Press: New York.

Rayner, K., Murphy, L., Henderson, J.M. and Pollatsek, A. (1989) 'Selective attentional dyslexia', *Cognitive Neuropsychology*, 6, 357–378.

Tallal, P. (1980) 'Auditory temporal perception phonics and reading disabilities in children', *Brain Language*, 9, 182–198.

Tallal, P. and Stark, R.E. (1982) 'Perceptual/motor profiles of reading impaired children with or without concomitant oral language deficits', *Annals of Dyslexia*, 32, 163–176.

Townsend, J.T. and Ashby, F.G. (1983) *Stochastic Modelling of Elementary Psychological Processes*. Cambridge University Press: London.

Vellutino, F.R. (1979) *Dyslexia: Theory and Research*. Massachusetts: Massachusetts Institute of Technology.

Wechsler, D. (1944) *The Measurement of Adult Intelligence: Third Edition*. Baltimore: Williams & Wilkins.

Williams, M. and LeCluyse, K. (1990) 'Perceptual consequences of a temporal processing deficit in reading disabled children', *Journal of the American Optometric Association*, 61, 111–121.

Willows, D.W. (1974) 'Reading between the lines: selective attention in good and poor readers', *Child Development*, 45, 408–415.

Witken, H.A., Dyk, R.B., Faterson, H.F., Goodenough, D.R. and Karp, S.A. (1962) *Psychological Differentiation*. New York: John Wiley & Sons

8 Attention and eye movements in reading

Alexander Pollatsek, Keith Rayner,
Martin H. Fischer and Erik D. Reichle

Introduction

The process of attending in the visual domain is most obviously carried out by moving the eyes, head and/or body so that the attended visual information is in the visual field, and preferably in the fovea. This overt process of orienting clearly does a considerable part of the job of controlling and scheduling the processing of visual information. Pointing the eyes to a location in space (**fixating**) serves two related attentional functions. First, visual information that does not hit the retina and is thus outside the field of vision is filtered out. Second, the decision of which information to put in the foveal region of central vision by fixating that region of space also serves a major attentional function: because acuity declines rapidly from the point of fixation, processing fine detail (such as reading text) must be done close to the fixation point.

When people read or view any static display, their eyes shift fixation location quite frequently. They do not move continuously, however, but move in a series of rapid, ballistic movements known as **saccades**. These saccades last in the order of 15–50 ms and serve the function of getting the eyes from point A to point B. No useful information is extracted during saccadic eye movements, and the duration of a saccade is merely an increasing function of its length. The eyes stay relatively still between these saccades, and these still periods are known as **fixations**. Fixations typically last between about 150 ms and 1 s, and for reading, most fixations are between about 150 and 500 ms, and the average is between about 200 and 300 ms, depending on the reader and the type of text being read. (For viewing pictures or scenes, the range of fixation durations is roughly the same as in reading, but the average fixation duration is about 100 ms longer than in reading.)

The fact that this change of eye position is so relentless suggests that attention in vision primarily works by moving the eyes. That is, it appears that the viewer extracts information from each fixation and, if some information can not be processed (or processed only with difficulty), the eyes can remedy the situation by directing central foveal vision to the spatial location of that information within a fraction of a second. In reading, the pattern of eye movements appears to be a direct window on what the reader is attending to and processing. In text, a majority of words are directly fixated (80 per cent of 'content words' and 25 per cent of 'function words') and almost all words receive a fixation that comes within about 3–4 characters of the word. Moreover, as we shall document, derived measures of reading performance indicate that there is a close relation between what is fixated and what is being processed. Thus, one might be tempted to conclude that attention in reading is synonymous with the overt pattern of eye fixations.

There is, however, a substantial literature indicating that there is a process of **covert** visual attention as well. One decoupling of covert attention and fixation occurs when you are attempting to deceive someone else about what you 'are looking at'. In those cases, you fixate a region of space that is not of interest, but move your attention away from the fixation point and to the object of real interest. This kind of movement of attention away from fixation has been examined in detail by several laboratory paradigms. In the simplest, **spatial cueing**, paradigm (Posner 1980), subjects are required to maintain fixation on the centre of a CRT (cathode-ray tube) display. A spatial location on the display is cued and then a target stimulus appears either in the cued location or a different location. Reaction time to the stimulus is decreased if it is in the cued location, indicating that covert spatial attention facilitated processing the target. Other experiments (e.g. Remington 1980) indicate that accuracy of identifying a target in the cued location is higher than in an uncued location.

The spatial cueing paradigm and related paradigms have been adapted to produce an explosion of knowledge in the last 15 years about the physiological correlates of covert visual attention and eye movement control. Visual stimuli are generally processed along two more or less anatomically and functionally discriminable pathways for location and identity of information (e.g., Ungerleider and Mishkin 1985; Van Essen and DeYoe 1995). The location of stimuli is registered in the dorsal (upper) pathway along the parietal lobes, while stimulus identity is analysed along a ventral (lower) pathway involving the temporal lobes. The former pathway is central to both eye movement control and covert spatial attention and includes area MT, the pulvinar, and the frontal eye fields. Cells in this dorsal pathway respond in anticipation of stimulation, suggesting an attentional function (Posner *et al.* 1987; Duhamel, Colby and Goldberg 1992), whereas cells along the ventral pathway are sensitive to stimulus attributes such as form or colour and change their activity in accord with the current stimulation and task demands (Moran and Desimone 1985; Spitzer, Desimone and Moran 1988).

Specifically, studies have shown that cells in the parietal pathway respond selectively either when a monkey is attending to a region of space and is about to fixate that region (Wurtz, Goldberg and Robinson 1980) or when it is attending to that region but is required to inhibit a saccade to the attended region. The data thus indicate that enhanced firing in the parietal lobe appears to be a marker for a process of covert attention that is prior to and can be independent of eye movements (as it appears without eye movements occurring). However, the pattern of data suggests that shifts of covert attention to a region of space naturally occur prior to the actual movement of the eyes and are only decoupled from overt eye movements when some other source of control (e.g. the frontal eye fields) intervenes to inhibit the eye movement.

Our knowledge about spatial attention is at present in a peculiar state. As indicated above, we have a great deal of knowledge about its physiological correlates and some excellent and sophisticated studies demonstrating it as a behavioural phenomenon. However, there is still little agreement about some of the basic properties of covert spatial attention. One issue is how the 'attentive region' is defined. Perhaps the most common view is that attention is like a 'spotlight' in which information within the spotlight region (presumably something like a circle or ellipse) is facilitated and/or information outside the spotlight is inhibited (e.g. Eriksen and Yeh 1985; LaBerge 1983). In some cases, the all-or-none metaphor of a spotlight is modified to there being a gradient of attention with a maximal value at the focus of attention (e.g. LaBerge and Brown 1989). In addition, the size of the area of the spotlight is thought by some to be under the control of the viewer like a 'zoom lens' (Eriksen and St James 1986). In still other views, attention is thought to be primarily based on object representations rather than spatial regions (Duncan 1984; Egly, Driver and Rafal 1994). We will not explore this issue in what follows but simply assume that attention can be allocated reasonably flexibly to some contiguous region of space. However, our treatment is compatible with an object-based view of attention as well.

A second issue is the **level of processing** that attention modulates. Some work suggests that spatial attention modulates relatively early 'perceptual' levels in the information stream (Hillyard *et al.* 1995) whereas other data indicate that such attention comes at a relatively late 'response selection' stage (Duncan 1980). A third issue is what attention does. A majority of the work has tacitly assumed that attention is an inhibition of input outside the attended region, an enhancement of information within the attended region, or both. However, some views of attention (e.g. Neisser 1967; Treisman and Gelade 1980; Ullman 1984) view attentional processing as a qualitatively different process than non-attended processing (e.g. combining visual features, executing serial 'visual routines', or performing 'analysis by synthesis'). For the most part, we will tacitly assume that covert spatial attention during reading merely serves a selection function.

We will return to these issues shortly. However, we wish to make a basic point when discussing covert attention in reading. Virtually all the studies carried out on covert spatial attention require the subject to maintain fixation while covertly moving spatial attention. This is a fairly unnatural situation, and thus one should exercise caution in generalising the findings from these studies to a dynamic task such as reading text. (These experiments also typically employ very simple visual displays, quite unlike text.) Moreover, these static paradigms do not naturally lead to exploring the issue of the functional significance (if any) of covert attention in a dynamic task such as reading (Fischer and Rayner 1993). Since the issue of the functional significance of covert attention in reading seems important, we would like to speculate a little about it before getting bogged down in the details of particular studies and paradigms.

As we indicated earlier, the eyes are moving about 4–5 times per second in reading and a majority of the words are fixated. Given that this overt attentional system is putting the fovea (the processor of fine detail) close to the region that is being processed, what would covert attention be plausibly needed for in reading? One possibility that we have mentioned earlier is that attention may help in the extraction of information about to be fixated because covert attentional shifts are likely to be more rapid than actual movements of the eyes. That is, if the reader finishes processing the fixated word (word *n*) early in a fixation, it would be functional to shift attention to the next word (*n* + 1) to allow efficient processing of that word prior to fixating it. The data of Wurtz *et al.* (1980), cited above, suggests that such attention shifts may be a natural precursor to many eye movements.

Another function of attention in reading could be related to the variability of saccadic programming. That is, the eyes do not necessarily go to where the brain has programmed them to go. In reading, it appears that the middle of a word appears to be the 'optimal location' for processing many words (O'Regan 1992). However, the eyes most frequently land between the beginning and the middle of a word (McConkie *et al.* 1988; Rayner 1979; Rayner, Sereno and Raney 1996), but the distribution of landing sites is in fact quite variable, with a non-negligible number of saccades landing on the spaces between words. The data are consistent with a model that assumes that (a) the reader attempts to fixate the middle of each word; (b) there is a bias to undershoot and land towards the beginning of the word; (c) the bias increases the further the 'launch site' of the saccade is from the target word; and (d) the variability increases the further the launch site is from the word (McConkie *et al.* 1988). This pattern of data suggests that readers may even fixate the 'wrong' word about 1–5 per cent of the time (i.e. not the one they intend to process). If so, then a major function of attention in a dynamic task like reading might be to 'correct' for these inaccuracies, whether large or small, and direct attention to the place on the page where the reader intended to fixate rather than to the actual fixation location.

Both of the above hypotheses – covert attention shifts being faster than eye movements and oculomotor noise – indicate why decoupling the centre of attention from the fixation point would be functional in a dynamic task such as reading. However, there is also the issue of the region that is attended to. In normal, single-spaced text, some of the letters in words above and below the line of text being read are in fact quite close to fixation and are often closer than some of the letters in the word that is fixated. If a major task of the reader on each fixation is to decode the currently fixated word (assuming no saccadic programming error), then inhibition of all other letters might be crucial to successful reading. Thus, a potentially important aspect of attention in reading might be the inhibition of information from words above and below the line of text currently being read.

Yet another possible function of attention in reading, related to the previous one, is the scheduling of information. In most languages, word order is crucial in understanding sentences. If attention were not deployed and if the decoding of words around fixation were done in parallel with words coming up to the 'sentence understander' in the order that they were decoded, then confusion could arise. For example, if word $n + 1$ was encoded before word n, then the reader might think word $n + 1$ occurred prior to word n. Or alternatively, if a word were encoded on one fixation and then re-encoded on the following fixation, the reader might think that the word appeared twice. Thus, spatial attention may plausibly play a crucial role in the 'scheduling' of information that is coming up to the central processor. That is, spatial attention may be the simplest mechanism that allows the spatial order of words on the printed page to be converted into the temporal order of the corresponding spoken discourse.

In summary, we have argued that in reading, the movement of the eyes probably does most of the work in selecting what information is to be processed at any given moment. As we shall argue shortly, visual acuity considerations sharply limit the region around fixation from which useful visual information can be extracted in reading. However, it appears that covert spatial attention may also play a considerable role in modulating how visual information is extracted from the printed page. As will become clear from our review below, we know quite a bit about the pattern of overt eye movements in reading but know considerably less about the role of covert attention.

Eye movements in reading: an overview

As we indicated above, a majority of the words in text are fixated as the eyes move across the printed page. We also indicated that what was fixated was closely related to what was being processed. We now will document these claims.

Some basic facts about fixations and saccades

The typical pattern of saccades across the printed page is from left to right (for English) with most words being fixated. However, as we indicated earlier, function words (which are frequent in the language and are often highly predictable) are often skipped. However, not all saccades in English are forward (i.e. left to right). For typical reading material, about 10–15 per cent of the saccades are **regressions** (i.e. go right to left). Most of these regressions are small (a character or two), but some are large and may go back to prior phrases or sentences. For the most part, readers are unaware of small regressive movements but are generally conscious of large regressions. In addition, of course, readers make large right to left **return sweep** saccades when they go from the end of one line to the beginning of the next. These sweeps are often complicated, as they may include an initial large saccade to about the third word on the line and then a smaller corrective saccade nearer to the beginning of the line. One interesting fact about reading connected discourse is that the first and last words on a line are often not fixated (Rayner 1978, 1998).

As mentioned earlier, invidual fixations are typically of the order of 200–300 ms. Individual saccades are typically about 5–9 characters. However, the variation in these measures is not random and tells us a great deal about the cognitive processes in reading. At present, however, there is considerable controversy about how to summarise the eye movement pattern in reading. Much of it revolves around the fact that words are not infrequently fixated more than once: Rayner *et al.* (1996), for example, found that 30 per cent of 5–9 letter words were fixated more than once, although these words were rarely fixated more than twice. The measures we prefer for analysing fixation durations are word-based and thus some additional definitions are needed.

One basic measure that we will use is the probability that a word is in fact ever fixated (or its complement, the probability that it is skipped). A second basic measure is the time spent on a word, given that it is fixated. The most commonly used measure is **gaze duration**, which is the sum of the durations of all fixations on a word before the reader fixates a subsequent word. That is, the gaze duration is the total time spent on a word on the **first pass** through that region of text. It does not include fixations on the word that occur as the result of regressing back to that word. Another commonly used measure is the **total time** on a word: the sum of the durations of all fixations on a word. For both measures, the means are computed only for those occasions when the reader fixates the word. That is, both the mean gaze duration and mean total time are averages conditional on the word being fixated.

There are also finer measures. One is the number of fixations on a word. Two other fixation measures are commonly used that may get at early processing on a word more directly than gaze duration. One is the mean **first fixation duration**, which averages the first fixation duration of multiple fixations and the only fixation duration if there is a single fixation. (Again, this measure is conditional on the word being fixated.) A related measure is the mean **single fixation duration**. This measures the mean fixation duration on a word, conditional on the word being fixated only once.

There is a close relation between eye behaviour and the text being processed

A major reason for introducing these measures is to document that eye behaviour is a sensitive function of the text being processed. For example, several studies show that there is a relationship between the frequency of a word in the language and the fixation time on a word (see Rayner and Sereno 1994 for a recent summary). (For most of the effects we will document, there are significant effects on both gaze duration and first fixation duration; to simplify matters, however, we will focus on gaze duration.) In natural language, of course, frequency is confounded with the length of a word – high frequency words tend to be short – but several experiments document that gaze durations are substantially shorter for high frequency words even when **word length** (i.e. the number of letters) is controlled (Inhoff and Rayner 1986; Rayner and Duffy 1986; Rayner *et al.* 1996). In contrast, the frequency of the word to the right of the fixated word does not influence fixation time (Henderson and Ferreira 1993; Rayner, Fischer and Pollatsek 1998). These findings are important for two reasons. First, they indicate that the text fixated is what is being processed. Second, it indicates that the information that is fixated (and presumably processed on that fixation) can influence the decision of when to move the eyes off a word. Thus, there appears to be a tight relationship between (a) what is fixated, (b) what is processed, and (c) the control of the eyes in reading. A caveat is in order, however. Logically, a demonstration of a relationship between the frequency of the word fixated and fixation time on the word only allows one to conclude that there is a close relationship between the text fixated and what is actually being processed on some fixations.

Word frequency is not the only variable that has an 'on-line' effect on the movement of the eyes through the text. Another variable that has been shown to have a major effect is the predictability of a word from sentence context. Typically, **predictability** is assessed by showing a group of subjects the sentence prior to the target word and asking them to predict the word that follows. Thus, this measure assesses how well the prior sentence context predicts the word (a) given time to make a conscious prediction and (b) without any physical information about the target word. Even though these two conditions are clearly different from those in reading text, predictability measured this way is a useful predictor of what occurs in reading. First, a more predictable word is skipped significantly more often than a less predictable word, even when the words are matched on frequency and length (Balota, Pollatsek and Rayner 1985; Ehrlich and Rayner 1981; Rayner and Well 1996). Moreover, gaze durations are shorter on predictable words than on unpredictable words on those occasions when they are fixated (Balota *et al.* 1985; Ehrlich and Rayner 1981; Zola 1984; Rayner and Well 1996).

Two other findings about the relationship of text characteristics to eye movements are worth noting. One is the effect of syntactic 'garden path' sentences (Frazier and Rayner 1982). That is, when readers encounter a sentence such as 'Since Jay always jogs a mile seems like a short distance to him', they experience difficulty immediately when they encounter the disambiguating word 'seems'. That is, sentences such as this 'lead readers down the garden path': readers initially misparse the sentence and, in this case, make 'a mile' the object of 'jogs'. However, when 'seems' is encountered, there is no way to incorporate it into that sentence structure and so the reader needs to reanalyse the sentence. Two points are worth noting about these garden path effects. First, the effects are often quite immediate, with lengthened fixation times on the disambiguating word and the word after, and regressions are often made back to earlier places in the sentences from one of these two locations. This indicates that the parsing mechanism is operating in fairly close temporal relation to the movement of the eyes. Second, the attempts to 'repair' the damage are relatively complex: sometimes the regressions go back to the beginning of the sentence, sometimes the reader maintains fixation at or near the disambiguating word and then goes on, and sometimes there are other, more complex patterns (Frazier and Rayner 1982).

Not all text processing operations necessarily have an immediate impact on eye movements, however. For example, the assignment of an antecedent to a pronoun usually appears to be delayed. The typical experimental paradigm for studying this phenomenon involves using gender stereotypical professions such as 'doctor' and 'secretary' and then placing either a 'he' or 'she' in the text that has to refer back to 'the doctor' or 'the secretary'. Delays are found when there is a mismatch (e.g. 'he' refers to 'the secretary'), but in most cases, this delay is not while fixating the region around the pronoun but somewhere in the region of the next 2–3 words (Ehrlich and Rayner 1983). This indicates that assignment of pronouns is probably not immediate and thus that the eyes are not waiting for all the possible linguistic operations to be carried out relevant to the fixated word before moving on.

To summarise, we have argued that there is a reasonably close relationship between the words in the text and the pattern of eye movements. In particular, how long a word is fixated and whether it is fixated or skipped is a function of its frequency in the language and its predictability from prior sentence context. Syntactic manipulations also influence the pattern of eye movements, as do 'higher-order' processing variables such as pronoun assignment. These findings all indicate that the eye movement system is an important part of the attentional system in reading: readers are fixating the word they are processing on an appreciable number of fixations.

Assessing covert attention in reading

None of the above data forces one to conclude that readers are **only** processing the fixated word, however. In fact, there is a large body of data indicating that this cannot be the case. One piece of data we have already presented argues strongly against that conclusion: more predictable words are skipped more often than unpredictable words. If skipping were merely a matter of guessing what the next word was, then it would not matter whether the word in the location of a pre-dictable word was that word or some other word. However, the data indicate that the skipping probability is dependent on the predictable word actually being in its expected location (Balota *et al.* 1985). In addition, when words are skipped, the duration of the fixation prior to the skip is inflated, indicating that processing of the skipped word is occurring on the prior fixation (Hogaboam 1983; Pollatsek, Rayner and Balota 1986). Hence, the skipping data indicate that the word to the right of fixation is being processed on at least some fixations, as its identity influences whether it is skipped or not. But is this the only occasion on which words other than the fixated word are processed?

A technique that has been developed to determine what information is actually processed by the reader on each fixation is the **moving window** paradigm (McConkie and Rayner 1975) and variants (Rayner 1975; Rayner and Bertera 1979). In a moving window experiment, the reader's eye movements are moni-tored and text is displayed on a CRT screen contingent on where the reader is fixating. Thus, for example, the experiment can be set up so that only the fixated word is normal and all other letters in the text are replaced by Xs (see Figure 8.1). Whenever the reader makes a saccade (either forwards or backwards), the display is changed and the new word that is fixated is now normal and all other words

The links between vision and cognition are critical

ONE-WORD WINDOW

Xxx xxxxx **between** xxxxxx xxx xxxxxxxxx xxx xxxxxxxx.
          *

Xxx xxxxx xxxxxxx **vision** xxx xxxxxxxxx xxx xxxxxxxx.
                   *

Xxx xxxxx xxxxxxx xxxxxx xxx **cognition** xxx xxxxxxxx.
                            *

TWO-WORD WINDOW (To right)

Xxx xxxxx **between vision** xxx xxxxxxxxx xxx xxxxxxxx.
          *

Xxx xxxxx xxxxxxx **vision and** xxxxxxxxx xxx xxxxxxxx.
                   *

Xxx xxxxx xxxxxxx xxxxxx xxx **cognition are** xxxxxxxx.
                            *

14-LETTER LEFT 14-LETTER RIGHT WINDOW (14L, 14R)

The links between vision anx xxxxxxxxx xxx xxxxxxxx.
          *

Xxx **xxxxs between vision and cognitiox** xxx xxxxxxxx.
                   *

Xxx xxxxx xxxxxxx **xxxion and cognition are criticax.**
                            *

4-LETTER LEFT 14-LETTER RIGHT WINDOW (4L, 14R)

Xxx xxxxx xxxxxxx **vision and cognitiox** xxx xxxxxxxx.
                   *

14-letter left 4-letter right window (14L, 4R)

Xxx **xxxxs between vision** anx xxxxxxxxx xxx xxxxxxxx.
                   *

Figure 8.1 Examples of moving window displays.

Note

The top line represents a line of text and the lines below represent how the line would be displayed in various window conditions. The asterisk below each line represents where the reader is fixating on each line and is not part of the experimental display. For the top three window conditions, we illustrate how the window changes through three successive fixations. For the bottom two conditions, we merely indicate what the window would be on the second of those three fixations.

(including the previously fixated one) are changed to Xs. In these experiments, a key manipulation is the size of the window – it can be defined either in terms of words, as in the above example, or in terms of the number of character spaces to the left and right of fixation. The material outside the window can also be manipulated – the letters in the text could not only be replaced by Xs, but by other letters or meaningless patterns, and the spaces between words could be preserved or mutilated.

Space does not permit a full summary of the findings of these experiments (see Rayner and Pollatsek 1989; Rayner 1993, 1995, 1998 for summaries), so we will confine ourselves to discussing the size of the window and only conditions in which the spaces between words outside the window are preserved as in Figure 8.1. The first question that one can ask using this technique is what the region is from which readers extract useful information (the **perceptual span**). This is measured by finding the smallest moving window such that reading is normal (i.e. normal speed and comprehension). For example, if reading were normal given the one word window shown in Figure 8.1, one could conclude that no useful information was extracted from outside the fixated word and that the perceptual span was one word. However, in such a one word window condition, reading rate declines by about 40 per cent, although comprehension is unaffected (Rayner *et al.* 1982). This indicates that subjects are processing more than one word on at least some fixations. In fact, McConkie and Rayner (1975) found that reading was normal when the window extended only 14–15 character spaces in both directions from fixation (the third window condition illustrated in Figure 8.1). Thus, the region from which useful information is extracted is relatively small, but extends beyond the fixated word.

McConkie and Rayner's findings place an upper bound on the size of the region from which useful information is extracted in normal reading. This region is most probably delimited by considerations of acuity, however, rather than by strategic considerations in reading. For example, Rayner and Bertera (1979) developed a **moving mask** paradigm which was the inverse of the moving window paradigm. In these experiments, subjects attempted to read when the characters around fixation were changed to a meaningless 'mask' and the outer portion of the text was left normal. In these conditions, when the central 13–17 characters around fixation were masked, subjects were virtually unable to extract any information about the text. In addition, in studies in which individual isolated words are placed in the parafovea with the closest letter 5 degrees to the right or left of fixation (the same visual angle as 15 character spaces in these experiments), subjects extracted no useful information about the letters in the words (Rayner, McConkie and Ehrlich 1978).

Thus, for reading in the conditions studied in these experiments, the outer limit from which information can be extracted appears to be about 15 character spaces or 5 degrees of visual angle. This figure may differ somewhat, depending on the size of the text, the font, or the writing system used (e.g. English vs Greek vs Hebrew vs Chinese). However, this figure is probably a good guide to what the outer limits of acuity are for textual information in English.

But is the reader really attending to all the information within this window? A series of follow-up experiments indicate that the actual region from which information is extracted is significantly narrower. First, it appears that no useful information is being extracted outside the line of text being read. Pollatsek *et al.* (1993) conducted a moving window experiment in which subjects read 15-line passages and all text below the line being read was mutilated. The text below the line being read was replaced either with (a) letters visually similar to those in the text, (b) letters visually different from those in the text, (c) Xs, or (d) text from a different passage. They found that the reading speed was essentially the same in all conditions as when there was no window (i.e. the 15-line passage was continually visible during reading). This indicates that information below the line is not processed during reading (see also Inhoff and Briihl 1991; Inhoff and Topolski 1992). We assume that if information below the line (which has not yet been processed) is not attended in reading, then information above the line (which has already been processed) is not attended either. Pollatsek *et al.* also found that information below the line was of little relevance in a visual search task involving the same materials when subjects were instructed to scan the lines from left to right as in reading. (For visual search involving downward vertical scanning patterns, information below fixation becomes relevant (Prinz 1984).) Thus, it appears that a narrowing of the attentional window to the line being processed is not limited to reading but may also occur in any task that calls for a scanning of a line of text or text-like characters (e.g. mathematical formulae).

Another set of studies investigated whether the window of attention is symmetric around fixation. McConkie and Rayner (1976) found that it was not, and that reading was unaffected when the moving window extended 4 characters to the left of fixation and 14 characters to the right of fixation (4L,14R), whereas reading was significantly disrupted for a (14L,4R) window (see Figure 8.1). This finding was extended by Rayner, Well and Pollatsek (1980) and Rayner *et al.* (1982). They showed that when the window was not restricted to the right that the reader was extracting no useful information to the left of the beginning of the fixated word and that they were extracting no information beyond word $N + 2$ (i.e. the word two to the right of the fixated word). Thus, during a fixation, readers appear to be merely attending to words N, $N + 1$, and $N + 2$, although they are probably not attending to all three words on all fixations.

This asymmetric pattern of attention, with a bias to the right visual field, is related to the direction of scanning through the text rather than to language specialisation of the left cortical hemisphere. Pollatsek *et al.* (1981) presented asymmetric windows to native Hebrew speakers reading either Hebrew or English. When they read Hebrew, they read normally with a (14L,4R) window, but were slowed down by a (4L,14R) window. When reading English, they showed the same pattern as native English speakers.

To summarise, moving window studies show that the useful information extracted from text is limited both by the pattern of eye movements and covert attention. That is, it appears that the region of useful information is limited to about 15 character spaces by acuity considerations of the visual system to the right and left of fixation. (Acuity falls off somewhat more steeply above and below fixation.) However, covert attention also influences what is processed: it appears that no information outside the current line of text is attended to nor is information to the left of the fixated word in a language that is read from left to right. It is interesting in this regard that one dyslexic reader that we studied (Rayner *et al.* 1989) was affected by window restrictions differently from normal readers. When the material outside the window was Xs, he exhibited better reading in the two word window condition (see Figure 8.1) than when the window was bigger or when reading normal text. However, when the 'words' outside the window were comprised of random letters that thus looked much more like text, constricting the window did not help him. It appeared that he had a selective attention deficit and did not naturally attend to a narrow region around the fixation point. The presence of a clearly demarcated area of text helped him to focus his attention. We should emphasise that he is the only such subject we have encountered, so that these kinds of selective attention problems are likely to be rare.

Another finding of moving window experiments and related experiments is important. Above we indicated that words to the right of fixation are sometimes processed completely and are skipped. However, information to the right of the fixated word serves another important function: it is sometimes incompletely processed, but this incomplete processing speeds processing when the word is fixated later. Such preview benefit has been shown in moving window studies, but it has been studied more carefully in a paradigm that is a variant of the moving window technique known as the **boundary paradigm** (Rayner 1975). In this technique, the display change affects only a single word which may be mutilated or distorted in a number of ways prior to the subject fixating that word. The distorted or mutilated **preview** of the word is then transformed to the **base word**: the word that belongs in the text when the subject's eyes cross an invisible boundary usually defined at or near the space preceding the target word (see Figure 8.2). In our example, the target word is **cake** but a number of possible preview words could be in the location of the target word before it is fixated. For example, the preview word could be the target word, a letter string that contains many of the same letters, a word that is semantically similar, or a word that is very different. More specifically, **preview benefit** is assessed by examining how much shorter fixation times are (usually gaze durations) when there is a similar preview in the target location than in a baseline condition in which there is a different preview (something like a very dissimilar word or a string of random letters).

The basic finding of these studies is that the preview benefit on the target word is greatest when the preview word is identical to the target, but that almost as much preview benefit occurs when the preview is visually similar (**cahc** in our example). (Several experiments indicate that what is crucial is that the preview and target share the first two or three letters.) This 'visual similarity effect', though, is at the level of abstract letters rather than visual features, because changing the case of all the letters from preview to target does not change the size of the preview benefit (McConkie and Zola 1979; Rayner, McConkie and Zola

Fixation N:

The baker rushed the wedding
cookies and <u>cahc</u> to the party.
    * |

Fixation N + 1:

The baker rushed the wedding
cookies and <u>cake</u> to the party.
    | *

Figure 8.2 An example of a boundary experiment.

Notes

The boundary (invisible to the subject) is indicated by the vertical line under the *d* in *and*. (The fixation points are indicated by asterisks and the target location by underlining.) Before the eyes cross the boundary, the preview string (*cahc* in the figure) is displayed. After crossing the boundary, the target word (*cake* in the example) is displayed. In the identical preview condition, *cake* would be the preview as well. Other types of preview conditions could be a semantically similar word (*pies*), a dissimilar word (*bomb*), or a random letter string (*tcib*). The data indicate that there is no difference between the latter three conditions.

1980). Sound coding is involved in preview benefit as well, as a homophone preview provides more benefit than another word that is equated with the homophone on visual similarity to the target word (Pollatsek *et al.* 1992; see also Henderson *et al.* 1995, for other evidence of sound coding). In contrast, there is no preview benefit when the preview is merely semantically similar (Rayner, Balota and Pollatsek 1986), suggesting that partial semantic features are not activated by the preview when the word is subsequently fixated.

Attention modulates the size of preview benefit: preview benefit depends on the difficulty of processing information in the fovea. This has been most directly shown by Henderson and Ferreira (1990) (see also Inhoff *et al.* 1989; Kennison and Clifton 1995) who manipulated both whether there was a preview of a target word or not and the difficulty of the prior word in the text. They found almost no benefit from a preview of the target word when the preceding word was low frequency, but found a normal preview benefit when the preceding word was high frequency. Rayner (1986) observed a similar effect with children. When fourth graders read age-appropriate material, their perceptual span was virtually the same as adults, whereas when they read material that was too difficult for them, their perceptual span was little more than a word, indicating that less information could be extracted from the parafovea when foveal processing was difficult.

One final issue concerns the use of parafoveal information. Specifically, Underwood and colleagues (see Everatt and Underwood 1992; Hyönä, Niemi and

Underwood 1989; Underwood, Bloomfield and Clews 1988; Underwood, Clews and Everatt 1990) have argued that semantic information from a parafoveal word influences where the reader's initial fixation lands in a word. They reported that the eyes move further into word $N + 1$ when the informative portion is located at the end rather than the beginning of the word. In this situation, presumably the reader's attention would move from the currently fixated word to the next word and assess where the informative information is located. However, neither Rayner and Morris (1992) nor Hyönä (1995) replicated the effect (and the effect was often either very small or not present in the experiments reported by Underwood and colleagues). At this point, it seems prudent to assume that semantic pre-processing of this sort does not occur.

To summarise our brief discussion of preview benefit, it appears that information from words to the right of fixation is often used as a preview that facilitates processing of the word when it is later fixated. To date, there is no evidence that semantic information is involved in integration of information across fixations, but it appears that both abstract letter codes and phonological codes are involved. Moreover, attention modulates the amount of information that is extracted from the parafovea.

The above studies delimit some aspects of attention during reading, but the picture is incomplete. First, they tell us that subjects sometimes attend to three words on a fixation (particularly if they are short) and that the difficulty of the foveal word modulates how much the reader attends to in the parafovea. But there may be other factors that modulate attention. Second, they tell us little about the time course of attention during a fixation. Because a fixation is relatively long (200–300 ms), it is plausible that attention could shift at least once within a fixation. The physiological data we discussed earlier suggested that, in static situations, a covert attentional shift to the region about to be fixated occurs prior to the eye movement. Does attention in fact shift rightward during a fixation in reading? If it does, how does it do so? Does it shift from word to word? Letter to letter? As we will see, we have very incomplete answers to these and other basic questions.

Does attention shift from letter to letter?

We have no clear evidence to answer this question when people read text. Slowiaczek and Rayner (1987) attempted to answer the question by sequentially masking letters at the rate of 10 ms per letter over the first 50 ms of a fixation. If people serially read letter by letter, then such a mask would not be disruptive if the characteristics of the mask coincided with the subjects' scanning rates and patterns. They found evidence for disruption, suggesting that subjects were not processing letters serially. However, this could have been because the timing or location of the masks did not coincide with the subjects' covert scanning patterns.

Most of the evidence from experiments where people process a single word at fixation, however, is consonant with Slowiaczek and Rayner's conclusion and indicates that all the letters in a word are read in parallel, at least for reasonably short words. Most notably, the well-known 'word superiority effect' (Reicher 1969) – the fact that letters in words can be identified more accurately than letters in isolation – argues for parallel processing of letters in words (see Carr and Pollatsek 1985 for a review of this literature and McClelland and Rumelhart 1981, and Paap *et al.* 1982, for two different models of parallel processing of letters within words). This conclusion is buttressed by evidence from LaBerge (1983), who has shown (using a probe technique similar to the Posner cueing paradigm discussed earlier) that the spotlight of attention during word processing is the entire word.

These experiments have all been carried out on relatively short words seen in isolation in a static viewing situation. Thus, we have little idea about the limits of parallel processing of letters within words and how letter information is integrated to identify words in a dynamic viewing situation. We have previously noted that words in text are not infrequently fixated twice. Thus, in some gross sense, words are commonly processed serially. However, we have little idea about how this process occurs. One possibility is that an earlier chunk of a longer word (such as its initial morpheme) may be processed on the first fixation and the rest of the word may be processed on the second fixation. Another possibility, however, is that the processing on each fixation is completely in parallel. That is, on the first fixation (which would typically be on the first half of the word), the reader may attempt to process all the letters in a word and may narrow down identification to a candidate set. The reader might then refixate the word towards the end, and again attempt to process the entire word and use that information to decide among the candidate set.

Do readers shift attention from word to word during a fixation?

The above evidence suggests that letters in words are processed in parallel and that readers do not serially scan through the letters using a shifting window of attention. However, there is little direct evidence to indicate whether words can be processed in parallel or not in reading. Our data on skipping strongly suggest that more than one word can be processed on a fixation, but that does not necessarily mean that two or more words are processed in parallel as fixations last 200–300 ms. The reader could first process the fixated word (word N), shift attention to word $N + 1$ and process it, and if those two words are processed rapidly, possibly shift attention again and process word $N + 2$. We have no direct evidence on this issue in reading, but there is some indication from a static paradigm that words cannot be processed in parallel. If a subject sees a display of 1–4 words arrayed around the fixation point and is asked to judge whether one of the words is an exemplar of some semantic category (e.g. animals), the time to respond is a serial function of the number of words in the display with a slope suggesting that it takes roughly 200–250 ms to examine each word to determine whether it is an animal or not (Karlin and Bower 1976; Pollatsek, Well and Gott 1978).

These experiments are certainly not definitive, but they suggest that it is difficult if not impossible to process unrelated words in parallel in a static situation. However, a different picture might be obtained with related words (as in text) and in a more dynamic viewing situation. For the sake of simplifying future discussion, though, we will tacitly assume that (a) letters in words are processed in parallel, and (b) attention moves sequentially across the page, word by word.

Level of attention in reading?

None of the above discussion directly speaks to the issue of the level at which attention is operating in reading and what functions it is serving. The simplest possibility is that spatial attention in reading serves mainly a filtering function: filtering out letters that do not belong to the word that the reader is currently trying to identify. A second possibility is that attention allows special processing routines to be directed at the attended word that aid in the parallel integration of the component letters. Obviously, these two possibilities are not mutually exclusive and the two mechanisms could be working together. The first possibility, however, suggests a relatively 'low level' filtering operation, whereas the second suggests a somewhat higher level of attentional processing.

Unfortunately, the present data do not allow us to draw any firm conclusions about how covert spatial attention operates in reading. The fact that irrelevant information to the left of the fixated word or below the line has no effect on reading, despite being potentially available in terms of visual acuity, suggests that it is filtered out at a relatively early level. This conclusion is buttressed by the finding mentioned earlier that in the experiment manipulating information below the line, reading was the same when the material was irrelevant text as it was when it was meaningless combinations of letters. If the material below the line were processed up to a relatively high level (such as words being identified) and then filtered out, one would expect more interference when the material below the line was irrelevant text. However, a similar moving window experiment has not been conducted on material to the left of fixation, so that material on the currently fixated line may be excluded by a somewhat higher-order process.

In fact, one piece of data suggests that material to the left of fixation may not always be irrelevant. The experiment (Balota *et al.* 1985) used the **boundary** technique, discussed above. In this experiment, the target word was not only a predictable word like **cake** in Figure 8.2, but it could also be a sensible but unpredictable word such as **pies**. Balota *et al.* found that when the highly predictable word, **cake**, was in the parafovea, it was skipped about 11 per cent of the time. When the reader skipped **cake** and **cake** was not subsequently altered, there were no regressions back to that region. However, when the preview word **cake** was changed to the target word **pies**, readers regressed back to it about 5 per cent of the time, or almost half the time that they skipped it. This indicates that the change was registered at least some of the time and thus that information to the left of fixation affects reading some of the time (Binder, Pollatsek and Rayner in press). Perhaps the moving window techniques mentioned earlier were not sensitive enough to pick up these small effects.

In this section, we have speculated on the role of attention in reading. We have focused on normal, skilled reading. However, we suspect that attentional processes operate in most dyslexic readers in the same manner as they operate in skilled readers. We believe, as will be documented in the next section, that for most dyslexic readers, the difficulties they have are associated with processing the word that they are currently fixating. While a few readers may have various types of attentional or perceptual deficits that result in reading problems, we suspect that most developmental dyslexic readers' problems are related to linguistic deficits (see Rayner and Pollatsek 1989). In the next section, we turn to the relationship between attention and eye movements in dyslexic readers.

Attention, eye movements and dyslexia

Recently, a number of researchers have made arguments to the effect that dyslexia is related to attentional deficits. Because these positions are discussed in detail in other chapters in this volume, we will not comment on them specifically. However, it is often suggested (see Farmer and Klein 1995) that attentional deficits have obvious implications for the eye movements of dyslexic readers. Thus, we will briefly discuss the characteristics of developmental dyslexic readers' eye movements.

It is a well-known fact that developmental dyslexics' eye movements while reading text are quantitatively different from those of normal readers (Rayner 1978, 1985, 1998): in comparison to normal readers, dyslexic readers' average fixation durations are longer, their average saccade length is shorter, and the average number of regressions is much larger. But such differences could be attributed to a number of different causal factors including visual persistence from prior fixations (as suggested by Farmer and Klein 1995; see p. 196 for further detail), difficulty processing the words in the text, and faulty control of the saccadic eye movement system. The point is that we cannot tell merely by examining the eye movements of dyslexic readers while they read. With respect to this latter issue, Pavlidis (1981, 1985) examined the eye movements of dyslexic readers when they were engaged in a non-reading sequential processing task. He appropriately noted that any study based on reading experiments alone would be open to a number of interpretations, and he reasoned that if the cause of dyslexia is due to an attentional or sequential processing disability, one would expect that such a disability would manifest itself not only in reading, but in other tasks in which attention or sequencing and eye movements are important. Thus he asked normal and dyslexic readers to maintain fixation on a target that jumped sequentially either from left to right or right to left across the screen. Pavlidis' primary finding was that when the target moved from left to right, dyslexic readers made significantly more right to left saccades than did the normal readers. He concluded that erratic eye movements (moving from right to left when the task calls for movements from left to right) are characteristic of dyslexic readers.

Pavlidis' results are consistent with some case studies (Ciuffreda *et al.* 1976; Pirozzolo and Rayner 1978; Zangwill and Blakemore 1972) in which dyslexic readers have been described as having a tendency to move their eyes from right to left during reading. However, on the basis of Pavlidis' (1981) original report, a number of attempts were undertaken to confirm his findings. None of these studies (Black *et al.* 1984; Brown *et al.* 1983; Olson, Kliegl and Davidson 1983; Stanley, Smith and Howell 1983) were able to replicate Pavlidis' findings: there was no indication in any of these studies that dyslexic readers differed from normal readers in the frequency of regressions when moving their eyes from left to right in Pavlidis' task. Other studies (Adler-Grinberg and Stark 1978; Eskenazi and Diamond 1983; Stanley *et al.* 1983) have also failed to find differences between normal and dyslexic readers' eye movement patterns in a visual search task.

Perhaps the easiest way to account for the discrepant findings between Pavlidis' research and the failures to replicate his work is that Pavlidis' subject-selection process somehow resulted in a larger number of dyslexic readers with visual deficits in his subject sample than is typical of the population of dyslexics (Pollatsek 1983; Rayner 1985). Some of the studies that generally failed to replicate Pavlidis' findings reported that a few of the subjects yielded results like those reported by Pavlidis.

We turn now to a hypothesis of Farmer and Klein (1995) regarding eye fixations of dyslexic readers. They proposed that dyslexics may have visual persistence from a prior fixation interfering with processing of the current fixation. This implies that (1) dyslexics' eye fixations when reading text may be longer than for normal readers, or (2) they make more fixations than normal readers. As we have noted, this is indeed true, but the reason for this is not at all clear and could be due to a number of factors. When dyslexic readers are given reading-age appropriate reading material, their eye movement characteristics do not differ from normal readers of that age (Pirozzolo 1979), whereas when normal readers are given text that is too difficult, their eye movement characteristics look very much like those of dyslexic readers (Rayner 1986). Furthermore, when dyslexic readers' eye movements are compared to those of reading-age control subjects, their average fixation durations and eye movement characteristics do not differ (Hyönä and Olson 1994, 1995). Finally, Hyönä and Olson found that the fixation durations of dyslexics and normal readers in visual search do not differ. If visual persistence (or some other low-level visual factor) were the problem, one would expect dyslexics' eye movement patterns to be different from normal readers regardless of the difficulty of the text. Thus, the most likely explanation for the majority of dyslexic readers' longer fixation durations when reading is that they are having difficulty processing individual words.

Farmer and Klein (1995) also suggested that dyslexic readers may process less parafoveal information on each eye fixation than normal readers. On this issue, there are some relevant data using the eye-contingent moving window paradigm. As we noted earlier, reading speed increases as the size of the window increases. This increase is the result both of shorter fixations and fewer fixations. Rayner *et al.* (1989) compared three dyslexic readers in the moving window paradigm with some normal readers. Figure 8.3 shows the reading rate as a function of window size for two of the dyslexic readers and the controls (the third dyslexic reader was discussed earlier and will be discussed further on p. 198). Although the dyslexic

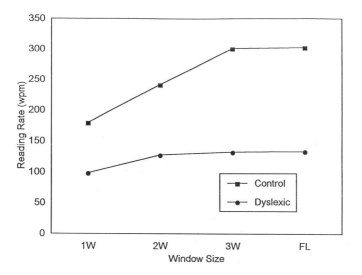

Figure 8.3   The effect of window size on reading rate for normal and dyslexic readers.

Notes

1W = 1 word;
2W = 2 words;
3W = 3 words;
FL = full line.

readers reached asymptote in reading rate with a two-word window whereas the normal readers did not reach asymptote until the window was three words, the general pattern is quite similar. These data thus indicate that the perceptual span of the dyslexic readers might be a bit smaller than that of normal readers; however, they do not necessarily mean that the cause of their reading difficulties is a 'parafoveal processing deficit'. In particular, as we noted earlier, when the fixated word is difficult to process readers obtain less parafoveal information than when the fixated word is easy to process (Rayner 1986; Henderson and Ferreira 1990). In other words, processing difficulty associated with the fixated word shrinks the size of the perceptual span.

These data lead us to believe that while the perceptual span may be somewhat smaller for dyslexic readers than for skilled readers, it is not because they process parafoveal information less effectively than normal readers, but rather it is due to the difficulty they are having processing the fixated word (see Rayner, Pollatsek and Bilsky 1995). Geiger and Lettvin (1987), however, proposed that the cause of dyslexia is that dyslexic readers process parafoveal information **more** effectively than normal readers; they suggested that dyslexics' efficient parafoveal processing interferes with foveal processing, leading to their reading problem. Indeed, Geiger, Lettvin and Fahle (1994) argued that dyslexic readers can markedly increase their reading ability by cutting a small window in an index card and moving the window across the text, reading the material inside the window.

However, there is considerable controversy concerning the basic result that dyslexic readers process parafoveal information more effectively than normal readers. Whereas Perry *et al.* (1989) reported results consistent with Geiger and Lettvin, others (Goolkasian and King 1990; Klein *et al.* 1990; Slaghuis, Lovegrove and Freestun 1992) were unable to replicate the main finding.

Finally, the third dyslexic subject reported by Rayner *et al.* (1989), who we commented on earlier, showed characteristics that are somewhat like those of Geiger and Lettvin's subjects: he could identify parafoveal words and letters better than normal readers; and, when reading with a moving window, he read better with a small window than with a large window, indicating that he has a selective attention deficit which makes it difficult for him to focus attention on the fixated word. However, as we noted earlier, we believe that he is very atypical of dyslexic readers.

An attempted synthesis and a model of eye movements in reading

We have attempted so far to summarise what is known about attention and eye movements in reading. In this last section, we will attempt to outline a model of eye movement control of reading. This model grows out of a model by Morrison (1984) that was influenced by the physiological work Wurtz *et al.* (1980) discussed earlier. A key assumption of the model is that words are identified one at a time with an attentional spotlight moving sequentially from word to word, with the signal to shift attention being the act of identifying the attended word (lexical access). We have earlier tried to argue that such an assumption is reasonable although certainly not forced by any existing data. A second key assumption of Morrison's model is that the shift of attention is the occasion for a programme being laid down to execute an eye movement to the next word (word $N + 1$).

These two assumptions correctly predict that fixation times will be influenced by word frequency, predictability and other variables that affect lexical access, but incorrectly predict (without further modification) that each word in the text will be fixated. Accordingly, Morrison used Becker and Jurgens' (1979) data from a simpler paradigm to make a critical assumption: eye movements can be programmed in parallel. Specifically, Morrison assumed that a later eye movement programme can cancel an earlier eye movement programme if the later programme is laid down soon enough after the earlier one. On the other hand, if the later programme is laid down after this 'critical period', both programmes are executed. This assumption predicts some important facts about word skipping in an elegant way. When processing of word N is finished, attention moves to word $N + 1$ and an eye movement programme is laid down to execute a saccade to word $N + 1$. However, if word $N + 1$ is short, frequent in the language, and/or predictable, processing of it will often be rapid so that attention will quickly shift to word $N + 2$, together with a programme to execute a saccade to word $N + 2$. Thus, Morrison's model correctly predicts that short, frequent and predictable words tend to be skipped.

This verbal model appears to be a good general framework for constructing a theory of eye movement control in reading. However, it has some problems. One is that it assumes that eye movements in reading are completely driven by lexical access. The work we reviewed on syntax and pronoun assignment argues that this assumption is oversimplified. However, in what follows, we will ignore effects due to processes such as these. Our rationale is twofold. First, our knowledge of how sentences are parsed and how text representations are constructed is very sketchy. Given that, it seems foolhardy to try to account for all such effects in any detail. Second, when multiple regression analyses are performed on fixation durations in reading, lexical variables account for a large percentage of the variance (Just and Carpenter 1980), indicating that a lexically driven model may account for what happens on most fixations. In fact, all of the higher-order effects we documented are effects of disruption (e.g. 'garden path' effects, difficulty in assigning antecedents to pronouns).

We think it is a reasonable hypothesis that the adaptation of Morrison's model that we propose below might be the 'normal' mode of eye control in reading and that higher-order influences only come into play when the reader is in a state of confusion. Then, the normal process is halted, the confusion repaired somehow, and normal processing resumed. As indicated above, the processes by which readers attempt to 'repair the damage' in garden path sentences are complex and variable. Thus, we have only attempted to model sentences in which readers do not regress backward beyond the fixated word. We are thus tacitly assuming that most interword regressions are due to confusions from attempting to build syntactic and text structures.

A second problem with Morrison's model is that it does not account for the 'foveal difficulty' effect discussed above: that less information is processed in the parafovea when the foveal material is difficult. Morrison's model predicts no such effect because it posits that attention goes to word $N + 1$ whenever word N is lexically processed. The time spent processing word $N + 1$ is thus the lag between the attention shift and the actual execution of the saccade, which will be independent of the difficulty of processing word N. Thus one needs to uncouple the attention shift from the saccadic programme if one is to explain the data. (This is unfortunate because this uncoupling loses some of the elegant simplicity of Morrison's model.)

Another limitation of Morrison's model is that it does not attempt to deal with the details of fixations within words. It makes no explicit statement about where fixations are directed in words nor does it acknowledge that words can be fixated more than once. Whereas we will attempt to explain refixations within words (see below), we will not attempt here to deal with the issue of where fixations land in words. We assume that the model of McConkie *et al.* (1988) discussed earlier is essentially correct: (a) readers programme the fixation to the middle of a word; but (b) there is a bias to undershoot the middle that increases as the launch site gets further from the word; and (c) random error also increases as the 'launch site' of the saccade gets further from the word. As we indicated earlier, a consequence of this is that the word that the reader intends to fixate is not always the word that is fixated. In our modelling efforts, we assume that the reader always lands on the word to which the saccade is programmed and hope that this is only a minor error.

Towards a model of reading

In our modelling efforts (Reichle *et al.* 1998), we have preserved the basic concept of Morrison's model. That is, we assume (1) readers attend to only one word at a time and (2) the signal to shift attention to the next word is lexical access of the attended word. However, we have complicated the model by postulating a **familiarity check** process, f, prior to lexical access, which is the signal to programme an eye movement. The rationale for this process is that the reader might not want to wait until lexical access is complete before deciding to move the eyes because eye movement latencies are relatively long (150–175 ms), even for very simple stimuli (Rayner *et al.* 1983). Thus, using a prior signal that indicates that lexical access is imminent (with high probability) might make for more efficient reading. We envision this familiarity stage to be related to lexical access and its completion may be triggered when the level of total excitation in the lexicon exceeds a threshold. (This idea resembles the 'compound cue' model that Ratcliff and McKoon (1988) used to explain lexical decisions and recognition judgements.)

   We postulate that both the lexical access stage (which controls attention shifts) and the familiarity check stage (which controls eye movement programming) are decreasing linear functions of the log of the frequency of a word in the language, and that the difference between them, l, is also a decreasing linear function of log frequency. The latter assumption allows us to account for the foveal difficulty effect: as the difference between the initiation of the eye movement programme and the attention shift increases, the reader spends more time processing the foveal word after the eye movement programme has been laid down and thus there is less preview benefit. We modelled the assumption of parallel eye movement programming by assuming that there are two stages in the eye movement programme: an initial labile stage m, in which a subsequent programme can cancel it and a later non-labile stage, M, which cannot be cancelled. We also added two assumptions about how predictability influences lexical access time and familiarity check time. First, we assumed that both these times were affected by p, where p is the probability that a word could be predicted from the prior sentence context. We obtained the p values by having a group of subjects – other than the readers – predict the words based on the prior sentence context; thus, these p values were not free parameters of the model. Second, we assumed that predictability affected the familiarity check and lexical access stages somewhat differently because we thought that the familiarity check stage was 'lower level' and would thus be less affected by context. To implement this intuition, we assumed that l was multiplied by $(1-p)$, but that f was only multiplied by $(1-0.5p)$. These functions relating predictability to processing time are admittedly crude, but were made in order to reduce the number of free parameters in the model.

Table 8.1 Observed and predicted values of gaze durations and probability of skipping for model 2c of Reichle *et al.* (1998) for five frequency classes of words

Frequency class	Mean frequency	Gaze duration		Probability of skipping	
		Observed	Predicted E–Z Reader 2c	Observed	Predicted E–Z Reader 2c
1	3	293	292	0.10	0.12
2	45	272	272	0.13	0.20
3	347	256	255	0.22	0.27
4	4 889	234	232	0.55	0.46
5	40 700	214	210	0.67	0.63

Notes

The best fitting parameters for this model are:

f_b (the intercept of the familiarity check) = 242 ms;

f_m (the slope of the familiarity check) = -17 ms;

Δ (the ratio of the duration of *l*, the difference between lexical access and familiarity check, to *f*, the familiarity check time) = 0.65;

m (the labile motor programming time) = 150 ms;

M (the non-labile motor programming time) = 50 ms.

We used this relatively simple model (model 2c in Reichle *et al.* 1998) to predict gaze durations and the probability of fixating words of five frequency classes for a corpus of data in which subjects read a set of sentences that were each on a single line of text (see Table 8.1). The model had five free parameters: a slope and an intercept for the linear function relating word frequency to the duration of the familiarity check stage, *f*, a simple multiplicative parameter, Δ, relating the familiarity check, *f*, to *l*, and parameters for the duration of the *m* and *M* stages. Note that the frequency of words and length of words is confounded in fitting *f* and *l* in order to reduce the number of free parameters.

As can be seen in Table 8.1, the initial fits were quite good. At least at this gross level, this model accounts for both how long people inspect words and how often they skip. We then went on to try to fit multiple fixations within words. We did so by trying what we viewed as the simplest possible assumption: that a refixation on a word is programmed automatically when the reader begins a fixation. This programme for a refixation, however, can be cancelled by the programme to move on to the next word (triggered by completion of the familiarity check stage) by exactly the same mechanism that produces skipping: a programme to fixate word $N + 2$ cancels the programme to fixate word $N + 1$. In fact, the addition of this assumption added no free parameters to the model. This revised model (model 3 in Reichle *et al.* 1998) successfully predicted the eye movement data at a more detailed level, predicting both gaze and first fixation durations and predicting the probability of refixating a word (see Table 8.2).

In a third stage of modelling (model 5 in Reichle *et al.* 1998), we added two new parameters to the model, not so much to improve the overall fits, but to make

Table 8.2 Observed and predicted values of gaze durations and individual fixations, probability of skipping, making a single fixation, and making two fixations for model 3 of Reichle *et al.* (1998) for five frequency classes of words

Freq. class	Mean freq.	Gaze durations		First fixation duration		Single fixation duration	
		Observed	Predicted	Observed	Predicted	Observed	Predicted
1	3	293	292	248	248	265	269
2	45	272	275	233	252	249	264
3	347	256	258	230	245	243	252
4	4 889	234	228	223	224	235	226
5	40 700	214	203	208	202	216	203

Freq. class	Probability of skipping		Probability of making a single fixation		Probability of making two fixations	
	Observed	Predicted	Observed	Predicted	Observed	Predicted
1	0.10	0.11	0.68	0.70	0.20	0.18
2	0.13	0.19	0.70	0.72	0.16	0.09
3	0.22	0.26	0.68	0.69	0.10	0.06
4	0.55	0.46	0.44	0.52	0.02	0.02
5	0.67	0.65	0.32	0.34	0.01	0.01

Notes
The best fitting parameters for this model are:
$f_b = 250$ ms; $f_m = 16$ ms; $M = 50$ ms; $m = 150$ ms; $\Delta = 0.50$. The times for the within-word mean labile and non-labile programming stages, r and R, are assumed to have the same values as m and M respectively. (See Table 8.1 for a definition of the parameters.)

the model more psychologically reasonable. These parameters modulated the speed at which the familiarity check stage and the lexical access stage could be completed as a function of the distance the word being processed was from the fixation point (the above models assumed that processing is as rapid when the word is in the parafovea as when it is fixated). The rationale for two different parameters was that we thought that the familiarity check process was relatively crude and would be slowed down less by increased distance from the fixation point than lexical access would. Without going into further details, the new fits of the model were as good as before they were added and also made better fits of certain sequential properties of the data.

To summarise, we feel that our modelling efforts provide a framework for evaluating eye movements and attention in reading. While all the assumptions may not be correct, it appears that a model that assumes that words are processed one at a time, with attention shifting from word to word gives a creditable account of reading in a model that posits psychologically reasonable lexical access times and makes reasonable assumptions about the latency of programming an eye movement. Again, we should note that this model is incomplete: (a) it does not account for how syntactic and text structure processing can influence eye movements (and presumably attention as well); and (b) it does not indicate how decisions to fixate a word are translated into spatial coordinates that guide where the eyes actually move to.

Summary

In this chapter, we have attempted to describe how eye movements and covert spatial attention operate in reading. The major findings are the following. First, the eyes fixate a majority of words in text and fixation times on words reflect linguistic properties of those words. This indicates that readers are often fixating what they are processing and that this processing influences the movement of the eyes. Second, readers attend to a relatively narrow region of text: the word they are fixating on and (at most) two words to the right. Moreover, the difficulty of processing the foveal word appears to modulate the size of the region that is attended to. Third, words to the right of fixation are used in two ways: they are sometimes completely processed and skipped, but often a word is partially processed and this partial processing aids processing of the word when it is later fixated. Moreover, we think the evidence indicates that the same principles apply to most dyslexic readers; while their eye movement patterns are somewhat different from those of normal readers, this is most plausibly ascribed to their problems with identifying the words they are currently fixating.

Many basic issues are still unresolved. While it is reasonable to assume that letters within words are processed in parallel whereas words are processed one at a time with attention shifting from word to word, the evidence is far from definitive. We have sketched a model of reading that synthesises all of the above ideas and provides a coherent framework for how cognition and covert attention and eye movements interrelate. Moreover, this model provides reasonable fits to existing reading data with a relatively small number of free parameters. Indeed, our modelling efforts have already led to some new insights concerning eye movements in reading and we are confident that much can be learned in the coming years.

Note

Preparation of this chapter was supported by Grant HD26765 to Keith Rayner and Alexander Pollatsek and by a Career Scientist Award (MH01255) to Keith Rayner.

References

Adler-Grinberg, D. and Stark, L. (1978) 'Eye movements, scan paths and dyslexia', *American Journal of Optometry and Physiological Optics*, 55, 557–570.

Balota, D.A., Pollatsek, A. and Rayner, K. (1985) 'The interaction of contextual constraints and parafoveal visual information in reading', *Cognitive Psychology*, 17, 364–390.

Becker, W. and Jurgens, R. (1979) 'An analysis of the saccadic system by means of double-step stimuli', *Vision Research*, 19, 967–983.

Binder, K.S., Pollatsek, A. and Rayner, K. (in press) 'Extraction of information to the left of the fixated word in reading', *Journal of Experimental Psychology: Human Perception and Performance*.

Black, J.L., Collins, D.W.K., DeRoach, J.N. and Zubrick, S. (1984) 'A detailed study of sequential saccadic eye movements for normal and poor reading children', *Perceptual and Motor Skills*, 59, 423–434.

Brown, B., Haegerstrom-Portnoy, G., Adams, A.J., Yingling, C.D., Galin, D., Herron, J. and Marcus, M. (1983) 'Predictive eye movements do not discriminate between dyslexic and normal children', *Neuropsychologia*, 21, 121–128.

Carr, T.H. and Pollatsek, A. (1985) 'Recognizing printed words: A look at current models. In D. Besner, T.G. Waller and G.E. MacKinnon (eds), *Reading Research: Advances in Theory and Practice* (vol. 5). Orlando, FL: Academic Press.

Ciuffreda, K.J., Bahill, A.T., Kenyon, R.W. and Stark, L. (1976) 'Eye movements during reading: case reports', *American Journal of Optometry and Physiological Optics*, 53, 389–395.

Duhamel, J.R., Colby, C.L. and Goldberg, M.E. (1992) 'The updating of the representation of visual space in parietal cortex by intended eye movements', *Science*, 255, 90–92.

Duncan, J. (1980) 'The locus of interference in the perception of simultaneous stimuli', *Psychological Review*, 87, 272–300.

Duncan, J. (1984) 'Selective attention and the organization of visual information', *Journal of Experimental Psychology: General*, 113, 501–517.

Egly, R., Driver, J. and Rafal, R.D. (1994) 'Shifting visual attention between objects and locations: Evidence from normal and parietal lesion subjects', *Journal of Experimental Psychology: General*, 123, 161–177.

Ehrlich, S.F. and Rayner, K. (1981) 'Contextual effects on word perception and eye movements during reading', *Journal of Verbal Learning and Verbal Behavior*, 20, 641–655.

Ehrlich, K. and Rayner K. (1983) 'Pronoun assignment and semantic integration during reading: Eye movements and immediacy of processing', *Journal of Verbal Learning and Verbal Behavior*, 22, 75–87.

Eriksen, C.W. and St. James, J.D. (1986) 'Visual attention within and around the field of focal attention: A zoom lens model', *Perception and Psychophysics*, 40, 225–240.

Eriksen, C.W. and Yeh, Y. (1985) 'Allocation of attention in the visual field', *Journal of Experimental Psychology: Human Perception and Performance*, 11, 583–597.

Eskenazi, D. and Diamond, S.P. (1983) 'Visual exploration of non-verbal material by dyslexic children', *Cortex*, 19, 353–370

Everatt, J. and Underwood, G. (1992) 'Parafoveal guidance and priming effects during reading: A special case of the mind being ahead of the eyes', *Consciousness and Cognition*, 1, 186–197.

Farmer, M.E. and Klein, R.M. (1995) 'The evidence for a temporal processing deficit linked to dyslexia: A review', *Psychonomic Bulletin and Review*, 2, 460–493.

Fischer, M.H. and Rayner, K. (1993) 'On the functional significance of express saccades', *Behavioral and Brain Sciences*, 16, 577.

Frazier, L. and Rayner, K. (1982) 'Making and correcting errors during sentence comprehension: Eye movements in the analysis of structurally ambiguous sentences', *Cognitive Psychology*, 14, 178–210.

Geiger, G. and Lettvin, J.Y. (1987) 'Peripheral vision in persons with dyslexia', *New England Journal of Medicine*, 316, 1238–1243.

Geiger, G., Lettvin, J.Y. and Fahle, M. (1994) 'Dyslexic children learn a new visual strategy for reading: A controlled experiment', *Vision Research*, 34, 1223–1233.

Goolkasian, P. and King, J. (1990) 'Letter identification and lateral masking in dyslexic and average readers', *American Journal of Psychology*, 103, 519–538.

Henderson, J.M., Dixon, P., Peterson, A., Twilley, L.C. and Ferreira, F. (1995) 'Evidence for the use of phonological representations during transsaccadic word recognition', *Journal of Experimental Psychology: Human Perception and Performance*, 21, 82–98.

Henderson, J.M. and Ferreira, F. (1990) 'Effects of foveal processing difficulty on the perceptual span in reading: Implications for attention and eye movement control', *Journal of Experimental Psychology: Learning, Memory and Cognition*, 16, 417–429.

Henderson, J.M. and Ferreira, F. (1993) 'Eye movement control during reading: Fixation measures reflect foveal but not parafoveal processing difficulty', *Canadian Journal of Experimental Psychology*, 47, 201–221.

Hillyard, S.A., Mangun, G.R., Woldorff, M.G. and Luck, S.J. (1995) 'Neural systems mediating selective attention', in M. Gazzaniga (ed.), *The Cognitive Neurosciences*. Cambridge, MA: MIT Press.

Hogaboam, T.W. (1983) 'Reading patterns in eye movement data', in K. Rayner (ed.) *Eye Movements in Reading*. New York: Academic Press.

Hyönä, J. (1995) 'Do irregular letter combinations attract readers' attention? Evidence from fixation locations in words', *Journal of Experimental Psychology: Human Perception and Performance*, 21, 68–81.

Hyönä. J., Niemi, P. and Underwood, G. (1989) 'Reading long words embedded in sentences: Informativeness of word parts affects eye movements', *Journal of Experimental Psychology: Human Perception and Performance*, 15, 142–152.

Hyönä, J. and Olson, R.K. (1994) 'Dyslexic and normal readers' eye movement patterns in reading, visual search and tracking', in J. Ygge and G. Lennerstrand (eds.), *Eye Movements in Reading*. London: Pergamon Press.

Hyönä, J. and Olson, R.K. (1995) 'Eye fixation patterns among dyslexic and normal readers: Effects of word length and word frequency', *Journal of Experimental Psychology: Learning, Memory and Cognition*, 21, 1430–1440.

Inhoff, A.W. and Briihl, D. (1991) 'Semantic processing of unattended text during selective reading: How the eyes see it', *Perception and Psychophysics*, 49, 289–294.

Inhoff, A.W., Pollatsek, A., Posner, M.I. and Rayner, K. (1989) 'Covert attention and eye movements in reading', *Quarterly Journal of Experimental Psychology*, 41A, 63–89.

Inhoff, A.W. and Rayner, K. (1986) 'Parafoveal word processing during eye fixations in reading: Effects of word frequency', *Perception and Psychophysics*, 40, 431–439.

Inhoff, A.W. and Topolski, R. (1992) 'Lack of semantic activation from unattended text during passage reading', *Bulletin of the Psychonomic Society*, 30, 365–366.

Just, M.A. and Carpenter, P.A. (1980) 'A theory of reading: From eye fixations to comprehension', *Psychological Review*, 87, 329–354.

Karlin, M.B. and Bower, G.H. (1976) 'Semantic category effects in visual word search', *Perception and Psychophysics*, 19, 417–424.

Kennison, S.M. and Clifton, C. (1995) 'Determinants of parafoveal preview benefit in high and low working memory capacity readers: Implications for eye movement control', *Journal of Experimental Psychology: Learning, Memory and Cognition*, 21, 68–81.

Klein, R., Berry, G., Briand, K., D'Entremont, B. and Farmer, M. (1990) 'Letter identification declines with increasing retinal eccentricity at the same rate for normal and dyslexic readers', *Perception and Psychophysics*, 47, 601–606.

LaBerge, D. (1983) 'Spatial extent of attention to letters and words', *Journal of Experimental Psychology: Human Perception and Performance*, 9, 371–379.

LaBerge, D. and Brown, V. (1989) 'Theory of attentional operations in shape identification', *Psychological Review*, 96, 101–124.

McClelland, J.L. and Rumelhart, D.E. (1981) 'An interactive activation model of context effects in letter perception: Part 1. An account of basic findings', *Psychological Review*, 88, 375–407.

McConkie, G.W., Kerr, P.W., Reddix, M.D. and Zola, D. (1988) 'Eye movement control during reading: I. The location of initial fixations on words', *Vision Research*, 28, 1107–1118.

McConkie, G.W. and Rayner, K. (1975) 'The span of the effective stimulus during a fixation in reading', *Perception and Psychophysics*, 17, 578–586.

McConkie, G.W. and Rayner, K. (1976) 'Asymmetry of the perceptual span in reading', *Bulletin of the Psychonomic Society*, 8, 365–368.

McConkie, G.W. and Zola, D. (1979) 'Is visual information integrated across successive fixations in reading?', *Perception and Psychophysics*, 25, 221–224.

Moran, J. and Desimone, R. (1985) 'Selective attention gates visual processing in extrastriate cortex', *Science*, 229, 782–784.

Morrison, R.E. (1984) 'Manipulation of stimulus onset delay in reading: Evidence for parallel programming of saccades', *Journal of Experimental Psychology: Human Perception and Performance*, 10, 667–682.

Neisser, U. (1967) *Cognitive Psychology*. New York: Appleton, Century Crofts.

Olson, R.K., Kliegl, R. and Davidson, B.J. (1983) 'Dyslexic and normal children's tracking eye movements', *Journal of Experimental Psychology: Human Perception and Performance*, 9, 816–825.

O'Regan, J.K. (1992) 'Optimal viewing position in words and the strategy-tactics theory of eye movements in reading', in K. Rayner (ed.), *Eye Movements and Visual Cognition: Scene Perception and Reading* (pp. 333–354). New York: Springer-Verlag.

Paap, K.R., Newsome, S.L., McDonald, J.E. and Schvaneveldt, R.W. (1982) 'An activation-verification model for letter and word recognition: The word superiority effect', *Psychological Review*, 89, 573–594.

Pavlidis, G.T. (1981) 'Do eye movements hold the key to dyslexia?', *Neuropsychologia*, 19, 57–64.

Pavlidis, G.T. (1985) 'Eye movement differences between dyslexics, normal, and retarded readers while sequentially fixating digits', *American Journal of Optometry and Physiological Optics*, 62, 820–832.

Perry, A.R., Dember, W.N., Warm, J.S. and Sacks, J.G. (1989) 'Letter identification in normal and dyslexic readers: A verification', *Bulletin of the Psychonomic Society*, 27, 445–448.

Pirozzolo, F.J. (1979) *The Neuropsychology of Developmental Reading Disorders*. New York: Praeger Publishers.

Pirozzolo, F.J. and Rayner K. (1978) 'The normal control of eye movements in acquired and developmental reading disorders', in H. Avakian-Whitaker and H.A. Whitaker (eds), *Advances in Neurolinguistics and Psycholinguistics*. New York: Academic Press.

Pollatsek, A. (1983) 'What can eye movements tell us about dyslexia?', in K. Rayner (ed.), *Eye Movements in Reading: Perceptual and Language Processes*. New York: Academic Press.

Pollatsek, A., Bolozky, S., Well, A.D. and Rayner, K. (1981) 'Asymmetries in the perceptual span for Israeli readers', *Brain and Language*, 14, 174–180.

Pollatsek, A., Lesch, M.F., Morris, R.K. and Rayner, K. (1992) 'Phonological codes are used in integrating information across saccades in word identification and reading', *Journal of Experimental Psychology: Human Perception and Performance*, 18, 148–162.

Pollatsek, A., Raney, G.E., LaGasse, L. and Rayner, K. (1993) 'The use of information below fixation in reading and in visual search', *Canadian Journal of Psychology*, 47, 179–200.

Pollatsek, A., Rayner, K. and Balota, D.A. (1986) 'Inferences about eye movement control from the perceptual span in reading', *Perception and Psychophysics*, 40, 123–130.

Pollatsek, A., Well, A. and Gott, R. (1978) 'Searching through words and non-words', paper presented at the Psychonomic Society Nineteenth Annual Meeting.

Posner, M.I. (1980) 'Orienting of attention', *Quarterly Journal of Experimental Psychology*, 32, 3–25.

Posner, M.I., Walker, J.A., Friedrich, F.A. and Rafal, R.D. (1987) 'How do the parietal lobes direct covert attention?', *Neuropsychologia*, 25, 135–145.

Prinz, W. (1984) 'Attention and sensitivity in visual search', *Psychological Research*, 45, 355–366.

Ratcliff, R. and McKoon, G. (1988) 'A retrieval theory of priming in memory', *Psychological Review*, 95, 385–408.

Rayner, K. (1975) 'The perceptual span and peripheral cues in reading', *Cognitive Psychology*, 7, 65–81.

Rayner, K. (1978) 'Eye movements in reading and information processing', *Psychological Bulletin*, 85, 618–660.

Rayner, K. (1979) 'Eye guidance in reading: Fixation locations within words', *Perception*, 8, 21–30.

Rayner, K. (1985) 'Do faulty eye movements cause dyslexia?', *Developmental Neuropsychology*, 1, 3–15.

Rayner, K. (1986) 'Eye movements and the perceptual span in beginning and skilled readers', *Journal of Experimental Child Psychology*, 41, 211–236.

Rayner, K. (1993) 'Eye movements in reading: Recent developments', *Current Directions in Psychological Science*, 2, 81–85.

Rayner, K. (1995) 'Eye movements and cognitive processes in reading, visual search, and scene perception', in J.M. Findlay, R. Walker and R.W. Kentridge (eds), *Eye Movement Research: Mechanisms, Processes, and Applications* (pp. 3–22). Amsterdam: North-Holland Press.

Rayner, K. (1998) 'Eye movements in reading and information processing: 20 years of research', *Psychological Bulletin*, 124, 372-422.

Rayner, K., Balota, D.A. and Pollatsek, A. (1986) 'Against parafoveal semantic pre-processing during eye fixations in reading', *Canadian Journal of Psychology*, 40, 473–483.

Rayner, K. and Bertera, J.H. (1979) 'Reading without a fovea', *Science*, 206, 468–469.

Rayner, K. and Duffy, S.A. (1986) 'Lexical complexity and fixation times in reading: Effects of word frequency, verb complexity, and lexical ambiguity', *Memory and Cognition*, 14, 191–201.

Rayner, K., Fischer, M.H. and Pollatsek, A. (1998) 'Unspaced text interferes with both word identification and eye movement control', *Vision Research*, forthcoming.

Rayner, K., McConkie, G.W. and Ehrlich, S.F. (1978) 'Eye movements and integrating information across fixations', *Journal of Experimental Psychology: Human Perception and Performance*, 4, 529–544.

Rayner, K., McConkie, G.W. and Zola, D. (1980) 'Integrating information across eye movements', *Cognitive Psychology*, 12, 206–226.

Rayner, K. and Morris, R.K. (1992) 'Eye movement control in reading: Evidence against semantic preprocessing', *Journal of Experimental Psychology: Human Perception and Performance*, 18, 163–172.

Rayner, K., Murphy, L.A., Henderson, J.M. and Pollatsek, A. (1989) 'Selective attentional dyslexia', *Cognitive Neuropsychology*, 6, 357–378.

Rayner, K. and Pollatsek, A. (1989) *The Psychology of Reading*. Hillsdale, NJ: Erlbaum.

Rayner, K., Pollatsek, A. and Bilsky, A.B. (1995) 'Can a temporal processing deficit account for dyslexia?', *Psychonomic Bulletin and Review*, 2, 501–507.

Rayner, K. and Sereno, S.C. (1994) 'Eye movements in reading: Psycholinguistic studies', in M.A. Gernsbacher (ed.), *Handbook of Psycholinguistics* (pp. 57–82). San Diego: Academic Press.

Rayner, K., Sereno, S.C. and Raney, G.E. (1996) 'Eye movement control in reading: A comparison of two types of models', *Journal of Experimental Psychology: Human Perception and Performance*, 22, 1188–1200.

Rayner, K., Slowiaczek, M.L., Clifton, C. and Bertera, J.H. (1983) 'Latency of sequential eye movements: Implications for reading', *Journal of Experimental Psychology: Human Perception and Performance*, 9, 912–922.

Rayner, K. and Well, A.D. (1996) 'Effects of contextual constraint on eye movements in reading: A further examination', *Psychonomic Bulletin and Review*, 3, 504–509.

Rayner, K., Well, A.D. and Pollatsek, A. (1980) 'Asymmetry of the effective visual field in reading', *Perception and Psychophysics*, 27, 537–544.

Rayner, K., Well, A.D., Pollatsek, A. and Bertera, J.H. (1982) 'The availability of useful information to the right of fixation in reading', *Perception and Psychophysics*, 31, 537–550.

Reicher, G.M. (1969) 'Perceptual recognition as a function of meaningfulness of stimulus material', *Journal of Experimental Psychology*, 81, 275–280.

Reichle, E.D., Pollatsek, A., Fisher, D.L. and Rayner, K. (1998) 'Toward a model of eye movement control in reading', *Psychological Review*, 105, 125–157.

Remington, R.W. (1980) 'Attention and saccadic eye movements', *Journal of Experimental Psychology: Human Perception and Performance*, 6, 726–744.

Slaghuis, W.L., Lovegrove, W.J. and Freestun, J. (1992) 'Letter recognition in peripheral vision and metacontrast masking in dyslexic and normal readers', *Clinical Vision Sciences*, 7, 53–65.

Slowiaczek, M.L. and Rayner, K. (1987) 'Sequential masking during eye fixations in reading', *Bulletin of the Psychonomic Society*, 25, 175–178.

Spitzer, H., Desimone, R. and Moran, J. (1988) 'Increased attention enhances both behavioral and neuronal performance', *Science*, 240, 338–340.

Stanley, G., Smith, G.A. and Howell, E.A. (1983) 'Eye movements and sequential tracking in dyslexic and control children', *British Journal of Psychology*, 74, 181–187.

Treisman, A.M. and Gelade, G. (1980) 'A feature-integration theory of attention', *Cognitive Psychology*, 12, 97–136.

Ullman, S. (1984) 'Visual routines', in S. Pinker (ed.), *Visual Cognition*. Cambridge, MA: MIT Press.

Underwood, G., Bloomfield, R. and Clews, S. (1988) 'Information influences the pattern of eye fixations during sentence comprehension', *Perception*, 17, 267–278.

Underwood, G., Clews, S. and Everatt, J. (1990) 'How do readers know where to look next? Local information distributions influence eye fixations', *Quarterly Journal of Experimental Psychology*, 42A, 39–65.

Ungerleider, L.G. and Mishkin, M. (1985) 'Two cortical visual systems', in D.J. Ingle, M.A. Goodale and R.J.W. Mansfield (eds), *Analysis of Visual Behavior*. Cambridge, MA.: MIT Press.

Van Essen, D.C. and DeYoe, E.A. (1995) 'Concurrent processing in the primate visual cortex', in M. Gazzaniga (ed.) *The Cognitive Neurosciences*. Cambridge, MA: MIT Press.

Wurtz, R.H., Goldberg M.E. and Robinson, D.L. (1980) 'Behavioral modulation of visual responses in the monkey: Stimulus selection for attention and movement', in J.M. Sprague and A.N. Epstein (eds), *Progress in Psychobiology and Physiological Psychology* (vol. 9). New York: Academic Press.

Zangwill, O.L. and Blakemore, C. (1972) 'Dyslexia: Reversal of eye movements during reading', *Neuropsychologia*, 10, 371–373.

Zola, D. (1984) 'Redundancy and word perception during reading', *Perception and Psychophysics*, 36, 277–284.

Index